George A. Sala

Dutch Pictures

with some sketches in the Flemish manner

George A. Sala

Dutch Pictures
with some sketches in the Flemish manner

ISBN/EAN: 9783337302184

Printed in Europe. USA, Canada, Australia, Japan

Cover: Foto ©Thcmas Meinert / pixelio.de

More available bcoks at **www.hansebooks.com**

DUTCH PICTURES;

With some Sketches in the Flemish Manner.

BY

GEORGE AUGUSTUS SALA,

*Author of " William Hogarth ;" the " Seven Sons of
Mammon ;" " A Journey Due North ;" " Twice
Round the Clock ;" &c., &c.*

" Vidi tantum . . . . . ."

LONDON :

TINSLEY BROTHERS,

CATHERINE STREET, STRAND.

1861.

CONTENTS.

PREFACE.

―――⁂―――

On the Batavian School of Delineation.

I THINK that of would-be epigramatic, alliterative, or simply clap-trap titles to books, we have had, of late years, satiety. Am I, in calling my volume "Dutch Pictures," adding but one more "taking" title to the list? Can "Dutch Pictures" have any more real meaning or significance than "Sand and Shells," "Patchwork," "Odds and Ends," "Olla Podrida," "Waifs and Strays," "Bubble and Squeak," or "Gammon and Spinach?" I hope to prove that I have had a definite object in attaching to these papers their present title, and that it is not, after all, grossly inappropriate.

I put "Dutch Pictures" at the head of my page for these reasons. First, because, unless I am much mistaken, the Batavian painters of the seventeenth century were remarkable for their careful delineation of the minutest objects in nature, animate and inanimate, bestowing infinite pains on the reproduction of, or the shadows and reflections in, pots and pans,—of the twigs in a birch-broom, of the texture of a carpet or a curtain, of the fat and lean of a loin of pork, of the knitted stockings of a fraw, of the red nose of a boor, of the peelings of carrots and turnips, of the plumage of a bird, of the veins in a cabbage, of the smoke from a tobacco-pipe. Next, because I have endeavoured, perhaps unsuccessfully, but always laboriously, to imitate with the pen what these ingenious artists have done with the pencil, and to bring to the description of the men and the manners of the times in which I have lived that minuteness—it may be pettiness of observation—which makes every Dutch Picture, to the meanest, curious, if not excellent. Let me not be mistaken by critics. There are Dutchmen and Dutchmen. There are the Teniers, the Gerard Douws, the Ostades, and the Metzus—the great makers of minutiæ, but surpassingly gifted likewise in skilful draughtsmanship, in harmonious composition, in brilliant colour, in delicate texture, in exquisite finish. Such admirable exemplars answer, perhaps, to our Goldsmiths, our Lambs, our Leigh Hunts, and our Washington Irvings. I will name no living writer for fear of being howled at. But there are Dutch painters of the second, the third, and the fourth rank. There are the Wouvermans', the Micris', the Breughels; there are, lower still, the Jan Steens and the Schkalkens; there are the Weenix's, the Van Huysums, the Vanvoorsts, and the Steenwycks. There may be mentioned, again, the jolly Jordaens, and the coarse but brilliant Adrian Brouwer. When the pearly tints of a Teniers, the wonderful light and shade of an Isaac Ostade, the matchless manipulation* of a Gerard Douw, are almost beyond price, collectors and curiosity-hunters can yet find a word of praise, and a corner in their cabinets, for the inferior works of the Dutch school—not gems, intaglios, or enamels, certainly, but rather buttons, and quaint carved toys, and tradesmen's tokens of art, which give them, so far as the limited capacity, but untiring industry, of the Dutchman went, his notion of the interior of a school-room, the economy of a kitchen, the jollity of a tavern, or the humours of a *kermesse.* What scenes analogous to those just mentioned I have witnessed at home or abroad, I have attempted to draw with pen and ink, slowly and carefully, in the Dutch manner; and if I

---

* I use the long word in preference to "handling," because the latter has been degraded and distorted by Art critics, who speak of mere coarse dash and vigour in a picture as "handling," whereas by "manipulation," I mean the pains-taking work of the pencil wielded by a highly educated hand.

have failed, it has been for lack of power, and not of will, or toil.

A favourite device adopted now a-days by those whose business it is to dissect a book, is to ask the author his reasons for writing, for publishing, or for republishing it. There is no easier cry than *cui bono?* and the response is not so very difficult. There is a story told of Mr. John Cooper the tragedian—who is facetiously supposed to be many hundred years old—stating that he once asked William Shakspeare why he drank so much soda-water and sal-volatile, to which the bard tranquilly replied, "Because I like it, John." I might retort, were I asked my reasons for putting forth these old pictures, of which the majority originally appeared in "Household Words" between the years 1851 and 1856, inclusive, and which are now reprinted by permission of Mr. Charles Dickens, that to do so suits my humour, my vanity, or my interest; but I have two more reasons, less egotistical and perhaps as valid. I wrote the stories in this book with the purpose of amusing my readers, and I hope that those who read them may derive some amusement from them now. I wrote the sketches and essays as studies of the manners I saw around me, and with the idea that they might not be without some interest when those manners had passed away. Both stories and sketches may be disfigured by errors of style, by involved and confused language, by repetitions, by inaccuracies, and by verbal affectations, involuntary, but not the less offensive. With respect to such blemishes, I have but one plea to offer, and to repeat—that there are Dutchmen and Dutchmen, and that to all painters are not given the magic *coup-d'œil* of Ostade, the unerring touch of Teniers.

I have heard that a politician once declared that had he not been bred up to the Quaker persuasion, he would surely have been a prizefighter. It is probable that, had I not drifted into authorship, I should have been a broker's man. I can even remember in early life once "taking stock" in a theatrical wardrobe, and once making out the Christmas bills for a fashionable tailor; and I can recall the delight with which, in a neat round hand, I expatiated upon "one demon's dress, complete," "six page's tunics and tights," and again upon "one best superfine Saxony broad cloth frock-coat, with silk sleeve and skirt lining, buttons and binding." On that same art of inventory-making, and stock-taking, I still take my stand. Whatever success I have to be thankful for in a life of incessant and painful labour—never without censure, seldom relieved by encouragement or praise—pursued in sickness and sorrow, in poverty and obscurity, has been due to the pen and the inkhorn of the inventory-maker, to persistence in describing the things I have seen, and to a habit of setting down the common things I have thought about them : exactly as they have been presented to me, and exactly as they have occurred.

GEORGE AUGUSTUS SALA.

Upton Court, Bucks,
September, 1861.

DUTCH PICTURES.

I.

THE SHADOW OF A DUTCH PAINTER.

YELLOW, thumbed, devastated by flies and time, stained with spots of oil and varnish, broken-backed, dog's-eared—a sorry, lazar-house copy, which no bookstall-keeper would look at, and at which the meanest of buttermen would turn up his nose—I have a book which I love. It is the Reverend Mr. Pilkington, his Dictionary of Painters. You know it, oh ye amateurs of the fine arts, seeking to verify the masters and the dates of your favourite canvasses! You know it, ye industrials of Cawdor Street, for it is your grand book of reference, when your journeyman artist Smith, only recently emancipated from limning "Red Lions," and making "Bulls" radiant with gold leaf, and then painting a Holy Family and affixing thereto the signature (pious fraud!) of Dominichino or Zurbaran, runs the risk, if to the signature he adds a date, of making a slight mistake in chronology, and dating his work fifty years or so before the painter's birth, or after his death. I have seen, ere now, an original Rembrandt (with a flourish to the R at which the boldest of sceptics would not dare to cavil), dated 1560. I know my Pilkington well, and of old, and I love it, for it is full of Shadows. I can keep good shadowy company with it; now with the cream — the R. A.'s of the old masters: Titian in the Mocenigo Palace receiving his pencil from the hands of Charles the Fifth, with a condescending bow; Rubens riding abroad with fifty gentlemen in his train; Raffaelle lying in state, with princes and cardinals around, and his glorious Transfiguration at the bed-head; now, with the less prominent celebrities: jovial, clever, worthless Adrian Brouwer; Gian Bellini, so meek, so mild, and so pious; honest Peter Claes, so great in painting pots and pans; stolid old Dirk Stoop the battle painter.

Turn again, Pilkington, and let me summon the shadow of Peter de Laar.

We are in Rome, in the year of grace sixteen hundred and twenty-three, and in a house in the Strada Vecchia. Light steals with no garish glitter, but with a chastened mellowed softness, through a solitary window into a grand old room. Not but what there are other windows, and large ones too: but they are all fastened and curtained up, that so much light as is needed, and no more, shall permeate into the painter's studio. Three large easels I see, and a smaller one, far off, in a corner, whereat a fair-haired boy is making a study, in chalk, from a plaster bust on a pedestal. There is a good store of old armour, old furniture, old tapestry scattered about, and, above all, an old painted ceiling, where a considerable contingent from Olympus once disported themselves upon clouds, but are well nigh invisible now through clouds of dust and smoke from this lower earth. In revenge for their forced obscurity above, the gods and goddesses have descended to the shelves, where, in plaster, and wanting some of them a leg or an arm, they are as beautiful, and more useful than above. The Venus of Milo stands amicably side by side with Actæon and his dogs, while in strange proximity is the horned Moses of Michael Angelo. There is a great velvet-covered silver-clasped book of " Hours " on a lectern of carved oak, and in an ebony cabinet, among strange poignards and quaint pieces of plate, are a few books: a copy of Livy with a passage kept open by an ivory rosary, some dog's-eared sketch-books, and a parchment-covered folio of St. Augustine's works, the margins scrawled over with skeletons and fragments of men with muscles in violent relief. Nor are these last the only muscular decorations of the apartment. One shelf is entirely devoted to a range of phials, containing anatomical preparations sufficiently hideous to the view; and there stands, close to a table where a serving lad with an eminently French face is grinding colours on a marble slab and humming an air the while, a horrible figure as large as life, from which the skin has been flayed off, showing the muscles and arteries beneath—a dreadful sight to view. It may be of wax or of plaster, but I would as soon not meet with it, out of a dissecting-room, or a charnel-house. A skeleton, too—the bones artistically wired together, and supported on a tripod —would show that the occupant of the apartment was not

averse from the study of osteology. This skeleton has no
head, the place thereof being supplied by a mask, a cardboard "dummy" of a superlatively inane cast of beauty:
the blue eyes and symmetrical lips (curved into an unmean-
ing and eternal simper), the pink cheeks, and silken dolls'
tresses, contrasting strangely with the terribly matter-of-fact
bones and ligaments beneath—the moral to my lady's looking-glass. This room might belong to a surgeon who is
fond of painting (for there are more bones, and one or two
real grinning skulls about), or to a painter who is fond of
surgery; for the anatomical drawings which crowd every
vacant place, which are scrawled on the walls and furniture
in chalk and charcoal and red cinnabar, bear trace of a
masterly eye and of an experienced hand. If the apartment
be the habitation of a painter, however, he is no poet, no
admirer of music, no gallant devoted to gay clothes, or delighting to serenade noble dames; for through the length
and breadth of the studio I can catch no glimpse of lute, or
plumed hat, or velvet mantle trailing on a chair—of sprucely
bound volume of Ariosto or Boccaccio, or, worse, of ribald
Aretin, of soiled glove, or crushed rose-bud, or crumpled
ribbon. The painter, if he be one, must be a grave, sedate
cavalier, and so, of a truth, he is. No one yet accused
Messire NICOLAS POUSSIN, to whom this studio belongs,
of gallantry, or verse-making, or lute-twanging, or flower-
seeking. He is a tall, well-made, personable gentleman,
prematurely grey, and of a grave presence. He wears a
justaucorps of black velvet, not quite innocent of paint-stains,
and a well-worn cap of red silk sits on his crisp and curled
locks. He carries palette on thumb and pencil in hand,

with which last he is busily calling up, on the canvass before him, a jovial, riotous, wine-bibbing, dishevelled crew of fauns satyrs, Bacchanals and Hamadryads, dancing, shouting, and leaping round a most disreputable-looking old Silenus, bestriding a leopard and very far gone in Grecian vintages.

Anon, the fair-haired boy quits the ˈroom, and, returning, announces that there is one below would speak with his master. The words are scarcely out of his mouth, when the stranger, of whom it is question, enters. With much creaking of shoes, and cracking of joints, and rustling of his brave garments, he advances to Poussin, and presents him with a packet of letters, which the painter receives with a grave reverence. This is Peter de Laar: here is his Shadow.

Take Sancho Panza's head; blend in the expression of the countenance the shrewd impudence of Gil Blas, the sententious yet saucy wit of Figaro, and the stolid humour of Molière's Sganarelle, yet leave the close-cropped bullet skull, the swarthy tint, the grinning ivories, the penthouse ears and twinkling little eyes of the immortal governor of Barataria ; mount this head on a trunk combining the strength and muscular development of Buonarotti's *torso*, with the exuberant rotundity of Falstaff; plant this trunk on the legs of Edward Longshanks, of the celebrated Mr. Carus Wilson, or of that member of the Daddy Longlegs family, whose inability or disinclination to perform his orisons led to his being precipitated down an indefinite number of stairs. Add to all this, arms always placed at distressingly eccentric angles to the body; feet, the toes of which are always turned in the contrary direction to that which they properly should be ; hands, with joints for ever cracking, with palms for ever smiting each other, with thumbs and fingers and wrists for ever combining themselves into strange gestures, into concentric balls of quaint humour; a nose which, when blown, resounds like a Chaldean trumpet in the new moon; moustaches fierce as those of the Copper Captain, long as those of a Circassian chieftain, twisted upwards like those of Mephistopheles in the outlines of Moritz Retsch. Cover this strange, joyous, bizarree, humourously awkward, quaint and *goguenarde* frame with habiliments so strangely cut, so queerly fashioned, of such staring colours, bespattered with such fantastic embroidery, that you know not whether to call them vulgar or picturesque, ridiculous or pleasing. Balance me this notable figure in any position out of his proper centre of gravity; make him sit on tables, or on easels, or on wainscot ledges, till Master Poussin has courteously signalled an easy chair to him; and even then let him sit on the back, the legs, the arms thereof, rather than sit as Christians are wont to repose. Let him do nothing as other men do; let him have a voice the faintest vibration of which, before ever he utters a word, shall make you hold your sides with laughter; let him have been born a low comedian, a mountebank, a merry-andrew, a jack-pudding, a live marionette, even as some men are born scoundrels, and some women queens. Let him have wit, talent, impudence (and monstrous impudence!), good-humour and versatility; let him be a joyous companion, a firm friend, indifferently moral, questionably sober, and passing honest; imagine him to be all these, and you have the shadow of Peter de Laar, the Dutch painter, better known in Pilkingtonian and auction room lore by the pseudonym given him by the Italians, with reference to his witty buffoonery, of *Il Bamboccio*.

Peter has come straight from dear old Amsterdam; from the sluggish canals, the square-cut trees, the washing tub-like luggers and galliots, the parti-coloured houses, the clean flag-stones, tulip-beds, pictorial tiles, multifarious wind-mills, pagoda hay-stacks, pickled gherkins, linsey-woolsey petticoats, and fat, honest, stupid, kind Dutch faces of the City of the Dykes and the Dams, to Rome. He has come as straight, moreover, as the governor of the Low Countries, as the police of M. de Richelieu in France, as a slender purse, and an inveterate propensity to turn out of the beaten track wherever there were pretty faces, good wine, or good company to be found, would allow him to progress. He is come to study landscape painting in Italy, and has brought letters of introduction to Poussin, from persons of consideration both in Holland and France. The great French painter receives him with cordiality. Wine and meats are brought in. Presently enter two friends of Poussin, both painters : Monsieur Sandrart, who has left but an unsubstantial shadow to us, and Monsieur Gelée, whose real appellation has also been forgotten, but who will live, I trust, as long as painting lives, under the title of Claude Lorraine. Peter de Laar is introduced to these worthies. They talk of things literary, of things pictorial, of the last scandal in the sacred college, of the last squib on the Corso, the last lampoon passed on Pasquin's statue, of the success of the Cavaliere Vandyck in England, of the probable jealousy thereat of the Cavaliere Rubens; of Gaspar Dughet—Nicolas's brother-in-law and pupil, who adopted his master's patronymic—and of his friendship with Albano. They are grave at first, but somehow Peter de Laar makes them all laugh. Then there are more wines and more meats, and considerably more laughter. Suddenly, from no man knows whither, Peter produces a fiddle. He plays once, and twice, and thrice, and again. He plays the good old airs of Holland, such as Teniers' vrows dance to, and Ostade's boors nod lazily to, guzzling beer the while ; such as the lady in the satin dress of Honthorst plays so sweetly to the cavalier in buff boots; such as the hurdygurdy players of Metzu and Jan Steen grind so piteously before cottage doors ; such as bring the tears into the eyes of the good company in the old house in the Strada Vecchia, though Peter de Laar be the only Dutchman present.

Peter can paint, and paint well, besides playing on the fiddle. He has a pretty hand, too, for turning verses—the more satirical the better. He is a good classic and inimitable story-teller, and a practical joker unrivalled for invention and audacity. He can smoke like a Dutchman, as he is, and sing in madrigals, and do tricks of legerdemain wonderful to look at. He is come to spend three months among the beautiful Italian scenery, but how long do you think he stops ? Five years. Soon the grave and sedate Nicolas Poussin, soon the saturnine Claude Gelée, yclept Lorraine, began to find that they cannot do without the sprightly Dutchman. He fiddles, or touches the viol di gamba or the harpsichord, before they set to work of a morning; he sings to them as he and they paint, or, while a tint is drying, or the sky is too overcast for him to paint the sunny landscapes by, he will throw his huge grotesque laugh-provoking limbs on a stool, and from one of the tomes in the ebon cabinet read forth in a bold strident voice the sounding prose of Livy that Master Poussin loves so well to listen to ; or he will " lisp in numbers," and clearing

away the dust and cobwebs from crabbed Basle or Haerlem
Latin characters—call forth joy and merriment from Master
Quintus Horatius Flaccus, and Master P. Virgilius Maro their
repositories.

But when work is over (Peter can work well and play
well), it is then that his supple joints, his joyous face, his
great hearty laugh come into full play.   It is in the wine-
shops, among the merry crowds on the Corso and the
Pincian Hill, in moonlight junketings among the ruins of
the Colliseum, in the gloomy Ghetto among the Jews, playing
them roguish tricks, that he earns his surname of *Il Bamboccio*, that he becomes the idol and the glory of the Italian
jokers and hoaxers.   We have been too much accustomed to
look at the Italians as a sentimental and romantic people ;
yet, in pure fact, few nations possess so much of the comic vein
A glance at the memoirs of Baldinucci, at the glorious reper-
tory of hoaxes to be found in the Decameron, at the infinity of
pantomimes, farces, and burlesques to which the little Venetian theatres gave birth ; or even at the buffooneries of that
superlative literary rascal, Peter Aretino, would prove the
contrary.   Punch came from Italy, so did Toby ; so did harlequin, columbine, clown, and pantaloon.   Fancy the stealing
of sausages and the animation of clock-faces to have had their
origins in the clime of Dante and Petrarch, oh, ye Della Crus-
cans, and readers of Rosa Matilda novels !   If orchards were
to be rifled, old ladies frightened, monks waylaid and enticed
to drink strong waters till they went home intoning profane
canticles to the great scandal of the monastic orders—who but
Il Bamboccio ?   If tradesmen's signs were to be altered, names
erased, obnoxious collectors of the salt-tax, to be tarred

and feathered, or any other achievements to be accomplished—who but *Il Bamboccio?* Like many practical jokers as famous, Peter de Laar not only enjoys the fame of what he does, but of a great deal of what he neither does do nor has any hand in doing. All the hoaxes, all the satires, all the practical jokes, all the caricatures, all the *concetti*, are credited to his account. Though he strenuously denies it, he is set down for certain as the heir-at-law to the celebrated Pasquin. If ever a pasquinade appears against a Cardinal, an epigram on a *Monsignore*, a couplet on love, politics, or divinity—who but *Il Bamboccio* is fixed upon as the culprit?

Every evening, after the heat of the day, when the dust is laid and the cool breezes come in refreshingly from the Campagna, the grandees of Rome come forth to walk on the Corso. Priests, gentles, noble ladies, *cavalieri serventi* and *patiti*, stately Cardinals in their coaches of scarlet and gold, drawn by eight mules a-piece, walk, ride, flirt, or decorously amble up and down. There are smiles, and jests, and smart witticisms, and brilliant skirmishes of gallantry round the ladies. One Friday, in the year 1624, at the very height and fashionable time of the promenade, a huge elderly ape, a white-headed, vicious, bushy-haired, villainous animal, which would be, perhaps, were he to stand upright, nearly as large as a man, appears at the further extremity of the Corso. Gravely he marches, looking slyly at the ladies under their veils, and grimacing horribly. Some laugh, some shriek, some cry that he has escaped from a menagerie. All at once, with an appalling scream and a chattering such as man never heard before, he stops opposite a richly-dressed lady, called La Parqueria, and, in defiance of all laws of politeness and etiquette, gives her a round of kisses in amazingly rapid succession ; then, turning on his tail, flies and is seen no more.

Now La Parqueria, I grieve to tell it, is rather more beautiful than good.   Scandal, busy at Rome as elsewhere, says naughty things of her with reference to a certain Cardinal.   Next day, on the statue of Pasquin appears a most abusive libel, called *il bracciamento*, in which, in reference to the occurrence of the day before, his Eminence the Cardinal is likened to an old ape.   The affair makes a furious noise in Rome ; and our friend Bamboccio is generally believed to know more about it than he cares to aver.   He drinks, and fiddles, and paints none the less, but he keeps his own counsel, goes home rather earlier of an evening, and never alone, and is heard to boast a good deal in public touching being cunning of fence.   As for the poor Parqueria, so great is the hubbub and ridicule, that she is obliged to leave Rome.   At this time of day it would scarcely bring Peter de Laar within the range of the batteries of the Holy Inquisition to say that he is the guilty party, the real monkey, and the author of the libel as well.   There is an obstinate old woman in Rome who is of the same opinion, and who avers, that with her proper eyes she saw the monkey assume the shape of Bamboccio, mount a horse, and gallop away at the top of his speed ; but she is at last persuaded that it was the devil she saw and not the Dutchman, and performs, in consequence, a Novena at the church of San Pancrazio.

Five years have nearly elapsed since Bamboccio's arrival at Rome, when he is one day agreeably surprised by the appearance of his brother, Roeland de Laar, who brings with him two more young Dutchmen (and famous ones), John and

Andrew Both, who are come to study landscape under Claude Lorraine. Roeland has journeyed hither with the intention of taking his brother back to his native country; but, after the manner of the hammer which was sent to fetch the chisel, and which, in turn, required the mallet to be sent after it, Bamboccio easily persuades his brother to stay in Rome, and the four painters agree to live merrily together. They take a roomy old house, and lead for upwards of a year the gayest, most jovial, yet most industrious bachelor life you can imagine. Alas, for the clouds that are so soon to overcast this fair sky!

One day, on a sketching excursion, and during Lent, after having filled their portfolios with sketches, they sit down by a running stream to eat their afternoon meal. The pie is good, and the wine is good, and the ample and hilarious enjoyment thereof does them, so they think, good too. Not so, however, thinks a shaven monk with a white, cowled blanket lashed round his waist by a greasy rope, feet very picturesquely sandalled but leaving something to be desired in the way of cleanliness, a thin lip, and an evil eye. He takes the artists roundly to task for eating meat in Lent, and threatens nothing less than to denounce them to the ecclesiastical authorities; whereupon Bamboccio abuses him with much humorous virulence.

"For a fellow," says Peter, "who recommends abstinence, you keep no Lent in wine, Father Baldpate, to judge by your ruby snout."

" Wine, in moderation, is sent by Providence for the use of man," answers the monk, sententiously.

"And water wherewith to dilute it," cries Bamboccio,

with an ominous glance at the running stream. "Did you ever do penance, old shaveling?"

"When I sin, as you do," responds the monk.

"Well," says Bamboccio, "you must have sinned during the last two minutes, and you shall do penance now. What say you, brothers?" he adds, turning to his three companions, and glancing at the stream again.

A clamorous cry of acquiescence in his proposition greets him. The monk endeavours to beat a retreat; but Peter, with a great Dutch oath, swears he shall do penance, and, catching him by the cowl and waistband, throws him clean into the water.

"When he has washed a few of his sins out," he says, laughing, "we will fish him out."

But the current is rapid and the stream is deep, and the monk never is fished out again. He is drowned.

Bamboccio and his accomplishes are in consternation; some counsel one thing, some another, but all at length agree to set off immediately on their return to Holland.

From that fatal day Peter de Laar becomes another man. The shadow of the monk is always before him. At Amsterdam, at Haerlem, at Dordt, at Utrecht, where his paintings are held in great request and are munificently paid for, he lives extravagantly, and is as boisterous a boon companion as of old; but his laugh loses its heartiness, and his eye grows dull and his cheek haggard. It is the Monk. He avoids the companions and accomplices of his crime, even his favourite brother Roeland.

In the year 1650, Andrew Both drowns himself in a canal at Venice. It is the Monk.

In the year 1660, John Both perishes in the water at Utrecht. It is the Monk.

In the year 1663, Roeland de Laar crossing a wooden bridge, the ass on which he is mounted stumbles : he is precipitated into the torrent beneath, and is drowned. It is the Monk.

In the year 1675, Peter de Laar having come to be more than sixty years of age, a miserable, infirm, sombre old man, ruined in health by excesses, impoverished in purse, eclipsed in fame by the rising star of Wouvermans, is found drowned in a well at Haerlem. It is the Monk.

So they that smite with the sword perish by the sword ; and I shut up Pilkington and the Shadows fade away.

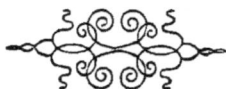

II.

THE SHADOW OF DAY AND NIGHT.

AS most of us have our Doubles, so, in many noticeable lives, there are a Day and Night so wonderfully contrasted, so strikingly opposed, so picturesque in their opposition to each other, that there can be few more remarkable subjects for consideration.

Let me recall a few such Days and Nights.

The weather is sultry, scorching, though there are banks of heavy clouds in the sky. A hot wind shakes the strangely-shaped leaves of gaunt trees fitfully to and fro, or agitates tufts of brushwood and furze, rankly luxuriant, which grow here and there on the grey rocks. There are sudden declivities, and more rocks beyond, furrowed, scarred, and seamed, by tears of brine. On every side beyond, as far as the strained eye can reach, is the interminable Sea. There are birds overhead with sullen flapping wings, and insects and reptiles of strange shape beneath. In a mean house, with whitewashed walls, and crazy Venetian blinds, with paltry furniture strangely diversified by rich pieces of plate and jewellers's ware, is a man in a bath, with a Madras handkerchief tied round his head. Anon he is dressed by his servants, with whom he is peevish and fretful. He grumbles with the coffee at breakfast, abuses his attendants, begins a dozen things and does not accomplish one. Now he is in his garden : you will observe that he is short, stout, sallow, and with a discontented expression of countenance. He wears a large straw hat, a white jacket and trousers, a checked shirt, and has a black handkerchief knotted round his neck. He takes up a book, and throws it down, a newspaper, and casts it aside. He is idle, and loaths his idleness. Through an open window you may look into his plain study, of which the walls are covered with striped paper. You may see hanging their a portrait of a little child, and a map of the world.

Who may this man be? What was he? A testy East India captain with a liver complaint, a disappointed Indigo planter, a crusty widower with a lagging Chancery suit? No. It is Night now, but Day was. Twelve years before, he stood on the steps of a throne in Nôtre Dame with the Pontiff of the Catholic church behind him, with the dignitaries of that church, the princes of his empire, the marshals of his armies, the sages of his tribunals, the ladies of his court, the flower of his subjects on his right hand and on his left. He was arrayed in velvet, satin and gold, laurels on his head and a sceptre in his hand. He was Napoleon the Great, Emperor and King; now he is the outlaw of Europe, the Ogre of his former subjects, the scoff of the Quarterly Review, the hated, bankrupt, captive, despot General Bonaparte, a prisoner at St. Helena, at the beck and call of an English orderly officer. The portrait of the little child is that of the King of Rome, whose melancholy Double, the pale young man in a white coat, is to be Metternichised in Vienna yonder, and the map is of the World which was to have been his inheritance.

Again. We are in the pit of an Italian theatre. Wax tapers, in bell-shaped shades, flare round the dress circle, for we are in the eighteenth century, and as yet gas and fishtail burners are not. Gaudy frescoes decorate the front of the tiers of boxes ; the palisade of the orchestra is surmounted with a spiked railing ; the occupants of the pit, in which there are no seats, wear cocked-hats and wigs ; and, in the dress circle, the beaux sport laced ruffles and sparkling-hilted swords, and the belles powder and patches. In one of the proscenium-boxes is the Grand Duke, sitting, imposing, in embroidery ; behind him are his suite, standing humble in ditto. The corresponding box on the other side of the proscenium is empty. The first act of the opera is over, and an intermediary ballet is being performed. An impossible shepherd, in blue satin trunks, a cauliflower wig, and carrying a golden crook, makes choregraphic overtures, to live with him and be his love, to an apocryphal shepherdess in a *robe Pompadour* and hair powder. You would see such a pair nowhere else save in Arcadia, or in Wardour Street, and in Dresden China. More shepherds and shepherdesses execute pastoral gambadoes, and the divertissement is over. Then commences the second act of the opera. About this time, verging on half-past nine in the evening, you hear the door of the vacant private box open. An easy chair is brought down to the front, and a book of the opera, a bottle of essences, and a golden snuff-box are placed upon the ledge before it. Anon enters unto these an infirm, staggering, broken-looking old man, with a splendid dress hanging in

C

slovenly magnificence on his half-palsied limbs. He has a
bloated countenance, marbled with purple stains, a heavy
eyelid and a blood-shoot eye that once must have been bright
blue. Every feature is shattered, weary, drooping, and flaccid.
Every nerve is unstrung: the man is a wreck, and an un-
sightly one. His flabby hands are covered with rings, a
crumpled blue ribbon crosses his breast, and round his neck
hangs another ribbon, from which dangles something that
sparkles, like a diamond star. Finally, he is more than
three parts inebriated. It is easy to understand *that* from
his unsteady hand, from the dozing torpor into which he
occasionally falls, from the querulous incoherence of his
speech, from the anxiety manifested by the thin, pale, old
men in uniform, with the cross of a commander of Saint
Louis, and the hard featured gentlemen with silver thistles in
their cravats, who stand on either side of their master, and
seem momentarily to fear that he will fall out of his chair.
The beaux and belles in the dress circle do not seem to
express much curiosity at the advent of this intoxicated
gentleman. They merely whisper " *E il Signore Cavaliere :*
he is very far gone to-night," or words to that effect. The
spectacle is no novelty. The opera is that most beautiful
one by Gluck, Orfeo. The Orpheus of the evening, in a
Grecian tunic, but bewigged and powdered according to
orthodoxy, is singing the sublime lament, " *Che farò senza
Euridice.*" The beautiful wailing melody floats upwards,
and for a moment the belles forget to flirt, and the beaux to
swagger. Cambric handkerchiefs are used for other purposes
than to assure the owner that the rouge on the cheeks holds
fast, and is not coming off. What is the slovenly magnifico

opposite the Grand Duke doing? During the prelude he was nodding his head and breathing stentoriously; but as the song proceeds, he sits erect in his chair; his blue eye dilates; a score of years of seams and furrows on his brows and cheeks vanish: he is a Man. But the strain concludes, and his Excellency bursts into a fit of maudlin weeping, and has recourse to the bottle of essences.

His excellency has not spent a pleasant day. He has been bullied by his chaplain, snubbed by his chamberlain, and has had a deadly quarrel with his favourite. Moreover his dinner has disagreed with him, and he has drunk a great deal more, both before and after it, than was good for him. Are these tears merely the offspring of whimpering drunkenness; or has the music touched some responsive chord of the cracked lyre, sent some thoughts of what he was through his poor hazy brain clouded with wine of Alicant and strong waters? Have the strains he has heard to-night, some mysterious connection (as only music can have) with his youth, his dead happiness, his hopes crushed for ever;—with the days when he was Charles Edward Stuart, pretending to the Crown of England; when he rode through the streets of Edinburgh at the head of the clans amid the crooning of the bagpipes, the shouts of his partisans, the waving of silken banners 'broidered by the white hands of noble ladies. " *Non sum qualis eram*," his chaplain will tell him; but, ah me! what a sorry evening is this to so bright a morning.

To come nearer home: the good Queen Anne reigns in England, and an enthusiastic phalanx of High Church ragamuffins have just been bellowing round the Queen's sedan chair, "God save your Majesty and Doctor Sacheverell."

Thre are a great many country gentlemen in town, for term is just on, and the cause list is full. A white haired patriarch in extreme old age, who has been subpœnaed on some trial, has strolled from Westminster Hall, and entered the House of Lords, where he stands peering curiously at the carved roof, the dingy tapestry, and scarlet covered woolsack. He is one of those men in whose whole apparel and bearing you seem to read farmer, as in another man's you will read thief. His snowy white locks, his ruddy, sunburnt, freckeld countenance carved into a thousand wrinkles, like a Nuremburg nut-cracker, tell of hale, hearty old age. You may read farmer in his flapped felt hat and long duffel coat; in his scarlet-flapped waistcoat and boots of untanned leather, his stout ashen staff, with a crutch and leathern strap. His full clear eye, his pleasant smile, his jaunty, though feeble bearing, say clearly farmer—a well to do, Queen-loving, God-fearing old agriculturist. His life has probably passed in peace and comfort; and when he dies he will sleep in the green churchyard where his fore-elders sleep. Here is a London gentleman who accosts him—a coffee-house wit, a buck skilled in the nice conduct of a clouded cane. He patronises the old farmer, and undertakes to show him the lions of the place. This is the door leading to my Lord Chancellor's robing room; from behind that curtain enters Her Majesty; there is the gallery for the peeresses; there the bar. Is he not astonished? Is not the place magnificent? Being from the country (" Shocking Bœotian," says the buck compassionately to himself) he has probably never been in the house of Lords before. The old man raises his stick, and points it, tremulously, towards where, blazing in crimson velvet, embroidery and gold, is the Throne. "Never," he answers, "since I sat in that chair!" The old farmer's Double was Richard Cromwell, whilom Lord Protector of England.

Here is a placid-looking little old man, trotting briskly down John Street, Tottenham Court Road. He is about seventy, apparently, but walks erect. He has a natty little three-cornered hat, a well-brushed black suit, rather white at the seams, grey silk stockings, and silver buckles in his shoes. Two powdered *ailes de pigeon* give relief to his simple good-humoured countenance, and his hair is gathered behind into a neat pigtail, which leaves a meandering line of powder on the back of his coat. His linen is very white, so are his hands, on one of the fingers of which he wears a ring of price. He lodges in a little street in the neighbourhood I have mentioned, pays his rent regularly, has frequent friendly chats with the book-stall keepers, to whom he is, an excellent customer, and with whom he is highly popular; pats all the children on the head, and smiles affably at the maid servants. The neighbours set him down as a retired schoolmaster, a half-pay navy purser, or, perhaps, a widower with a small independence. At any rate, he is a pleasant body, and quite the gentleman. This is about the close of his Day. Would you like to know his Night? Read the Old Bailey Sessions Paper: ask the Bow Street officers, who have been tracking him for years, and have captured him at last; who are carrying him handcuffed to Newgate, to stand his trial for Murder. His double was Governor Wall, commandant of Goree, who was hanged for the murder of Serjeant Armstrong, whom he caused to be flogged to death; very strongly adjuring the negro who inflicted the torture, to cut the victim's liver out.

But I should never end were I to notice a tithe of the Days and Nights that flit across this paper while I write. A paralytic old octogenarian, drivelling, idiotic, and who, of all the passions of his other self has preserved but one,—the most grovelling avarice,—hobbles across a room, and, glancing at himself in a mirror, mutters, " That was once a man." The man was John Churchill, Duke of Marlborough. A moping invalid, imbecile and speechless, dozing in an arm-chair, sees a servant endeavouring to break an obstinate lump of coal in the grate : " It's a stone, you blackguard ! " he cries; and these are the first words he has spoken for years—the first that have passed his lips since the Day shone no more on Jonathan Swift, Dean of St. Patrick's. Anon a shrivelled little dotard, with a bald head and a yellow face, clad in a nightcap, drawers, and slippers, comes grimacing to my desk, and tells me that although it is Night now, he, Louis the Fourteenth, had his Day—*Ludovicus Magnus :* of the Porte St. Denis : Louis le Grand in the Gallery of Versailles : in a towering perruque and high-heeled shoes, giving laws to princes. A mincing gentleman in powder, with an olive or rather seagreen complexion, with a sky-blue coat, a waistcoat lined with rose-coloured satin, and silk stockings, and with an air something between a dandy and a dancing-master, tells me that, when alive, he lived over an upholsterer's shop, in the Rue St. Honoré; that he was frugal, just and incorrup-tible; that he was beloved by his landlord and landlady; but that he had a Double of the Convention and of the Com-mittee of Public Safety; a Double who swam in the blood of all that was great and noble in France ; a Double whose name was Maximilian Robespierre.

O Day and Night, but this is wondrous strange !

III.

MY philosophy makes no pretence to be elucidative or doctrinal; it is humbly suggestive. I do not presume to explain or to advise; I only crave the liberty, timidly and respectfully, to hint.

My philosophy, like the attire of a beggar, is ragged. It is disjointed, threadbare, looped and windowed with the holes that have been picked in it; patched, pinned instead of buttoned; flimsy and unsubstantial, and, consequently, undeserving (as all rags must be) of respect. But it may serve to wile away some ten minutes or so, even as a tattered little wretch was wont, in the days of long stages, to amuse the outside passengers by keeping pace with the "spanking tits," for the contingent reversion of a halfpenny; and as, in our own times, forlorn little street "Arabs" turn the somersaults known as "cartwheels" in the mud, for the amusement of the occupants of omnibus "knifeboards."

I have been philosophising lately, after my poor manner, on the dualities of men and women, of the faculty we all have, more or less, for casting our skin—for being one man abroad and another, at home; one character for the footlights, and

another, for the greenroom; of the marvellous capacity with
which we are all gifted, in greater or smaller proportions, for
playing a part, and, not only for playing one radically and
fundamentally different from the part we enact in private life,
but for playing it simultaneously with the other, and for being
(to use a very trite and imperfect Malapropism) two gentlemen
at once. Everybody, so it seems to me, can be, and is, somebody else.

You know this already, you may say, reader; but you
will not be angry with me for telling you what you knew
before. To be told what we know, flatters our self-love, and
makes us think, with some self-gratulation, of what sharp
fellows we are; but to be told that which we don't know
generally wounds our vanity or excites our scepticism, and
inclines us to a suspicion that our informant, although doubtless a well-informed person, is playing upon our credulity or
making sport of our ignorance. You will, perhaps, object
that in my theory of corporeal duality (I don't hint at the
duality of the mind, for that is a subject above my reach,
and above my ken), I am but giving another name to the
hypocrisy of mankind. But the duality I mean is not always
hypocritical. The double man is frequently unconscious of
his duality. He is as sincere in one part as he is in the
other, and believes himself just as firmly to be the person he
is representing, as an accomplished actress, such as Miss
O'Neil, would shed real, scalding tears, and sob out words
that came really from the heart; or as tipsy Manager Ellis-
ton, in the height and glory, the tinsel and Dutch metal
intoxication of a cardboard coronation, thought himself
George the Fourth in reality, and blessed his people with

vinous solemnity and sincerity. If people would place a little more credence in this duality, this Siamese-twin quality of their neighbours and of themselves, they would be more tolerant; they would not accuse of unblushing disregard of truth the gentleman who, when they had knocked at his door, entered his hall, and felt his oilcloth beneath their very feet, called, himself, over the bannisters, that he was not at home. Mr. Smith, they might thus reason, the working, novel-writing, statistic-hatching, or simply lazy and dun-hating Mr. Smith, may certainly be, and is, on the first floor landing; but the other Mr. Smith, his double, who has time to spare, and likes morning calls, and can conveniently settle the little bill his visitors may have called about, is not at home. He is a hundred miles away. He has just stepped out. It is uncertain when he will return. Duality, properly understood, would, like charity, cover a multitude of sins.

Some men are double willingly, knowingly, and with pre-meditation—they can be both wolves and lambs; and with these duplex persons, most frequently the lamb's face is the mask, and the wolf's the genuine article. Many put on masquerade knowingly but *un*willingly, and curse the mask and domino while they wear them. A great many wear double skins unconsciously, and would be surprised if you were to tell them that they once were some one else than what they are now, and that they have still another skin beneath the masquerading one. Of such is the ploughboy, over whose uncouth limbs has been dragged, slowly and painfully, a tightly fitting garment of discipline and drill. Of such is the schoolmaster who has a cricket-loving, child-petting, laughter-exciting, joke-cracking skin for inmost covering, but is swathed without in parchment bands of authority and stern words — bands scribbled over with declensions and perfects forming in *avi,* stained with ink, dusty with the powder of slate pencils, stockaded with *chevaux-de-frise* of cane and birch. There is the duality donned by the exigency of position. The fat man who knows himself inwardly, and is notoriously at home a ninny, yet, awake to the responsibility of a cocked hat and staff and gold laced coat, frowns himself into the semblance of the most austere of beadles, is a most double-faced individual. Necessity is the mother not only of invention, but of duality in men; and habit is the great wet nurse. She suckles the twins, and sends them forth into the world.

Look at Lord de Rougecoffer, Secretary of the department of State for no matter what affairs, and see how double a man habit has made him. To look at him, throning on the Treasury bench, you would think that nothing less than the great cauldron of broth political could simmer and bubble beneath his hat, and that the domestic *pot-au-feu* could find no place there. To hear him pleading with all the majesty of official eloquence the cause of tapeism, irremediably crushing into an inert and shapeless mass her Majesty's Opposition on the other side of the house (he has been crushed himself, many a time, when *he* sat opposite, and is none the worse for the crushing at this hour); sonorously rapping the tin box of office, zealously coughing down injudicious grievance-mongers, nay, even winking at his subordinates while they imitate the cries of the inferior animals, for the better carrying on of the Government of which he is a member : To watch the wearying and laborious course of his

official life, the treadmill industry to which he is daily and
nightly doomed, the matter-of-fact phraseology and action to
which he is confined ; to observe all this you might think that
he was a mere incarnation of Hansard's Debates, Babbage's
calculating machines, and Walkingame's Tutor's Assistant,
indefinitely multiplied ; that his bowels were of red tape, his
blood of liquified sealing-wax, his brain a pulp of mashed blue-
books. Yet this Lord de Rougecoffer of Downing Street, the
Treasury bench, and the division-lobby, this crusher of Opposition and pooh-pooher of deputations, and stifler of grievances,
has a Double in Belgrave Square, enthusiastically devoted to
the acquisition of Raphaels, Correggios, Dresden china and
Etruscan vases; a Double so thoroughly a *magister coquinæ*
that he seriously contemplates writing a cookery-book some
day, at his leisure—but he will know no leisure, on this side
the grave, until he is made a Peer, or is paralysed—a Double
enjoying Punch, and with an acknowledged partiality for
Ethiopian serenaders; a Double at a beautiful park down in
Hampshire, who is regarded as an oracle on all matters
connected with agriculture by ill-used and ruined gentlemen
with top-boots and heavy gold chains; who has a taste
almost amounting to a foible for the cultivation of exotic
flowering plants; a Double who is the delight of the smaller
branches of a large family; who can do the doll trick to a
nicety, make plum-puddings in his hat, cut an orange into a
perfect Chinese puzzle of shapes, and make as excellent a
" back " at leap frog as any young gentleman from the ages
of eight to twelve, inclusive, could desire. The Lord in
Downing Street rolls out statistics by the column; the Lord
in Belgrave Square is an indifferent hand at counting at

counting at whist, and never could understand a betting-book. The Lord in private life is a nobleman of unimpeach-able veracity, of unquestioned candour and sincerity, and enjoys the possession of an excellent memory; the Lord in St. Stephen's confidently affirms black to be white, shuffles, prevaricates, and backs out of obligations in an unseemly manner, and has a convenient forgetfulness of what he has said or done, and what he ought and has promised, to say or do, which is really surprising.

Habit gives a double cuticle to Mr. John Trett (of the firm of Tare and Trett) of the city of London, ship-broker. One Mr. Trett is a morose despot, with a fierce whisker, a malevolent white neckcloth, and a lowering eye. He is the terror of his clerks, the bane of ship-captains, the bugbear of the Jerusalem coffee-house. His surly talk is of ships that ought not to have come home in ballast, and underwriters on whom he will be " down ;" of confounded owners, of freights not worth twopence, of ships gone to the dogs, and customers not worth working for. He is a hard man, and those who serve him, he says, do not earn their salt. He is a tempe-rate man, and refuses chop-and-sherry invitations with scorn. He is a shabbily dressed man, and groans at the hardness of the times; yet he has a double at Dalston worth fifty thousand pounds, the merriest, most jovial, chirruping, middle-aged gentleman, with the handsomest house, the most attached servants, the largest assortment of comic albums and scrap books, and the prettiest daughters that eyes could wish to behold. He is something more than an amateur on the violoncello, although Giuseppe Pizzicato, from Genoa, was last week brought to Guildhall, at the complaint of Mr.

Treet's double, charged with outraging the tranquillity of Copperbottom Court, Threadneedle Street, where the ship-brokers have their offices, by the performance of airs from Don Giovanni on the hurdy-gurdy. East of Temple Bar Trett abhors the juice of the grape; at Dalston he has an undeniable taste for old Port, and is irresistible in the pro-position of " another bottle." It is quite a sight, when he insists on fetching this same "other bottle" from some peculiar and only-to-himself known bin, to see him emerging from the cellar beaming with smiles, cobwebs, and old Port wine. He is an excellent father, a liberal master, a jewel of a man at Dalston : only beware of him in Copperbottom Court. Temple Bar is the scarifier that performs the flaying operation upon him, and trust me, the under city skin is a rough and a hard one.

When you walk into Lincoln's Inn old square, and up the rotten staircase (worn with despairing client's footsteps) of No. 202; when you read on a scowling door an inscription purporting that it is the entrance to Messrs. Harrow and Wrench's offices; when, opening that door, which creaks on its hinges as though clients were being squeezed behind it, you push open the inner portal of baize, which yields with a softness equal to the velvet of a cat's paw; when you have waited a sufficient time in the outer office, and shuddered at the pale and sallow-visaged runners, and the ghastly Law Almanack, like Charles the First's death warrant, in a black frame, and listened to the grim music of the busy-writing clerks, scoring the doom of clients on parchment cut from clients' skins, with pens trimmed from clients' feathers, with ink distilled from clients' blood, tempered with the gall of law (as all these matters appear to you); when you are at last admitted to the inner sanctum, and to an interview with Mr. Harrow; when, as a debtor, you have begged for time, for lenity, for mercy, and have been refused; or, as a creditor, listened to Mr. Harrow's bland promises to sell Brown up, to seize Jones's sticks, to take care that Smith does not pass his last examination, to serve Tompkins with a *ne exeat*, and to sue out process of outlawry against Robinson; when you have paid a bill of costs, or have been presented with one which you have not the remotest chance of paying; when you have sustained all the misery and madness of the law's delay, and all the insolence of the office, you will very probably descend the staircase, commending the whole temple of injustice, cruelty, and chicane, to Ahriman and other demoniacal persons. Mr. Harrow will seem to you an embodied ghoul; Mr. Wrench, a vampire, with a whole faggot of legal sticks and staves through what *ought* to be his heart, but *is* a rule to show cause. The scribbling clerks, the tallow-visaged runners, the greasy process-servers, the villainous bailiff's followers snuffing up the scent of a debtor to be trapped from the instructions of a clerk—all these will appear to you cannibals, blood-suckers, venomous reptiles, hating their fellow-creatures, and a-hungered for their entrails. Yet, all these useful members of society are dualities; they have all their doubles. Mr. Harrow leaves his inexorable severity, his savage appetite for prey on his faded green-baize table. In Guildford Street, Russell Square, he gives delightful evening parties, loses his money at cards with charming complacency, and is never proof against petitions for new bonnets from his daughters, for autumn excursions from his wife, for ten-pound notes from his son at Cambridge. Mr. Wrench (who more particularly looks after the selling-up and scarifying business) is an active member of the Society for the Prevention of Cruelty to Animals, and is quite a "Man of Ross" among the poor crossing-sweepers in the neighbourhood of his residence. The chief clerk (who has the keenest nose and sharpest talon for a recalcitrant bankrupt of any managing clerk in the square) keeps rabbits, portioned his laundress's daughter when she married, and always weeps when he goes to the play, and the "Rent Day" is performed. The clerks who write the doom of clients, the runners, the process-servers, leave their deadly cunning, and remorseless writs, and life-destroying processes in their desks and blue bags and greasy leathern pouches; they leave their skins behind too; and, after office-hours, are joyous boon companions, irreproachable husbands in small suburban cottages, sweethearts leaving nothing to be desired, free-hearted roysterers always willing to be their twopence to another's twopence, men and brothers feeling another's woe, hiding the faults they see, showing mercy, inter-aiding and assisting each other. And, believe me, this species of duality is not the most uncommon. The butcher is, nine times out of ten, kind-hearted and peaceable at home; Sanson, the executioner, had a passion for the cultivation of flowers, and played prettily on the piano; General Haynau, I dare say (for the sake of argument, at least), was a "love" of an old gentleman in private life, with *such* "loves" of grey moustachios, and *so* full of anecdote! * Do you think the tiger is always savage

* I really met the General at a German watering place, and found

and brutal in domestic life; that the hyena does not laugh good-humouredly in the bosom of his family; that the wolf can't be sociable? No such thing. I dare say that clouds do sometimes obscure the zoological felicity; that Mrs. Tiger occasionally complains, should the antelope be tough or the marrow scanty; that Miss Hyena may lament the hardness of the times and the scarcity of carrion; and that Mr. Lupus may do worse than he expected during the winter; but I think the wild beasts can't be always howling, and yelling, and craunching, and tearing at home?

We grow so accustomed to see people in one character and costume, that we can scarcely fancy the possibility of that duality they certainly possess. For us the lion must be always lying in a hole under a rock, waiting for a traveller. We ignore his duality, the lion at home. We have grown so accustomed to a Mr. Phelps in a spangled Roman toga, or a Mr. Buckstone in a skyblue coat and scanty nankeen trousers, that we can't fancy those admired actors in private life, save in theatrical costumes, asking for beer in blank verse, in the first case; throwing the spectators in convulsions of laughter by poking the fire, in the second. We so mix up double men, and double dresses, and double avocations, that we fail to recognize even persons with whom we are familiar when they have laid the state dress and state character aside, and walk abroad plain men. We see a quiet-looking gentleman in plain black cheapening asparagus in Covent Garden Market, and we are told that he is the Speaker of the House of

him the pet of the table-d'hôte, and an immense favourite with the ladies. He once won a very large sum at Hombourg, and on his departure, gave a handsome percentage of his winnings to the poor.

Commons. Where are his bagwig, and his mace, that he should use as a walkingstick, or, at least, carry under his arm like an umbrella? Where is his three-cornered hat, with which he accomplishes those curious hanky-panky tricks in counting members? We are shewn a stout gentleman in a white hat and a cut away coat close to a handsome quiet-looking man, smoking a cigar, and are told that one designed the Crystal Palace, and that the other raised the Britannia Bridge.* Where are their compasses, their rules, their squares? Why don't they walk about the streets with their hands thrust in their waistcoats, their hair thrown back, and their eyes in a fine frenzy rolling? Without going quite so far as the boy who believed that every judge was born with a wig on his head and ermine on his shoulders, can you, can I, fancy a judge in a jacket and wide-a-wake hat? or, again, a judge in opera tights and a crush hat exchanging fisticuffs with a dandy in the stalls of Her Majesty's theatres? Is there not something incongruous and inharmonious in the realization of the picture of an archbishop in a linsey-woolsey nightcap? We can fancy a burglar cleaning his dark lantern, oiling his centre-bit, loading his pistols; but can we fancy him tending his sick wife, or playing with his children?

It may be the ruling habit, after all, and not the ruling passion, that is strong in death. The schoolmaster who directed his school to "dismiss;" the judge who sent the jury to consider of their verdict; the warrior who murmured *tête d'armée;* the mathematician who gave the square of twelve; the jester who said "drop the curtain; the farce is over;" all these responded more to some watchword of habit,

* R. S., ob. 1859.

D

than of a predominant passion. Doctor Black, though an excellent schoolmaster, can hardly be said to have had a *passion* for teaching boys their accidence; it was, perhaps, more the habit of the judge to sum up evidence for the jury, than his passion; although Napoleon certainly had a passion for war, the mathematican (I forget his name) was habituated to arithmetrical exercises, and gave the square of twelve through the force of habit; and as for the jester, as for Francis Rabelais, he was, for all his strange wild talk, a just and pious man; and it must have been the form, rather than the spirit, of a jest that he is said to have uttered in his last moments. Among the instances where the ruling passion does really seem to have been strong in death, those of the miser who wished the candle to be extinguished, as "he could die in the dark;" and the Highland Cateran* who objected to extreme unction as an "unco' waste of ulzie;" seem to me the most worthy of notice, though I am afraid the foundation on which their authenticity rests is rather dubious.

* Rob Roy

IV.

THE GOLDEN CALF.

READER, were you ever in—
I have a difficulty in expressing the word. Four little letters would serve my turn; but I dare not—this being above all for Household eyes—write them down. I might say Tophet, Hades, the place that is said to be paved with good intentions, the locality where old maids lead specimens of the simious race, Purgatory, L'Inferno, Tartarus; the debateable land where Telemachus (under the guidance of good Archbishop Fénélon, taking the pseudonym of Mentor) went to seek for Ulysses; all sorts of things; but, none of them would come up in terseness and comprehensiveness to the name the place is really called by, and which it is really like.

Readers, were you ever in Bartholomew Lane in the city of London. There is the wall of the Bank of England; there the Rotunda with those pleasant swing doors that with their "out" and "in" seem to bear the converse of Dante's immortal inscription; for who enters there takes Hope along with him—the hope of the residuary legatee, and the executor, and the dividend warrant bearer, and the government annuitant. There are the men who sell the dog-collars; the badly painted, well varnished pictures (did ever anybody buy one of those pictures, save perhaps a mad heir, frantic with the vanity of youthful blood to spend the old miser his grandfather's savings, and by misuse to poison good?); the spurious bronze sixpenny popguns; and the German silver pencil cases. There, above all are sold those marvellous pocket-books, with metallic pages, everlasting pencils, elastic straps, snap-locks, almanacs of the month, tables of the eclipses of the moon, the tides, the price of stamps, compound interest, the rate of wages, the birthdays of the Royal Family, and the list of London bankers—those pocket-books full of artful pockets—sweetly smelling pouches—for gold, silver, or notes, that suggest inexhaustible riches; and that a man must buy if he have money, and very often does buy, being without, but hoping to have some. I have such a pocket-book to this day. It is old, greasy, flabby, white at the edges now; but it burst with banknotes once—yea, burst —the strap flying one way and the clasp the other; and on its ass-skin opening pages were memoranda of the variations of the funds. There in the distance is Lothbury, whose very name is redolent of bullion—the dwelling-place of the golden Jones and the Loyds made of money; of auriferous gold-heavers in dusky counting-houses, who shovel out gold and weigh sovereigns until their hands become clogged and clammy with the dirt of dross, and they wash them perforce. There is the great Mammon Club, the Stock Exchange, where bulls and bears in white hats and cutaway coats are now frantic about the chances of the Derby favourite, and the next pigeon match at the Red House; now about three and a quarter for the account and Turkish scrip; now about a "little mare," name unknown, that can be backed to do wonderful things, anywhere, for any amount of money; but who allow no one to be frantic within the walls of their club under a subscription of ten guineas per annum; tarring, feathering, flouring, bonneting, and otherwise demolishing all those who dare to worship Mammon without a proper introduction and a proper burnt-offering. All Bartholomew Lane smells of money. Orange tawny canvas bags; escorted Pickford vans with bullion for the Bank cellars; common-looking packing-cases full of ingots that might turn Bethnal Green into Belgravia; bankers' clerks with huge pocket-books secured by iron chains round their bodies, holding bills and checks for thousands; stockbrokers, billbrokers, sharebrokers, money-brokers' offices; greasy men selling Birmingham sovereigns for a penny a piece (and a wager, of course); auctioneers, at the great roaring mart, knocking down advowsons and cures of souls to the highest bidder: there is gold everywhere in pockets, hearts, minds, souls, and strengths—gold, " bright and yellow, hard and cold "—gold for bad and gold for good,—

> " Molten, graven, hammer'd and roll'd,—
> Heavy to get, and light to hold,
> Now stamped with the image of Good Queen Bess,
> . And now of a Bloody Mary."

But how about the place I did not care to name? This. Little reck the white-neckclothed clergymen, so demure, so snug, so unimpeachable in umbrella; the old ladies in their gray shawls and coal-scuttle bonnets; the young spend-thrifts flushed with the announcement of so much money

standing in their names in Consols, and eager to find bro-
kers to sell out for them ; the anomalous well-dressed,
watch-chained, clean-shaven class, who seem to make it a
pretext for having " business in the city " to consume
bowls of soup at the Cock in Threadneedle Street, or sandwiches and sherry at Garraways ; — little do these harmless votaries of Mammon know of the existence of a sul-
phureous subterranean in the vicinity, where Mammon strips
off his gold-laced coat and cocked hat; sends Dei Gratiâ
packing ; and puts on his proper livery of horns and hoofs
and a tail ; where the innoxious veal pie in Birch the pastrycook's window in Cornhill casts off its crust—has four legs,
horns, and a yellow coat, and stands on a pedestal—the
Golden Calf—in—the place I won't mention to ears polite.

Under Capel Court, where the lame ducks, the disem-
bodied spirits of ruined stockbrokers hover, like phantoms,
on the banks of the Styx with no halfpenny to pay their
ferry-boat over, there is a staircase—foul, stony, precipitous
and dark—like one in a station-house or the poor side of a
debtors' prison.   Such establishments have no monopoly of
underground staircases like these that lead from life and
liberty to squalor, misery, and captivity.   At the bottom of
the staircase there is a board which some misanthropic brewer
has cast into the pit (hoping to find it eventually), relative to
entire porter and sparkling ales.   Placards also, telling of
wines and spirits, are as distinct as the gloominess of a place
rivalling a coal-cellar in obscurity and a bear-pit in savagery,
will allow them to be.   This place is a public-house and—
well, let us compromise the matter, and call it Hades.

You have very little opportunity of judging what the

place is like inside. You only know that it is dark and full
of smoke and men. Walls, bar, chairs, tables, drinking-
vessels must be of little account when the noblest study of
mankind—being, as it is well known, man—man, compasses
you round about, a smoking, drinking, whiskered, hoarse,
squabbling, shrieking crowd. Here a boastful buck, all
rings and rags. Here rags in their unadulterated condition,
but laced with grease and slashed with prospectuses and
share-lists. Here roguery, in luck, with clothes all too new,
and that will become old before their time, acting the cheap
Amphytrion in beer and pipes. Here carcasses without
gibbets and gibbets without carcasses looking hungrily upon
those who feed. Here utter broken-down misery: hunger
that was once well-fed—that has lent to many, but is
ashamed to borrow; perfect poverty that has no game up—
no little caper—that is not fly to anything—that has no
irons in the fire—that knows no parties—that can put you
up to no first-rate moves—that is not waiting for a chance
or to see its way, or something to turn up, but is only too
glad to warm itself at an eleemosynary fire, and inhale the
fumes of other men's tobacco, and wrap itself as in a garment with the steam of the fried onions of the more prosperous, and brood quietly in a corner of this Bartholomew
Lane Hades, ever remembering that it is a beggar, and that
it was once worth a hundred thousand pounds.

You that have heard of commercial manias, and that they
are periodical, don't believe in their transient nature. There
is always a Mania. Speculation never lulls. When thousands are shy, sixpence halfpenny offers. Mammon tempers
the wind to the shorn speculator. There is always some-

thing up. Thus in this Hades when railways are flat, there is always something to be done in gold mines. When the auriferous veins run short, there are nice little pickings to be got out of amalgamated companies for the exploitation of coal; strata of which are always found in the very nick of time somewhere where they were never heard or dreamed of before. Should the yield of the black diamond prove unremunerative, a rich vein of lead is sure to turn up at those famous Pyngwylly-Tuddyllyg mines in Wales, where lead has been promising for so many years, and has swallowed up so many thousand pounds in red gold, and driven so many Welsh squires to madness, or the Bankruptcy Court. Copper (somewhere between Honolulu and Vancouver's Island), or quicksilver (anywhere in the Sou-west-by-eastern latitudes) can scarcely fail when lead is scarce. When metals are at a discount, Land Companies; Emigration Companies; Extra-Economical Gas Companies, to give consumers gas (in their own pipes) at a penny farthing per thousand feet; Economical Funeral Companies—a shroud, a leaden coffin, mutes with silk scarves, gloves, hatbands, cake and wine, and a tombstone surmounted by a beautiful sculptured allegory of the three Graces inciting the trumpet of Fame to sound the praises of the domestic Virtues—all for three pound ten; Economical Hotel Companies—beds free, breakfasts gratis, wax candles for nothing, and no charge for waiters—Loan Societies, lending any amount of money on personal security at nominal rates of interest; Freehold Land and Building Societies, by subscribing to which (no fines, no stoppages, no entrance money), parties can become their own landlords—dwelling in houses as big as that once occupied by Count

Walewski at Albert Gate, and walking fifty miles per diem, if they choose, on their own land—in the short space of three months from day of enrolment; Guarantee Societies for securing merchants and bankers against dishonest clerks, landlords from non-rent paying tenants, sheep from the rot, pigs from the measles, feet from corns, drunkards from red noses, and quiet, country parsonages from crape-masked burglars. Such, and hundreds more such companies are always somehow in the market, suspectible of being quoted, advertised, and bruited about in Hades. There are always sufficient of these evanescent specs afloat for appointments to be made between dingy men; for pots of beer to be called for on the strength of; for letters to be written (on the first sheet of the half quire of sleezy post, purchased with borrowed halfpence from the cheap stationer—he who also sells greengrocery and penny blacking—in Stag's Head Court); for the pot-boy to be importuned for wafers; for a Post-office Directory of the year before last to be in immense request; for postage-stamps to be desired with a mad unquenchable (ofttimes hopeless) longing; for pipes to be lit, and the unwonted extravagance of another screw indulged in; for pens to be anxiously bitten, gnawed, and sucked; for the thick black mud at the bottom of the greasy, battered inkstand to be patiently scraped up, as if there were indeed a Pactolus at the bottom; for intricate calculations to be made with scraps of chalk, or wet fingers on the dinted table—the old, old, flatteringly fallacious calculations that prove with such lying accuracy that where there are no proceeds the profits must be necessarily very large: that two and two infallibly make five, and that from a capital of nothing, interest of at least seventy

per centum per annum must immediately accrue; for those
worn, tattered, disreputable old pocket books at whose existence I have already hinted to be unbuckled and disembowelled;
for the old dog's-eared bundles of foolscap to be dug up from
the recesses of the old scarecrow hat with the crape round it
—the hat that certainly holds, in addition, the lamentable
ninepenny cotton pocket-handkerchief full of holes, and perhaps the one black worsted glove without finger-tops; and
not impossibly the threepen'north of boiled beef for to-night's
supper; for, finally the "party" to be waited for—the party
who has money, and believes in the scheme; the party who
is seldom punctual, and sometimes fails altogether in keeping
his appointment—but when he does come produces a plea-
surable sensation in Hades by the sight of his clean shirt, un-
patched boots, nappy hat and watchchain :—who cries out
with a loud confident voice, "What are you drinking, gentlemen? Beer? Psha—have something warm;" and orders
the something warm; and throws down the broad, brave five
shilling piece to pay for it; and, with his creaking boots, his
shining jewellery, and big cigar-case (to say nothing of that
new silk umbrella, which did it belong to the speculator in
the blue goggles and check trousers opposite would be in less
than half-an-hour safe in the Times office in Printing House
Square, in the shape at least, of a five and sixpenny advertisement of the "Putative nephews and Cousins-german Tontine
and Mutual Assurance Company," provisionally registered),
infuses unutterable envy of gold into ragged Hunger yonder,
who whispers to unquenched Thirst his neighbour, that Tom
Lotts has got hold of another good card, and what a lucky
fellow he is !

Moons and stars! can anything equal the possessed state of mind of a man with a scheme? A man walks about, pulls his hair, talks folly, writes nonsense, makes a fool of himself about a fair woman. He falls enamoured of a picture, an opera tune, a poem with a new thought in it. A friend's goodness moves him quite to forget his own, till the friend turns out a rascal. A new country, city, house may engross all his admiration, observation, appreciation, till he becomes immensely bored; but give him a scheme—a project, that he thinks he can make his fortune by. Set up *that* Golden Calf on the altar of his heart, and you will never find him writing letters to the Times to complain of the length of Mammon's liturgy, as some short-breathed Christians do of that of the Church of England. Twenty full services a day will not be too much for him. As he walks the streets, his scheme precedes him as the pillar of cloud and fire went before the Israelites of old. When he reads the share list in the newspapers, the market prices of his company stand out in highest altitude of relief, and quote themselves in letters of burnished gold. It is a fine day in November when his scheme is at premium; it freezes in July when it is a discount. There are no names in the Court Guide so aristocratic as those in his committee (with power to add to their number). He envies no one. Nor dukes their gilded chariots, nor bucks in the parks their hundred guinea horses, nor members of clubs their Pall Mall palaces, nor M.P.'s their seats in the House; nor peers their robes, nor earls their yachts, nor mayors their chairs, nor aldermen their turtle, nor squires their broad lands, parks, and deer; nor judges their old port; nor college dons their claret and red mullet; nor bankers their parlours;

nor old ladies their dividends. All these things and more
will belong to him when his scheme pays. The rainbow
waistcoats in the shops are ticketed expressly for his eye, to
fix themselves on his remembrance till the project succeeds,
and he can buy them. Mr. Benson is now manufacturing
gold watches, Mr. Hoby boots, Mr. Sangster jewelled walk-
ing-sticks ; Mr. Hart is new painting the Trafalgar at Green-
wich, redecorating the Collingwood room, and bottling milk
punch by the thousand dozen ; Messrs. Hedges and Butler
are laying down Champagne and Johannisberger ; Messrs.
Fortnum and Mason are importing truffles, *pâté-de-foie-gras*,
Narbonne honey, Belgian ortolans, edible birds'-nests, and
Russian caviare ; Messrs. Laurie are building carriages with
silver axle-boxes, and emblazoned hammer-cloths ; Messrs.
Day and Scott are training two-year-olds at Newmarket ; all
expressly for him when his scheme comes into its property,
and he has twenty thousand pounds to spare in trifles. For
that good time coming, Mr. Cubitt is running up a few nine-
storied houses or so down Kensington way ; some half dozen
members of parliament—all staunch conservatives, of course,
as befits men of property—are thinking seriously of accepting
the Chiltern Hundreds ; and two or three peers of the realm
are going to the dogs as fast as they can, in order to be sold
up, and their estates, country houses, manorial rights disposed
of (in good time) to the lucky possessor of the successful
scheme. Which is the philosopher's stone. Which is the
latch-key to Thomas Tiddler, his ground, Which, even in
abeyance, even in the topmost turret of a castle in the air,
can yet comfort, solace, soothe the schemer, making him forget hunger, thirst, cold, sleeplessness, debt, impending death.

Which is Alnaschar's basket of glass, and is kicked down
often into the kennel, with a great clatter, and ruin of tum-
blers, pepper-casters, and hopes.   Yet to have a scheme, and
to believe in it, is to be happy.   Do you think Solomon de
Caux, crazy, ragged, in the Bicêtre, did not believe that his
scheme would triumph eventually, and he be sent for to Versailles, while the mad-house keeper and all unbelievers in
steam engines were to be conveyed incontinently to the gallies?
Do you think that that poor worn-out loyal gentleman, the
Marquis of Worcester, cared one jot for the hundreds of
thousands of pounds he had lost in the king's service, while
he yet had schemes and inventions, which *must* at last turn
out successful, and bring him fame and fortune?   Do you
think that the alchemists grudged their patrimonies smould-
ered away in the crucible; or that the poor captain, who
imagined if he did not perfectly invent the long range, was
not comforted even on his death-bed, by the persuasion that
the Great Mogul, the Grand Serag, the King of Oude, the
Lama of Thibet, or the Tycoon of Japan, must come before
life was extinct, and buy the great invention, though English
Boards of Ordnance, and European potentates looked coldly
upon it, for millions sterling, down?   Do you think that
Corney O'Gripper yonder, though ragged and penniless, is not
happy while he has some old "schame" to propound, or some
new one to perfect?

Corney has a most puissant and luxuriant head of hair—
the only thing that is rich about him.   It is a popular belief
that Corney scratches his various "schames" ready made out
of this head of hair as the cock in the fable did the pearl.
At all events his long fingers are continually busied in the

tufted recesses of his head-thatch, and as he scratches he pro-
pounds. His attire is very bad, but black. In his very worst
phase of costume he was never known to wear any waiscoat
than a black satin one, any coat but a swallow tail. Both
these articles of apparel show much more of the lining than is
consonant with our received notions of taste in costume.
From one imputation, however, they must be exempt.
Numerous as are their crevices and gaps they never disclose
the existence of such an article as a shirt. On wet days
the soles of his boots whistle like blackbirds, or (occasionally)
oysters. He wears a black stock, the original satin fabric of
which has gone away mournfully into shreds, and shows a
dingy white substance beneath, wavering in appearance between sackcloth and buckram. It is rumoured that Corney
O'Gripper has been a hedge schoolmaster, a coast-guardsman,
an illicit whisky-distiller, a guager, a sapper and miner, a
pawnbroker, a surgeon on the coast of Africa, a temperance
lecturer, a repealer, a fishmonger, a parish clerk, an advertis-
ing agent, a servants' registry office-keeper, a supercargo, a
collector of rents, a broker's man, an actor, a roulette table-
keeper on a race-course, a publican, a betting office-keeper, an
itinerant, a lawyer's clerk, a county court bailiff, and a life
assurance actuary. He confesses himself to have been a
"tacher;" also to having been in America, where he did
something considerable in town-lots, in the bank-notes known
as shin plaisters, and where he was blown up in a Mississippi
steam-boat; also to having passed twice through the Insolvent
Court. His present profession, and one that he glories in, is
that of a "promoter." A promoter of what? Companies.
He knows of a Spanish galleon sunk in the bay of Vera Cruz,

in Admiral Hosier's time, with two millions five hundred and
seventy thousand pounds sterling in doubloons, pillar dollars,
and golden candlesticks destined for the chapel of our St. Jago
of Compostella, on board. A joint stock company is just the
thing to fish her up, and secure a bonus of two hundred and
forty per cent. to every one of the shareholders. He only
wants a few good men to complete the list of directors of the
Great Female Moses Company, or Emporium of Ladies'
Ready-made Wearing Apparel Society. Lend him sixpence
and he will be enabled provisionally to register the Curing
Herrings on the North-west Coast of Ireland Company. He
is to be managing director of the Persons-condemned-to-
Capital-Punishment Life Assurance Society; he promoted the
Joint Stock Housebreakers' Investment Company ; the Naval,
Military, European, and General Pickpockets' Savings Bank
and Sick Fund; the Amalgamated Society for binding and
illustrating Cheesemongers' and Trunkmakers' Wastepaper ;
the Mutual Silver Snuff-box Voting Company ; the Bank-
rupts' Guarantee Fund ; and the Insolvents' Provident Institution. But the world has dealt hardly with him. No sooner
has he promoted companies and set them on their legs, than
solicitors have flouted, directors repudiated him. He has
nothing left now but his inextinguishable brogue, and his
inexhaustible invention. He will go on promoting till he
goes to utter penury, brokendownedness, and the workhouse ;
and let me whisper it to you, among all the wild, impossible,
crazy " schames " to which the tufted head of Corney O'Gripper has given birth, there have been some not quite wanting
in feasibility and success. There are at this moment companies with lofty-sounding names—with earls for chairmen ;

companies that spend thousands a year in advertisements, and have grand offices in Cannon Street and branch offices in Waterloo Place—that were in the origin promoted by this poor ragged creature, who is not too proud to sit on the tap-room bench in the Hades under Capel Court : who is only too happy to borrow ninepence, and who sleeps no one knows where, and feeds on fried fish, baked potatoes, saveloys, penny ham sandwiches and meat pies, when he is lucky enough even to be able to procure those simple viands.

Thus wags the world in the place I do not care to name. I wonder what should set—humph—Hades—running in my head this evening, and move me to descant upon it, for it is more than a year agone since I was there. What have the pewter pots, the rank tobacco, the shabby men, the fried beef-steaks and onions, the rummers of spirits and the sawdust of that old English Inferno in common with the pier-glass and arabesque decorated café, the marble table and crimson velvet couches where I sit—the opal-like scintillating glass of absinthe I am imbibing on the great Paris Boulevard, hard by the Café de l'Opéra? I have not been to the Bourse to-day, though I know *that* great screaming, tumbling, temple of Mammon well, and of old : its hot, reeking atmosphere, the snow storm of torn scraps of paper on its pavement ; the great inner and outer rings where the bulls and bears offer, refuse, scream, and gesticulate at each other like madmen ; the lofty galleries where crowds of idlers, mostly in blouses, lounge with crossed arms over the balustrades, lazily listening to the prodigious clamour that rises to the vaulted roof— the Kyrie Eleison of the worshippers of Mammon ; the deceptive frescoes on the cornices that look so like bas-reliefs ; the ushers in uniform darting about with the course of exchange lists; the municipal guards and gendarmes; the nursery maids and children that come here for amusement (where will not nursery maids and children come?), the trebly serried ranks of private carriages, fiacres and cabriolets in the place outside. No, I have not been to the Bourse. I sit quietly smoking a penny cigar and imbibing eight sous worth of absinthe preparatory to going to my friend Madame Busque's to dinner. Whatever can put Hades into my head this December evening I wonder?

This. The *café* where I sit (I was all unconscious of it before) is Hades; and in its pier-glassed precincts from five to seven every evening, sometimes later, the adorers of the Golden Calf go through their orisons (oh forgive me if I am free-tongued!) like the very deuce. For know you that, the Bourse being closed, the gaping for gain is by no means closed in the hearts of men. They rush to this *café*, hard by the Passage de l'Opéra and get up a little Bourse of their own—an illegitimate Bourse be it understood, and one, when its members are detected in speculating, treated with considerable severity by the government. Before I have been in the place ten minutes Sebastopol has been taken,—retaken—the allies defeated—kings and emperors assassinated twenty times over. Bank notes, Napoleons, and five franc pieces are strewn on the table amidst absinthe glasses, dominoes, decanters, and cigar ends. Moustachioed men lean over my shoulder and shake pencils at their opposite neighbours fiercely. Seedy men sit silent, in corners; prosperous speculators pay with shining gold. Shrieks of *vingt-cinq, trente, quatre-vingt-cinq* are bandied about like insults.

E

It is the old under-Capel-Court Inferno with a few moustaches, some plate-glass, and a ribbon or two of the Legion
of Honour; and as I finish my absinthe in the din, I seem
to see the Golden Calf on the marble, plate-covered counter,
very rampant indeed.

V.

A NEW RAILWAY LINE.

IF I succeed in the object I have proposed to myself in this paper, I shall consider that I am entitled to the gratitude of all poets, present and to come. For I shall have found them a new subject for verse: a discovery, I submit, as important as that of a new metal, or of a new motive power, a new pleasure, a new pattern for shawls, a new colour, or a new system of philosophy. No member of the tuneful craft; no gentleman whose eyes are in the habit of rolling in a fine frenzy; no sentimental young lady with an album will deny that the whole present domain of poetry is exhausted :—that it has been surveyed, travelled over, explored, ticketed, catalogued, classified, analysed and used up to the last inch of ground, to the last petal of the last flower, to the last blade of grass. Every poetical subject has been worn as threadbare as Sir John Cutler's stockings. The sea, its blueness, depth, vastness, raininess, freedom, noisiness, calmness, darkness, and brightness; its weeds and waves and finny denizens; its laughter, wailings, sighings, and deep bellowings; the ships that sail, and the boats that dance, and the tempests that howl over it; the white winged birds that skim above its billows; the great whales, and sharks, and monsters, to us yet unknown, that disport themselves in its lowest depths, and swinge the scaly horrors of their folded tails in its salt hiding places; the mermaids that ply their mirrors, and comb their tresses in its coral caves; the sirens that sing fathoms farther than plummet ever sounded; the jewels and gold that lie hidden in its caverns, measureless to man; the dead that it is to give up :—the Sea, and all pertaining to it, have been sung dry these thousand years. We heard the roar of its billows in the first line of the Iliad, and Mr. Mugg, the comic singer, will sing about it this very night at the North Woolwich Gardens, in connection with the Gravesend steamer, the steward, certain basins, and a boiled leg of mutton.

As for the Sun, he has had as many verses written about him as he is miles distant from the earth. His heat, brightness, roundness, and smiling face; his incorrigible propensities for getting up in the east and going to bed in the west; his obliging disposition in tipping the hills with gold, and bathing the evening sky with crimson, have all been sung. Every star in the firmament has had a stanza; Saturn's rings have all had their posies, and Mars, Venus and Jupiter, have all been chanted. As for the poor illused Moon, she has been ground on every barrel-organ in Parnassus since poetry existed. Her pallid complexion, chastity or lightness of conduct, treacherous, contemplative, or secretive disposition, her silvery or sickly smile, have all been over-celebrated in verse. And everything else belonging to the sky—the clouds, murky, purple, or silver lined, the hail, the rain, the snow, the rainbow, the wind in its circuits, the fowls that fly, and the insects that hover—they have all had their poets, and too many of them.

Is there anything new in poetry, I ask, to be said about Love? Surely that viand has been done to rags. We have it with every variety of dressing. Love and madness; love and smiles, tears, folly, crime, innocence, and charity. We have had love in a village, a palace, a cottage, a camp, a prison, and a tub. We have had the loves of pirates, highwaymen, lords and ladies, shepherds and shepherdesses; the Loves of the Angels and the Loves of the New Police. Canning was even good enough to impress the abstruse science of mathematics into the service of Poetry and Love; and to sing about the loves of ardent axioms, postulates, tangents, oscillation, cissoids, conchoids the square of the hypothenuse, asymptotes, parabolas, and conic sections—in short, all the Loves of the Triangles. Doctor Darwin gave us the Loves of the Plants, and in the economy of vegetation we had the loves of granite rocks, argillaceous strata, noduled flints, blue clay, silica, quartz, and the limestone formation. We have had in connection with love in poetry hearts, darts, spells, wrath, despair, withering smiles, burning tears, sighs, roses, posies, pearls and other precious stones; blighted hopes, beaming eyes, misery, wretchedness, and unutterable woe. It is too much. Everything is worn out. The whole of the flower-garden, from the brazen sunflower to the timid violet, has been exhausted long ago. All the birds in the world could never sing so loud or so long as the poets have sung about them. The bards have sung right through Lemprière's Classical Dictionary, Buffon's Natural History, Malte-Brun's Geography—for what country, city, mountain, or stream, remains unsung?—and the Biographie Universelle to boot. Every hero, and almost every scoundrel, has had his epic. We have had the poetical Pleasures of Hope, Memory, Imagination, and Friendship; likewise the Vanity of Human Wishes, the Fallacies of Hope, and the Triumphs of Temper. The heavenly muse has sung of man's first disobedience, and the mortal fruit of the forbidden tree, that brought Death into the world and all our woes. The honest muse has arisen and sung the Man of Ross. All the battles that ever were fought—all the arms and all the men—have been celebrated in numbers. Arts, commerce, laws, learning, and our old nobility, have had their poet. Suicide has found a member of the Court of Apollo musical and morbid enough to sing self-murder; and the Corn Laws have been rescued from Blue Books, and enshrined in Ballads. Mr. Pope has called upon my Lord Bolingbroke to awake, and "expatiate free o'er all this scene of man;" and the pair have, together, passed the whole catalogue of human virtues and vices in review. Drunkenness has been sung; so has painting, so has music. Poems have been written on the Art of Poetry. The Grave has been sung. The earth, and the waters under it, and the fearsome region under that; its " adamantine chains and penal fires;" its "ever burning sulphur unconsumed," its " darkness visible," its burning marl and sights of terror. We have heard the last lays of all the Last Minstrels, and the Last Man has had his say, or rather his song, under the auspices of Campbell. Money has been sung. We have had "Miss Kielmansegg and her golden leg," likewise " a song of sixpence." The harp that once hung in Tara's halls has not a string left, and nobody ought to play upon it any more.

Take instead, oh ye poets, the wires of the Electric Telegraph, and run your tuneful fingers over the chords. Sing the poetry of Railways. But what can there be of the poetical, or even of the picturesque, element in a Railway? Trunk lines, branch-lines, loop-lines, and sidings; cuttings, embankments, gradients, curves, and inclines; points, shuntings, switches, sleepers, fog-signals, and turn-tables; locomotives, break-vans, buffers, tenders, and whistles; platforms, tunnels, tubes, goods-sheds, return-tickets, axle-grease, cattle-trains, pilot-engines, time-tables, and coal-trucks; all these are eminently prosaic matter-of-fact things, determined, measured and maintained by line and rule, by the chapter and verse of printed regulations and bye-laws signed by Directors and Secretaries, and allowed by Commissioners of Railways. Can there be any poetry in the Secretary's office; in dividends, debentures, scrip, preference-shares, and deferred bonds? Is there any poetry in Railway time—the atrociously matter-of-fact system of calculation that has corrupted the half-past two o'clock of the old watchman into "two-thirty?" Is Bradshaw poetical? Are Messrs. Pickford, or Chaplin and Horne poetical? How the deuce (I put words into my opponent's mouths) are you to get any poetry out of that dreariest combination of parallel lines, a railroad;—parallel rails, parallel posts, parallel wires, parallel stations, and parallel termini?

As if there could be anything poetical about a Railroad! I hear Gusto the great fine art critic and judge of Literature say this with a sneer, turning up his fine Roman nose meanwhile. Poetry on a Railway! cries Prosycard, the man of business—nonsense! There may be some nonsensical verses or so in the books that Messrs. W. H. Smith and Sons sell at their stalls at the different stations; but Poetry on or in the Railway itself—ridiculous! Poetry on the Rail! echoes Heavypace, the commercial traveller—fudge! I travel fifteen thousand miles by railway every year. I know every line, branch, and station in Great Britain. I never saw any poetry on the Rail. And a crowd of passengers, directors, shareholders, engine-drivers, guards, stokers, station-masters, signal-men, and porters, with, I am ashamed to fear, a considerable proportion of the readers of " Dutch Pictures," seem to the ears of my mind, to take up the cry, to laugh scornfully at the preposterous idea of there being possibly any such a thing as poetry connected with so matter-of-fact an institution as a Railway, and to look upon me in the light of a fantastic visionary.

But I have tied myself to the stake; nailed my colours to the mast; drawn the sword and thrown away the scabbard : in fact, I have written the title of this article, and must abide the issue.

Take a Tunnel—in all its length, its utter darkness, its dank coldness and tempestuous windiness. To me a Tunnel is all poetry. To be suddenly snatched away from the light of day, from the pleasant companionship of the fleecy clouds, the green fields spangled with flowers, the golden wheat, the fantastically changing embankments,—now geological, now floral, now rocky, now chalky ; the hills, the valleys, and the winding streams ; the high mountains in the distance, that know they are emperors of the landscape, and so wear purple robes right imperially; the silly sheep in the meadows, that graze so contentedly, unwotting that John Hinds the butcher is coming down by the next train to purchase them for the slaughter-house ; the little lambs that are not quite up to

railway-trains, their noise and bustle and smoke, yet, and that
scamper nervously away, carrying their simple tails behind
them ; the sententious cattle that munch, and lazily watch
the steam from the funnel as it breaks into fleecy rags of
vapour, and then fall to munching again ;—to be hurried
from all these into pitchy obscurity, seems to me poetical and
picturesque in the extreme. It is like death in the midst of
life, a sudden suspension of vitality—the gloom and terror of
the grave pouncing like a hawk upon the warmth and cheerfulness of life. Many an ode, many a ballad could be written
on that dark and gloomy tunnel — the whirring roar and
scream and jarr of echoes, the clanging of wheels, the strange
voices that seem to make themselves heard as the train rushes
through the tunnel,—now in passionate supplication, now in
fierce anger and loud invective, now in an infernal chorus of
fiendish mirth and demoniac exultation, now in a loud and
long-continued though inarticulate screech—a meaningless
howl like the raving of a madman. To understand and appre-
ciate a tunnel in its full aspect of poetic and picturesque horror,
you should travel in a third-class carriage. To first and sometimes to second-class passengers the luxury of lamplight is by
the gracious favour of the Directors of the company condescendingly extended ; and in passing through a tunnel they are
enabled dimly to descry their fellow-travellers ; but for the
third-class voyager darkness, both outer and inner, are provided—darkness so complete and so intense, that as we are
borne invisibly on our howling way, dreadful thoughts spring
up in our minds of blindness ; that we have lost our sight
for ever ! Vainly we endeavour to peer through the darkness,
to strain our eyes to descry one ray of light, one outline—

be it ever so dim—of a human figure; one thin bead of day upon a panel, a ledge, a window-sill, or a door. Is there not matter for bards in all this?—in the length of the tunnel, its darkness and clamour; in the rage and fury of the engine eating its strong heart, burnt up by inward fire like a man consumed by his own passions; in the seemingly everlasting duration of the deprival from light and day and life; but a deprival which ends at last. Ah, how glad and welcome that restoration to sunshine is! We seem to have had a sore and dangerous sickness, and to be suddenly and graciously permitted to rise from a bed of pain and suffering, and enter at once into the enjoyment of the rudest health, with all its comforts and enjoyments, with all its cheerful pleasures and happy forgetfulness of the ills that are gone, and unconsciousness of the ills that are to come, and that *must* come, and surely.

Whenever I pass through a tunnel I meditate upon these things, and wish heartily that I were a poet, that I might tune my heart to sing the poetry of railway tunnels. I don't know whether the same thoughts strike other people. I suppose they do,—I hope they do. It may be that I muse more on tunnels, and shape their length and blackness, and coldness and noise, to subjects fit to be wedded to immortal verse; because I happen to reside on a railway, and that almost every morning and evening throughout the week I have to pass through a tunnel of prodigious length,—to say the truth, nearly as long as the Box Tunnel, on the Great Western Railway. Morning and night we dash from the fair fields of Kent,—from the orchards and the hop-gardens,— from the sight of the noble river in the distance, with its boats and barges and huge ships, into this Erebus, pitch

dark, nearly three miles long, and full of horrid noises.
Sometimes I travel in the lamp-lit carriages, and then I find
it poetical to watch the flickering gleams of the sickly light
upon shrouded figures, muffled closely in railway rugs and
mantles and shawls,—the ladies, who cower timidly in corners ; the children, who, half-pleased, half-frightened, don't
seem to know whether to laugh or cry, and compromise the
matter by sitting with their mouths wide open, and incessantly asking why it is getting dark, and why there is such a
noise.   Sometimes, and I am not ashamed to confess, much
more frequently, I make my journey in the poor man's
carriage—the " parly, " or third-class.   In that humble
" parly " train, believe me, there is much more railway
poetry attainable than in the more aristocratic compartments.
Total darkness, more noise (for the windows are generally
open, and the reverberation is consequently much greater),
more mocking voices, more mystery, and more romance.   I
have even gone through tunnels in those vile open standing-
up cars, called by an irreverant public " pig-boxes," and
seemingly provided by railway directors as a cutting reproach
on, and stern punishment for, poverty.   Yet I have drunk
deeply of railway poetry in a " pig-box."   There is something grand, there is something noble ; there is something
really sublime in the gradual melting away of the darkness
into light ; in the decadence of total eclipse and the glorious
restoration of the sun to his golden rights again.   Standing
up in the coverless car you see strange, dim, fantastic,
changing shapes above you.   The daylight becomes irriguous,
like dew, upon the steam from the funnel, the roofs of the
carriages, the brickwork sides of the tunnel itself.   But

nothing is defined, nothing fixed; all the shapes are irresolute, fleeting, confused; like the events in the memory of an
old man. The Tunnel becomes a phantom tube — a dry
Styx—the train seems changed into Charon's boat, and the
engine-driver turns into the infernal ferryman. And the end
of that awful navigation must surely be Tartarus. You think
so, you fancy yourself in the boat, as Dante and Virgil were
in the Divine Comedy; ghosts cling to the sides, vainly
repenting, uselessly lamenting; Francesca of Rimini floats
despairing by; far off, mingled with the rattle of wheels, are
heard the famine-wrung moans of Ugolino's children. Hark, to
that awful shrilly, hideous, prolonged yell—a scream like that
they say that Catherine of Russia gave on her deathbed, and
which, years afterwards, was wont to haunt the memories of
those that had heard it. Lord be good to us! there is the
scream again; it is the first scream of a lost spirit's last
agony; the cry of the child of earth waking up into the Ever
and Ever of pain; it is Facinata screaming in her sepulchre
of flames—no, it is simply the railway whistle as the train
emerges from the tunnel into sunlight again. The ghosts
vanish, there are no more horrible sights and noises, no flying
sparks, no red lamps at intervals like demon eyes. I turn
back in the "pig-box," and look at the arched entrance to
the tunnel we have just quitted. I seemed to fancy there
should be an inscription over it bidding all who enter to leave
Hope behind; but instead of that there is simply, hard by, a
placard on a post relative to cattle straying on the railway.

A railway accident! Ah, poets! how much of poetry
could you find in that, were you so minded! Odes and ballads, sapphics, alcaics and dactylics, strophes, chorusses and

semi-chorusses might be sung—rugged poems, rough as the rocky numbers of Ossian, soothing poems, " soft pity to infuse," running " softly sweet in Lydian measure" upon the woes of railway accidents, the widowhoods and orphanages that have been made by the carelessness of a driver, a faulty engine, an unturned " point," a mistaken signal. Think of the bride of yesterday, the first child of our manhood, the last child of our age, think of the dear friend who has been absent for years, who has been estranged from us by those whispering tongues that poison truth, and is coming swiftly along the iron road to be reconciled to us at last. Think of these all torn from us by a sudden, cruel, unprepared-for death ; think of these, falling upon that miserable battle-field, without glory, without foes to fight with, yet with fearfuller, ghastlier hurts, with more carnage and horror in destruction than you could meet with even on those gory Chersonean battle-fields after storms of shot and shell, after the fierce assaults of the bayonet's steel, and the trampling of the horses, and the stroke of the sharp sword. There are bards to wail over the warrior who falls in the fray, for the horse and his rider blasted by the crimson whirlwind. There are tears and songs for the dead that the sea engulfs, to cradle them in its blue depths till Time and Death shall be no more. There are elegies and epitaphs and mourning verses for those that sleep in the churchyard, that have laid their heads upon a turf, that eat their salad from the roots, that dwell with worms, and entertain creeping things in the cells and little chambers of their eyes. There is poetry even for the murderer on his gibbet ; but who cares to sing the railway victim ? who bids the line restore its dead ? who adjures the engine to bring back the true and brave? They are killed, and are buried; the inquest meet; the jurymen give their verdict, and forget all about it two days afterwards. Somebody is tried for manslaughter and acquitted, for, of course, there is nobody to blame? It is all over, and the excursion train, crammed with jovial excursionists, sweethearts, married couples, clubs of gay fellows, laughing children, baskets of prog, bottles of beer, and surreptitious, yet officially connived at, pipes; the engine dressed in ribbons, the stoker—Oh, wonder!—in a clean shirt; the excursion train, I say, rattles gaily over the very place where, a month since, the Accident took place; over the very spot where the earth drank up blood, and the rails were violently wrenched and twisted, and the sleepers were ensanguined, and death and havoc and desolation were strewn all around, and the wild flowers in the embankment were scalded with the steam from the shattered boiler.*

Can you form an idea, poets, of an haunted line? Suppose the same excursion train I was speaking of to be on its way home, late at night, say from Cripplegate-super-mare or Buffington Wells. Everybody has enjoyed himself very much—the children are tired, but happy. The bonnets of the married ladies have made their proper impression upon the population of Cripplegate-super-mare, and they are satisfied with them, their husbands, and themselves. The married gentlemen have found out of what the contents of the black bottle consisted—they smoke pipes openly now, quite

* Lest I should be suspected of having endeavoured to make " capital" out of recent catastrophes I may be allowed to state that this paper was written nearly seven years ago.

defiant, if not oblivious, of bye-laws and forty-shilling fines.
Nobody objects to smoking—not even the asthmatical old
gentleman in the respirator and the red comforter—not even
the tall lady, with the severe countenance and the green
umbrella, who took the mild fair man in spectacles so sharply
to task this morning about the mild cigar which he was
timidly smoking up the sleeve of his poncho. Even the
guards and officials at the stations do not object to smoking
One whiskered individual of the former class, ordinarily the
terror of the humble third-class passenger, whom he, with
fierce contempt, designates as " you, sir," and hauls out of
the carriage on the slightest provocation, condescends to be
satirical on the smoke subject; he puts his head in at the
window, and asks the passengers " how they like it—mild or
full flavoured ? " This is a joke, and everybody, of course,
laughs immensely, and goes on smoking unmolested. Bless
me ! how heartily we can laugh at the jokes of people we are
afraid of, or want to cringe to for a purpose.

Surely a merrier excursion train than this was never due at
the Babylon Bridge Station at " eleven-thirty." Funny stories
are told. A little round man, in a grey coat, and a hat like
a sailor's sings a comic song seven miles long, for he begins
it at one station and ends it at another seven miles distant.
A pretty, timorous widow is heard softly joining in the chorus
of " tol de rol lol." A bilious man of melancholy mien,
hitherto speechless, volunteers a humourous recitation, and
promises feats of conjuring after they have passed the next
station. Strangers are invited to drink out of strange bottles,
and drink. Everybody is willing to take everybody's children on his knee. People pencil down addresses by the

lamplight, and exchange them with people opposite, hoping that they shall become better acquainted. The select clubs of jolly fellows are very happy—they even say " vrappy." There is laughing, talking, jesting, courting, and tittering. None are silent but those who are asleep. Hurrah for this jovial excursion train, for the Nor-Nor-West-by-Eastern Railway Company, its cheap fares and admirable management !

Suppose that just at the spot where this allegro train now is, there occurred the great accident of last July. You remember, the excursion train, through some error, the cause of which was unfortunately never discovered, ran into the luggage train ! the driver and stoker of the former were dashed to pieces—thirty-three persons were killed or wounded. Suppose some man of poetical temperament, of fantastic imagination, of moody fancies were in the carriage of this merry train to-night, looking from the window, communing with the yellow moonlight, the light clouds placidly floating along the sea of heaven as if sure of a safe anchorage at last. He knows the line, he knows the place where that grim accident was—he muses on it—yes ; this was the spot, there lay the bodies.

Heavens and earth ! suppose the lines were haunted ! See, from a siding comes slowly, noiselessly along the rails the PHANTOM TRAIN ! There is no rattle of wheels, no puffing and blowing of the locomotive, only from time to time the engine whistle is heard in a fitful, murmuring, wailing gust of sound ; the lamps in front burn blue, sickly lambent flames leap from the funnel and the furnace door. The carriages are lamplit too, but with corpse candles. The carriages themselves are mere skeletons—they are all shattered, dislocated, ruined, yet, by some deadly principle of cohesion,

they keep together, and through the interstices of their cracking ribs and framework you see the passengers. Horrible
sight to see ! Some have limbs bound up in splinters, some
lie on stretchers, but they have all Faces and Eyes : and the
eyes and the faces, together with the phantom guard with
his lantern, from which long rays of ghastly light proceed ;
together with the phantom driver, with his jaw bound up ;
the phantom stoker, who stokes with a mattock and spade,
and feeds the fire as though he were making a grave ; the
phantom commercial travellers wrapped in shrouds for railway rugs ; the pair of lovers in the first-class coupé locked
in the embrace of death in which they were found after the
accident, the stout old gentleman with his head in his lap,
the legs of the man, the rest of whose body was never found,
but who still has a face and eyes, the skeletons of horses in
the horseboxes, the stacks of coffins in the luggage vans (for
all is transparent, and you can see the fatal verge of the embankment beyond, through the train). All these sights of
horror flit continually past, up and down, backwards and
forwards, haunting the line where the accident was.

But, ah me ! these are, perhaps, but silly fancies after all.
Respectability may be right, and there may be no more
poetry in a railway than in my boots. Yet I should like to
find poetry in everything, even in boots. I am afraid railways are *ugly*, dull, prosaic, straight ; yet the line of beauty,
Hogarth tells us, is a curve, and curves you may occasionally
find on the straightest of railways—and where beauty is,
poetry, you may be sure of it, is not far off. I am not
quite sure but you may find it in ugliness too, if there be
anything beautiful in your own mind.

F

VI.

WANT PLACES.

I CAREFULLY peruse every day the "Want Places" columns of the *Times* newspaper. As I shall presently shew, I happen to know most of the advertisers, and intend to introduce them to public notice. The ladies first:—

AS HOUSEKEEPER to a nobleman or gentleman, a respectable middle-aged party, fully conversant with her duties. Unexceptionable references. Address—K. G., 3, Preserve Street, Piccallilly Gardens.

Mrs. Barbara Blundy is the "party." She is fond of mentioning, casually, that she was born in eighteen hundred and twenty, but she is, at least, fifty; stiff, starch, demure. Two bands of well-pomatumed brown hair, and two thin pendants of corkscrew ringlets, stand perpetually on duty, on either side of her severe cap, caparisoned with grey ribbons of price; Mrs. Blundy's keys and keybasket are her inseparable companions. She carries the one, and she jingles the others, with an inflexible rigidity of purpose. Her dress is of iron grey, and in it, with her iron keys, she looks like the gaoler, as she is, of the pickles and preserves; the Charon of the still-room, the Alecto of the linen-chest, the Megæra of the housemaids, the Tisiphone of domestic economy. From her waist descends a silken apron of rich but sober hues, supposed to have been originally a genuine Bandanna handkerchief, one, indeed, of a set presented to her by General Sir Bulteel Bango, K.C.B., formerly colonel of the Old Hundredth regiment (raised by Colonel Sternhold in sixteen hundred and ninety-one, and known in the Low Country campaigns as Hopkins's foot). Mrs. Blundy wears a spray of ambiguous transparencies, accepted, by a great exertion of faith by those who pay her court, to be Irish diamonds; but which bear a stronger resemblance to the glass drops of a byegone girandole. Afternoon and evening she dons a black, stiff, rustling, silk dress —like a board, as I have heard ladies say. None of your fal-de-ral lavender boots, but rigid, unmistakeable shoes of Cordovan leather, with broad sandals, and stout soles. No gewgaws, or vain lappets for Mrs. Blundy, when it pleases her to walk abroad; but a severe, composed, decorous, comfortable, grey plaid shawl, a real sable muff (how the cook envies it!), a drawn silk bonnet, black kid gloves of staunch Lamb's Conduit Street make, and the keys in a reticule, like a silken travelling-bag. On Sunday evening she sweeps round the corner to chapel, and " sits under " the Reverend Nahum Gillywhack (of Lady Mullington's connection), and afterwards, perchance, condescends to partake of a neat supper of something warm at Mr. Chives's, formerly a butler, but now a greengrocer (and a widower), in Orchard Street.

When Mrs. Blundy is " suited " in a nobleman's or gentleman's family—as she was at Lady Leviathan's, in Plesiosaurus Square—she becomes a fearful and wonderful spectacle. She moves down the back stairs with the dignity of a duchess who has come that way by mistake. Yet she is profoundly humble. She hopes (oh, how humbly!) that she knows her place. To see her curtsey to Lady Leviathan you would imagine that she was wont to stand on a descending platform instead of on a square of carpet—so low did she bend. Mrs. Blundy considered Miss Poonah (governess to the Honourables Bovina and Lardina Lambert, her ladyship's eldest daughters) as a very well behaved "young person," highly accomplished, no doubt; but with a want of "moral fitness;" an ambiguous expression which told immensely with the schoolroom maid, who stated that it exactly tallied with her opinion of Miss Poonah, who was, *she* should say, a "stuck up thing."

Mrs. Blundy left Lady Leviathan's in consequence of a " difficulty" with the lady's maid respecting Mr. Chives.

Mrs. Blundy is not "suited" just now, and she is temporarily residing at a serious butcher's, in a narrow court, behind a great church, at the West End, wherein Mr. Cuffe, the beadle, not unfrequently condescends to insert his gold-laced person, and to purchase a plump chump chop, or a succulent lamb's fry. When Mrs. Blundy is "suited" (which will be soon, for her references are unexceptionable), she will rule the roast as completely as ever. She practises, perhaps unconsciously, Frederic Barbarossa's maxim—" Who can dissimulate can reign." She will bully the still-room maid, and the footman, and Heaven only help the housemaids! The terrible lectures they will have to endure on the sinfulness of ribbons, and the " unloveliness of lovelocks," the perdition of jewellery ! The dismal anecdotes they will have to endure of errant housemaids who, disregarding the advice of their pastors and friends—the housekeepers—fell into evil ways, and were afterwards seen walking in the Park on Sunday, with fourteen flounces one above the other, and leaning on the arms of Life-Guardsmen. All this will be, as it has been before, when Mrs. Blundy is "suited."

To be housekeeper to a duchess is the culminating point of Mrs. Blundy's ambition. To dine with the groom of the chambers, and my lord duke's steward—to have her own still-room footman behind her own still-room chair—to hear the latest Court news from her grace's lady's maid, or from Monsieur Anatole, the hair-dresser, invited in to partake of a glass of "London particular" Madeira. These, with the comfortable perspective of a retiring pension, or of a stately superannuation at his grace's great show-house in Hampshire; with rich fees for shewing Claudes and Petitots, Sèvres porcelain and Gobelin tapestry, to visitors. Any duchess, therefore, who may want such a person, will know where to apply.

A S HOUSEKEEPER to a Single or Invalid Gentleman, a Single Person of experience. Can be highly recommended. Address, Alpha, at Mr. Mutts, 72, Kingsgate Street, Holborn.

Attached relatives and friends of Sir Dian Lunes, Bart.— who, beyond occasional aberrations and delusions respecting his head being a beehive, and himself heir to the throne of Great Britain, is a harmless, helpless, paralytic, bedridden old gentleman enough—may be safely assured that Alpha is the housekeeper for him—Alpha, otherwise represented by Miss Rudd.

Mr. Mutts, trunkmaker, of Kingsgate Street, Holborn, knows Miss Rudd. Does he *not?* Ugh! Who but a meek, quiet, little, widowed, trunkmaker, with three daughters (grown up, and all inclined to redness at the nose), would know that terrible female, half as long as he has done? She

lodges with him in the frequent intervals between her situations.
" Hang her, she *do*," say Mutts to himself, as he is busy at
work.   And, as he says it, he gives a nail, which he fancies
has a Ruddish appearance, such an exasperated rap, that
Grapp, his apprentice, begins rapping at *his* nails, in
professional emulation, harder than ever ; and the two
between them engender such a storm of raps that Mr. Ferret,
the surly attorney opposite, sends across with his compliments,
and really he shall be obliged to indict Mr. Mutts for a
nuisance—indeed he shall.

Miss Rudd—she is tall, lanky, and bony ! She has some
jet ornaments, in heavy links, about her neck ; but, resembling
the fetters over the gate of the Old Bailey, they have not a
decorative effect.   She wears a faded black merino dress, the
reflections from which are red with rust.   Her feet are long
and narrow, like canoes.   Her hands, when she has those
hideous black mittens on, always remind me of unboiled
lobsters.

When Judith Jael Mutts, aged twenty-three years, tells
her father that Miss Rudd—having left Mrs. Major Morpuss's
family, in consequence of the levity of Miss Corpus, that
lady's niece—is, pending her acceptance of another engagement,
coming to stay a week in Kingsgate Street, the poor man breaks
out into a cold perspiration—yet his daughter Judith always
adds, " Really Miss Rudd is such a superior person, and has
so strict a sense of her moral mission, that we should all be
benefited (a glance at Mutts over his Sunday newspaper) by
her stay."   Mutts knows that it is all over with this said
newspaper during Miss Rudd's stay, which, though announced
as to be only of a week's duration, he knows, from sad

experience, will, very probably, be indefinitely protracted. Miss Rudd's moral mission ordinarily involves an unusual tartness of temper in Mr. Mutt's three amiable daughters; it makes—on the general question of theology at meal times, and extra exposure to being "worreted"—Grapp's, the apprentice's, life a temporary burden to him. There is no rest for Mr. Mutts while the single gentleman's housekeeper is good enough to lodge with him. He is in daily perturbation lest Miss Rudd should take his state of widowerhood as a state of sin; and, willing or not willing, marry him severely. With what alacrity he carries the notification of Miss Rudd's wishes to Printing-House Square! How devoutly he hopes that the advertisement will be speedily answered!

Not only to Sir Dian Lunes, but to Thomas Tallboys, Esq. (known, when in the House, from his taciturnity, as "Mum" Tallboys), Miss Rudd would be an eligible retainer. That stiff, stern, melancholy, silent, man would find a treasure in her. Trestles, the footman, who is more than half-brother to a mute, would have a grim and silent respect for her. Her lank canoe-like shoes would go noiselessly about the stairs; into Mr. Tallboys's ghastly dining-room, where there is a Turkey carpet, of which the faded colours seem to have sunk through the floor, like spectres; into the study, where there are great bookcases of vellum bound volumes, which seem to have turned pale with fright at the loneliness of their habitation, a view of the Street of Tombs at Pompeii, and a model of an ancient sarcophagus—the study where every morning she would find Mr. Tallboys in a dressing-gown, like a tartan winding sheet, with a bony paperknife cutting the leaves of the Registrar-General's returns, which he will have sent to him

weekly; into the silent kitchen, where an imposing and
gleaming *batterie de cuisine* (never used but twice a year) blinks
lazily at the preparations for his daily chop; into the mournful
housekeeper's room, garnished with unused sweets and
condiments; into the strange crypts and vaults of the silent
cellar, would Miss Rudd roam noiselessly, gloomily. Mr.
Tallboys will, after she has served him for a year, have the
highest respect for her. "She is a person," he will write to
his friend Colonel Vertebra, judge advocate of the colony of
Kensalgrenia, "of singular discretion and reticence." When
he dies, he will leave her a considerable sum in those mortuary
securities, South Sea annuities. Then, perhaps, she will
espouse the grim Mr. Trestles, and conduct a dreary lodging-
house in some dreary street adjoining an obsolete square; or,
adhering to celibacy, retire to a neat sarcophagus cottage in
the Mile-End Road, or the vicinity of Dalston.

It is a mistake to suppose that a single gentleman's
housekeeper proceeds uniformly to her end—which is
naturally connected with the probate duty—by means of
coaxing, complaisance, and general sycophancy. Such means
may be employed in certain cases, where the patient—like a
man who has been addicted to opium-eating—cannot be kept
up to the mark without doses of his habitual medicine, flattery.
But, in nine cases out of ten, the successful treatment is
composed of tyranny and intimidation. A proper impression
once implanted in the mind of the single gentleman that his
housekeeper is indispensable to his health and comfort, and
she is safe. Her knees need be no longer hinged, her neck
corrigible, her tongue oiled. The little finger of the domestic
becomes a rod of iron, with which the celibatarian may be

scourged, or round which he may be twisted at will. How many fierce major-generals there are, once the martinets of garrisons, who are now the submissive Helots of cross old women who cannot spell! How many Uncle Toms crouch beneath the lash of a female Legree, whom they feed and pay wages to! This is human nature. We know that we can turn Legree out of doors, and break her cowskin over her back, to-morrow; but we don't do anything of th sort.

There are many other housekeepers who want places just now. There is Mrs. Muggeridge, who is not too proud to seek a domestic appointment, in which the high art of the housekeeper is joined to the more homely avocations of the cook. As cook and housekeeper, Mrs. Muggeridge will suit genteel families in Bloomsbury and Russell Squares, Gower Street, Mornington Crescent, or Cadogan Place. She would be just the person for the upper end of Sloane Street. She has a neat hand in cutting vegetable bouquets for garnishing, out of carrots, turnips, and parsnips; also for the decorated frills of paper round the shankbones of legs of mutton and the tops of candlesticks. She can make gooseberry fools, custards, and jellies; but, if trifles or Chantilly baskets are in question, they must be procured from the pastrycook; fo. Mrs. Muggeridge is genteel, but not fashionable. She is a stout, buxom woman, very clean and neat; and, to see her going round to her various tradespeople in the morning with her capacious basket and store of red account books, is a very cheerful and edifying spectacle. Mrs. Muggeridge has a husband—a meek man with a grey head and a limp white neckcloth—who is head waiter at a large hotel; but he is seldom seen at home, and is not of much account there when he is.

Then there is Mrs. Compott, who is desirous of obtaining a situation as housekeeper in a school or public establishment. and who would not object to look after the linen department, Mrs. Compott is a very hard, angular, inflexible woman, with a decidedly strong mind. She is not exactly unfeeling, but her sensibilities are blunted—not to say deadened—by the wear and tear of many boys; and such a tough integument has been formed over her finer feelings as might be supposed to be possessed by a Scotch assistant surgeon in the navy after a sharp sequence of cock-pit practice. At Mr. Gripforth's academy for young gentlemen, Hammersmith, she would be an invaluable scholastic housekeeper and matron. The little maladies to which shool-boys are liable;—such as chicken-pox, hooping-cough, chilblains, ringworm, boils, chapped hands and cuts—all of which ailments she classes under the generic term of "rubbage"—she treats with sudden remedies, generally efficacious, but occasionally objected to by the patient. Mr. Katarr, the visiting apothecary —a fawn-coloured young man in a shiny macintosh, very harmless, and reputed to sustain nature by the consumption of his own stock of cough lozenges, humected with rose water—has a high opinion of Mrs. Compott. " I will send Tumfey," he says to the principal, " another bottle of the mixture; and that, with Mrs. Compott's good care, will soon bring him round." Have you never known a Mrs. Compott? In your young days, at Mr. Gripforth's academy, at Miss Whalebone's preparatory establishment, or Doctor Rubasore's collegiate school; where it was so essential that the pupils

should be sons of gentlemen, and where you had that great
fight with Andy Spring the pork-butcher's son? Can't you
remember your sycophancy to that majestic domestic for jam
and late bread and butter? You could not crawl lower, now,
for a Garter or a tide-waiter's place. Don't you yet feel a sort
of shudder at the remembrance of Mrs. Compott's Saturday
night's gymnastics with the towel, the yellow soap, the hard
water, and—horror of horrors—the small tooth comb?

Mrs. Compott is always a widow. Mr. Compott was
"unfortunate," and had "a house of his own once;" but
what his misfortunes or his house were is as mysterious as a
cuneiform inscription. Mrs. Compott very often contracts a
second marriage, and becomes Mrs. Gripforth or Mrs. Rubasore. But for such an alliance it would be inexplicable to me
what that rugged, inflexible, terrible personage the schoolmaster's wife could originally have been; or how indeed schoolmasters themselves find time and opportunity to court wives.
I never knew a young lady who kept company with a schoolmaster, nor was I ever at a scholastic wedding. Others may
have been more fortunate.

The schoolmaster's housekeeper would not mind under-
taking the superintendence of a public establishment, which
may mean Somerset House, an union workhouse, a female
penitentiary, or a set of chambers in the Adelphi. But she
is not to that manor born: the orthodox public housekeeper
is a widely different functionary. Such public establishments
as chambers, public offices, warehouses, &c., are peculiarly
adapted to Mrs. Tapps, married, but without incumbrance;
entertaining, indeed, a small niece, but who is so far from
being an incumbrance that she does, on more or less com-

pulsion, as much work as a grown-up housemaid. Mrs. Tapps is a cloudy female, with a great deal of apron, living chiefly underground, and never without a bonnet. What her literary attainments (if any) may be I am unable to say; but for all catechetical purposes she is profoundly ignorant. She knows positively nothing upon any subject holding with the external world; less (if that were possible) about any of the lodgers or occupants of the house she dwells in. "She can't say:"—"she don't know, she's sure:"—"she's not 'aweer,'" and so on to the end of the chapter. "She'll ask the landlord." The landlord is her Alpha and her Omega. The landlord is the Grand Thibetian Llama of her creed— as mysterious and as invisible—the Cæsar to whom all appeals must be made. The landlord is all Mrs. Tapps knows or seems to know anything of. Her niece Euphemia is also naturally reserved; of a timidity moving her to violent trembling and weeping when addressed, and afflicted more- over with an impediment in her speech. All you ordinarily see of her is a foreshortened presentment as she is scrubbing the doorsteps or the stairs—all you hear of her are the slipshod scuffling of her shoes about the house, and her stifled moans in the kitchen when being beaten by her aunt for black- leading her face instead of the stove. Mr. Tapps is a postman, or an *employé* in the docks, or a railway porter, or engaged in some avocation which necessitates his coming home every night very dirty and tired. He smokes a strong pipe and studies yesterday's newspaper till he goes to bed; but however Mrs. Tapps, and her neice, and the gaunt grey cat, and the long lean candle with the cauli- flower wick, pass their time during the long winter evenings in the silent kitchen in the empty house is beyond my comprehension.

There is another public establishment which boasts a housekeeper—I mean a theatre. Spruce visitors to the boxes, jovial frequenters of the pit, noisy denizens of the gallery, little deem of, if they did they would care as little about the existence of a dingy female, "Mrs. Smallgrove, the housekeeper," a personage well known to the stage-doorkeeper and the manager, and the chief of that sallow, decayed, mysterious band of women called "cleaners," who poke about the private boxes and pit benches with stunted brooms and guttering candles during rehearsals, and who are dimly visible in dressing-rooms and dark passages. The people behind the scenes, actors, musicians, workmen, are conscious of the existence of these functionaries, but scarcely more. They are aware of Mrs. Smallgrove, but they do not know her. It is a question even if they are familiar with her name. She superintends the lowering of the grim brown Holland cloths over the gay decorations after the performances. Where she lives is a mystery—somewhere underneath the "gravetrap" in the mezzanine floor, or high in the tackled flies, perhaps. No man regardeth her; but, when the last actor is descending from his dressing-room at night, when the last carpenter has packed up his tools to go home, the figure of the theatrical housekeeper is descried duskily looming in the distance—covering up the pianoforte in the green room, or conferring with the fireman amidst the coils of the engine hose, or upon the deserted stage, which, an hour ago, was joyous with light and life and music. When the Theatre Royal, Hatton Garden, has a vacancy for a housekeeper it is through some occult influence—some application totally independent of the three-and-sixpenny publicity—that Mrs. Smallgrove is inducted into this situation. She may have been a decayed keeper of a wardrobe, a prompter's wife fallen upon evil days, a decrepit ballet mistress. But what her antecedents have been is doubtful, likewise the amount of her salary.

A S NURSE in a Nobleman's or Gentleman's Family, a Person of great experience in the care of Children. Can be highly recommended by several families of distinction. Address P., care of Mr. Walkinshaw, Trotman's Buildings, Legg Street Road, S.

As nurse! For what enormous funds we can draw on the bank of Memory on the mention of that familiar word! With the Nurse are connected our youthful hopes and fears—our earliest joys, our earliest sorrows. She was the autocrat of our nonage. Her empire over us commenced even before memory began. When Frederick the Great tempted the soldier on guard to smoke a pipe, adding that he was the king, what was the reply of the faithful sentinel? "King," he said, "be hanged, what will my captain say?" So, when even the parental authority winked at our infantile shortcomings, the dread thought, "What will nurse say?" shot through our youthful minds; and the parental wink, although it might be urged in alleviation, could not purchase impunity.

Charles Lamb, in one of his delightful Essays, says, that if he were not an independent gentleman he would like to be a beggar. Alexander of Macedon expressed a somewhat analogical wish in reference to Diogenes in his tub. Thus, to come farther down, and nearer home, I may say that next to being the Marchioness of Candyshire, I should like to be the Marchioness of Candyshire's nurse. I will not enlarge

on the gorgeous estate of the monthly nurse in an aristocratic family, on her unquestioned despotism, her unresisted
caprices, her irreversible decrees, her undisputed sway over
Baby, her familiarity with the most eminent of the Faculty,
and the auriferous oblations offered to her in the shape of
guineas in the christening cup, because the lady of Trotman's
Buildings is the nurse I propose to sketch, not a lunar but a
permanent nurse, one of the arbiters of the child's career,
from its emancipation from the cradle to its entrance into the
school-room.

And surely, when we hear so much of what schoolmasters and mistresses have done towards forming children's
minds; when old Fuller bids us remember " R. Bond, of
Lancashire," for that he had the " breeding the learned
Ascham," and " Hartgrave in Brundly school, because he
was the first did teach worthy Dr. Whitaker," and " Mul-
grave for his scholar, that gulf of learning, Bishop Andrews;"
when we are told what influence this first schoolmistress had
towards making Hannah More a moralist, or that poor dear
governess L. E. L. a poetess, should we not call to mind what
mighty influences the nurse must have had in kneading the
capacities, and after-likings and after-learnings of the most
famous men and women? What heroes and statesmen must
have learnt their first lessons of fortitude and prudence on
the nurse's knee—what hornbooks of duty and truth and
love and piety must have been first conned under that homely
instructress? On the other hand, what grievous seeds
of craven fear, and dastardly rebellion, and hypocrisy and
hate, and stubborn pride must have been sown in the child's
first nursery garden by the nurse? Shakspeare, who never

overlooked anything, was mindful of the nurse's mission : you
may turn up in his works a score of quotations on the nursery
head without trouble ; and (most ludicrous descent of analogy)
even that American showman had some shrewd knowledge of
the chords that are respondent in the human heart, when he
foisted an old black woman on his countrymen as Washington's nurse.

Mrs. Pettifer, now desirous of an engagement in a family
of distinction, must have been originally, I take it, a nursery-
maid; but if ever lowliness were her " young ambition's
ladder," she now decidedly—

> " — looks in the clouds, scorning the base degrees
> By which she did ascend."

Between her and nursery-maids there is a yawning gulf as
impassable as Niagara in a cock-boat. " Bits of girls,"
" trumpery things," thus she characterises them. She over-
flows with the failing by which angels are said to have fallen
—pride. There is no humility, real or simulated, about her.
She knows her place thoroughly; but she knows that place
is to command, to reprimand, to overawe high and low, from
the Marchioness of Candyshire to Prue the smallest maid,
who is the slave of her gunpowder tea-pot and a bond servant to her arrowroot skillet.

At the Marchioness of Candyshire's (where we will suppose her, for the nonce, to be installed), at that imposing
town house in Great Gruffin Street, Brobdignag Square,
about which Messrs. Gunter's myrmidons are always hanging
with green boxes; where the clustered soot from bye-gone
flambeaux in the iron extinguishers on the area railings is

eloquent of entertainments past; and where the harlequinaded hatchment of Goliath the last Marquis (a sad man for chicken-hazard) hints what a great family the Candyshires are. Here, in this most noble mansion, from the nursery wicket to the weathercocks over the chimney cowls, Martha Pettifer is Empress and Queen. The lower suites of apartments she condescendingly concedes to the Marquis and Marchioness for balls, dinners, and similar trifles; but hers are the flight of nursery stairs, both back and front; hers the airy suite of upper rooms; hers the cribs, cradles, and tender bodies of the hopes and pride of Candyshire.

The youthful Earl of Everton, aged four, Lord Claude Toffie, aged three, Ladies Dulciana and Juliana Toffie, aged two years and eight months, respectively, are her serfs, vassals, and villains. Over them she has all rights of soccage, jambage, free warren, turbary, pit and gallows (or rather corner and cupboard), and all other feudal and manorial rights. Lord Candyshire, a timid marquis with a red head, manifestly afraid of his own footman—who was expected to do something great in the House on the Bosjesman Bishoprics (additional) Bill, but did not—is admitted to the nursery on sufferance; and gives there his caresses with perturbation, and his opinions with deference. Lady Candyshire—a superb member of the female aristocracy (you remember her portrait by Flummery, R.A., as Semiramis), and whom her cousin and former suitor Lord Tommy Fetlock frequently offers to back in the smoking-room of his club as " game " to " shut up " any number of ladies-in-waiting in a snail's canter—is subdued and complaisant in the nursery. She

G

has an uneasy consciousness that she is not quite mistress there; and though Mrs. Pettifer is not at all like Semiramis, and no Flummery, R.A., ever dreamt of taking her portrait, the Marchioness defers to her, and bears with her humours, and bends to her will. As for the Candyshire carriage, sleek horses, tigerskin hammercloth, coachman's wig, footman's batons, and herald painting, they are quite as much Mrs. Pettifer's as her ladyship's. If the youthful scions of that illustrious house are to take, according to her sovereign will, an airing in the Park, and the Marchioness is desirous of attending a meeting of the ladies' committee of the Penitent-Cannibals Society, she may take the brougham; Martha Pettifer must have the great body vehicle. If, on the other hand, a visit is to be made to Mr. Manismooth, the dentist's, Martha boldly usurps the close carriage, and, bleak as may be the day, and lowering the clouds, leaves her mistress to shift for herself—even when Lord Candyshire (whose silent services at the House of Lords involve the carrying about of a huge mass of papers) has bespoken the curly-wigged coachman and the horses for the conveyance of himself and blue-books to Westminster. As to poor Mademoiselle Frileuse, the thin Swiss governess, with her charge, Lady Ariadne Toffie, aged eleven, she may take what vehicle she can procure.

Martha Pettifer, notwithstanding her high estate of carriage, and curly-wigged coachman and batoned footman, does not ape the apparel of an aristocrat. There is no mistaking her for a marchioness; she is above that. She towers high among the youthful Candyshires, erect and stately, comfortably clad in woollen and stout silk. At shops and exhibitions, at the gate of that favourite resort of the juvenile aristocracy, the Zoological Gardens in the Regent's Park, you may see the great Candyshire carriage standing; or you may watch it rolling leisurely through Hyde Park, the Candyshire children looking as beautiful and as delicate as only British children can look. Aristocratic mammas pass by in their carriages and remark, with languid complacency, how well the dear children look, and what a treasure Lady Candyshire must have in her nurse.

Which is best, think you, Mademoiselle Frileuse, to be— after a tedious intellectual training which may fit you to become a duchess, inasmuch as you are expected to impart it to a young lady who may be a duchess some day—a governess, with forty pounds a year " salary," or to be Mrs. Pettifer, a nurse, with fifty pounds a year " wages " ? Have you a tithe as much authority over your pupil as she has over her nurslings ? Can you command the footmen, and make the nursemaids tremble ? Does the Marchioness defer to you, and say, " Mademoiselle, I dare say you know best, therefore do as you like." Can you contradict the doctor, the mighty Sir Paracelsus Powgrave, and make poor little Mr. Pildrag, the apothecary, shiver in his cloth boots when he comes to lance the children's gums ? Are all your lingual skill, your drawing, your painting, your harp and pianoforte cunning, your geography, your use of the globes, and your rudiments of Latin, held as of half so much account as Mrs. Pettifer's experiences in the administration of a foot-bath, in the virtues of lambs' wool socks, in the efficacy of a Dover's powder ? You are to teach the children the learning which is to fortify their minds, the graces which are to adorn their persons for the tournament of the world ; but yonder illiterate woman who gives the children their physic, superintends their washing and dressing, and cuts their bread and butter, thinks and knows herself to be infinitely superior to you : " a bit of a governess, indeed ! "

There are nurses in all grades and conditions of life who want places just now, but they all, on a correspondingly descending scale, are fashioned after the Pettifer model. Some are temporary and some permanent; some ready to take the child from the month, some preferring the care of children of more advanced growth. Then there is the transition nurse—half nurse, half nursemaid, and not averse to subsiding into the anomalous position of a " young-ladies' maid." There are nurses of tender hearts apt to conceive an affection for their charges quite as ardent as that which a mother ever had for her own children ; who grieve as passionately when they are separated from them as those good Normandy women do who take the babes from the Foundling Hospital in Paris. Such nurses will, after lapses of long years, and from immense distances, suddenly start up looking as young, or rather as old as ever, and shed tears of delight at the sight and speech of their nurse-children, grown men and women, now, with children of their own to nurse. Woe is me that there should be found, among this apparently simple-minded and affectionate class, persons who make of their once state of nursehood a kind of prescriptive ground for future claims. " Nurses ! " says my friend Brown, with a groan, " I've had enough of 'em. My mother had thirteen children, and I have had seven of my own ; and every now and then I am beset with importunate old women curtseying, hang 'em, and saying, ' Please, sir, I nursed you,' or, ' Please, sir, I was master Tommy's nurse;' and who expect five shillings and a pound of green tea."

Then there is Mrs. Crapper, whom I may characterise as the "back streets nurse," who is strictly temporary, and whose connection lies chiefly among small tradesmen and well-to-do mechanics. She dwells somewhere in Drury Court, or Carnaby Street, Golden Square, or Denmark Street, Soho, in a many-belled house, over a chandler's shop, or a bookstall, perhaps. The intuitive prescience of being wanted possessed by this woman is to me astonishing. She never requires to be " fetched" like the doctor—apparently so, at least. She seems to come up some domestic trap. There she is at her post, with a wonderful freemasonic understanding with the doctor, and the Registrar of Births, and the undertaker, and the sexton, and all the misty functionaries, whisperingly talked of but seldom seen, connected with our coming in and going out of the world. For Mrs. Crapper is as often an attendant upon the sunset as upon the sunrise of life.

There is also the Indian Nurse, the Ayah, a brown female in crumpled white muslin, who comes over, with her nurse child, or *baba*, with Mrs. Captain Chutney in the Puttyghaut East Indiaman, or with the widow of Mr. Mofuzzle of the civil service overland. Her performances in England are chiefly confined to sitting upon the stairs, shivering and chattering her teeth pitiably, and uttering heart-rending entreaties to be sent back to Bengal. Back to Bengal she is sent in due time, accordingly, to squat in a verandah, and talk to her *baba* in an unintelligible gabble of Hindostanee and English, after the manner of Ayahs generally.

There is a lady of the nurse persuasion who does not want a place in the *Times*, but who is not above wanting nurse children. The custom of putting children out to nurse is decidedly prevalent. The present writer was "raised" in this manner. I have no coherent remembrance of the lady, but I bear yet about me an extensive scar caused by a humorous freak of hers to tear off a blister before the proper time. She also, I understand, was in the habit of beating me into a very prismatic condition, though, to do her justice, she distributed her blows among her nurse children and her own with unflinching impartiality. The termination of my connection with her was caused by her putting me into a bed with two of her young charges who were ill of the measles; following out a theory she entertained, that it was as well that I should catch that complaint then as in after days; on which occasion I was rescued from her and conveyed home, wrapped up in blankets. I have also an indistinct remembrance of having been, in some stage of my petticoathood, introduced to a young gentleman in a trencher cap and leather breeches, on the ground that he had been my foster-brother. Carrying memory farther back, and remembering sundry cuffs and kicks, and mutual out-tearings of handfuls of hair, I had some faint idea that I really had been acquainted with the young gentleman at some time or other.

The person who takes children out to nurse resides at Brentford, or at Lewisham, or Sydenham. Her husband may be a labourer in a market-garden, or a suburban omnibus driver, or a river bargeman. She may be (as she often is) a comely, kindly, motherly woman, delighting to make her little knot of infants a perfect nosegay of health, and beauty, and cleanliness; or she may be (as she very often is, too) an ignorant, brutish, drunken jade; beating, starving, and neglecting her helpless wards, laying in them the foundation of such mortal maladies, both physical and moral, as years of afternurture shall not assuage. And yet we take our nurses, or send our babies to nurse, blindfold, although we would not go out partridge shooting with a gun we had bought of Cheap Jack, or adventure our merchandise in a ship of which we knew not the name, the tonnage, or the register.

One more nurse closes my list—the hospital nurse. Mrs. Pettifer's high-blown pride may have, from over distension, at length broken, and the many summers she has floated "in a sea of glory," may, and do, find a termination sometimes in the cold, dull, dark pool of an hospital ward. Yet power has not wholly passed away from her; for, beyond the doctors, to whom she must perforce be polite and submissive, and the students, whom she treats with waggish complacency, she is supreme over all with whom she comes in contact. Mrs. Pettifer, formerly feared and obeyed by the Candyshire vassalage, is here Nurse Canterbury or Nurse Adelaide, still feared, still obeyed in Canterbury or Adelaide Ward. Controller of physic, of sweet or bitter sauce for food; smoother of pillows, speaker of soft or querulous words, dispenser of gall or balsam to the sick, she is conciliated by relatives, dreaded or loved by patients. I often think, when I walk through the long, clean, silent wards of an hospital (nothing, save the lower decks of a man-of-war, can come up to hospital order, neatness, and cleanliness) watching the patients quietly resigned, yet so expressively suffering, the golden sunlight playing on their wan faces, the slow crawling steps of the convalescents, the intermittent cases sitting quietly at their beds' foot, waiting patiently till their time of torture shall come ;—hearing the monotonous ticking of the clock, the slow rustling of the bed-clothes, the pattering foot of the nurse as she moves from bed to bed, consulting the paper at the bed-head as to the medicine and diet, and slowly gurgling forth the draught : I often think of what an immense, an awful weight of responsibility hangs in this melancholy abode upon the Nurse. The doctor has his vocation, and per-forms it. He severs this diseased limb, and binds up that wound. The physician points out the path to health, and gives us drugs like money to help us on our way. But it is for the nurse to guide the weary wanderer; to wipe the dust from his bleared eyes and the cold sweat from his brow; to moisten his parched lips; to bathe his swollen feet : to soothe and tend and minister to him until the incubus of sickness be taken off and he struggle into life a whole man again.

Sometimes the hospital nurse is not an aristocrat in deca-dence, but a plebian promoted. Often the back streets nurse, at the recommendation of the doctor, changes the venue of her ministrations from Carnaby Street to Saint Gengulphus's or Saint Prude's. The hospital nurse is ordinarily hard-work-ing, skilful, placable, and scrupulously cleanly; but she has, too frequently, two deadly sins. She drinks, and she is accessible to bribery; and, where bribery begins, extortion, partiality, and tyranny, to those who cannot bribe, soon fol-low. I wish I could acquit the hospital nurse of these weak-nesses, but I cannot.* And this is why I hail as excellent

---

* This paper was first published in 1853 ; since that time many bene-ficial changes have been made in the system and practice of hospital nursing.

and hopeful the recent introduction into some hospitals of superintendent nurses, called Sisters, superior in intelligence and education to the average class of attendants.

As nursery-maid ; as nurse-girl ; as wet-nurse (" with a good," &c., a lady generally sensitive as to diet, and whose daily pints of porter are with her points of honour) ; as school-room-maid : all these "want places" speak for themselves. They are buds and offshoots and twigs of the nurse-tree proper, and as such are highly useful, each in their distinctive sphere, but beyond that they do not call for any detailed notice here.

VII.

MORE PLACES WANTED.

A S LADY'S-MAID, a young person who has lived in the first
families, and can have four years's good character. Fully under-
stands dressmaking, hair-dressing, and getting up fine linen. Address
Miss T., Bunty's Library, Crest Terrace, Pimlico.

Miss Fanny Tarlatan, the young lady in quest of a situation, does not reside at Bunty's library. Mr. Bunty and Mr.
Bunty's wife are only friends of hers. Mr. Bunty is tall
and stout, with a white neckcloth, and is very like a clergyman, with a dash of the schoolmaster and a smack of the
butler. Mrs. Bunty is an acrid lady in ribbons, with a
perpetual smile for lady customers; which would be a little
more agreeable if it did not twist her neck, and screw her
mouth up, and twist her body over the counter. At
Bunty's library are three-volume novels bound in dashing
cloth; and Bunty's library is carpeted; and in the centre
thereof is a great round table groaning beneath the weight of
ladies' albums, and works of genteel piety, and treatises
written with a view to induce a state of contentment among
the rural population (hot-pressed and with gilt edges),

together with neatly stitched pamphlets upon genteelly religious and political subjects, and handsomely clapsed church services, with great red crosses on their backs and sides.

No; Miss Tarlatan does not live at Bunty's; but she is an old colleague of Mrs. Bunty's (once Miss Thorneytwig, my Lady Crocus's waiting woman), and calls her Matilda, and is by her called "Fanny," and "Dear Girl;" and therefore she gives Bunty's library as an address; it being considered more aristocratic than Tidlers' Gardens; where, in the house of Mrs. Silkey, that respectable milliner and dress-maker, Miss Tarlatan is at present staying.

She can dress hair, make dresses, and perfectly under-stands getting up fine linen. The French *coiffeur* is still a great personage; but his services are now-a-days often sup-plied by the lady's-maid; and there are many fair and noble ladies who are not too haughty to employ Miss Tarlatan, and go, resplendent from her skill, into the presence of their sovereign, or into the melodious vicinity of the singers of the Italian opera. Also to wear ball and court dresses made, not by the pallid workwomen and "first hands" of the great millinery establishments of the West-End, but by the nimble fingers of Fanny Tarlatan. Also to confide to her sundry priceless treasures of Mechlin and Brussels, Honiton and old point, or "Beggar's lace," sprigged shawls and veils, and such marvels of fine things, to be by her got up. All of which proceedings are characterised by the great millinery establishments, by the fashionable *blanchisseus de fin*, and by M. Anatole, *coiffeur*, of Regent Street, as atrocious, mean, stingy, avaricious, and unjustifiable on the part of miladi;

but which, if they suit her to order and Miss Tarlatan to
undertake, are in my mind, on the broad-gauge of free trade,
perfectly reasonable and justifiable. Some ladies make a
merit of their Tarlatanism, stating, with pride, that their
maids " do everything for them ; " others endeavour uneasily
to defend their economy by reference to the hardness of the
times, to their large families, to the failure of revenue from
my lord's Irish estates, to the extravagance of such and such
a son or heir, or to Sir John having lost enormously in railways or by electioneering. One lady I have heard of who
palliated all domestic retrenchments on the ground of having
to pay so much income-tax. Unhappy woman !

Hairdresser, dressmaker, getter-up of fine linen ; skilled
in cosmetics and perfumes ; tasteful arranger of bouquets ;
dexterous cleaner of gloves (for my lady must have two pairs
of clean gloves a-day and, bountiful as may be her pin-money,
you will rarely find her spending seven-hundred and thirty
times four shillings per annum in gloves) ; artful trimmer of
bonnets ; clever linguist ; of great conversational powers in
her own language ; of untiring industry, cheerfulness, and
good temper—all these is Fanny Tarlatan, aged twenty-
eight. I have a great respect for Fanny Tarlatan, and for
the lady's-maid, generally, and wish to vindicate her from
the slur of being a gossiping, tawdry, intriguing, venal
waiting-maid, as which she is generally represented in novels
and plays, and similar performances.

Fanny is not without personal charms. She has ringlets
that her lady might envy, and the comely good-humoured
look which eight-and-twenty is often gilded with. She has
been resolute enough to steel her heart against the advances

of many a dashing courier, of many an accomplished valet, of many a staid and portly butler. She does not look for matrimony in the World of Service. Mr. Whatnext, at the Great Haberdashery Palace, Froppery House, head man there, indeed (though Mr. Biggs, my lord's gentleman, has sneeringly alluded to him as a "low counter-jumper"), has spoken her fair. Jellytin, the rising pastrycook at Gunter's, has openly avowed his maddening passion, and showed her his savings'-bank book. But that did not dazzle her; for she too has a "little bit of money of her own." Her revenues chiefly lie, not in her wages—they are not too ample— but in her perquisites. Lawyers would starve (figuratively, of course, for 'tis impossible for a lawyer to starve under any circumstances) on the bare six and eightpences—it is the extra costs that fatten. Perquisites are Fanny Tarlatan's costs. To her fall all my lady's cast-off clothes. Their amount and value depend upon my lady's constitutional liberality or parsimony. A dress may be worn once, a week, a month, or a year before it reverts to the lady's-maid. So with gloves, shoes, ribbons, and all the other weapons in the female armoury, of which I know no more than St. Anthony did of the sex—or that Levantine monk Mr. Curzon made us acquainted with, who had never *seen* a woman. Old Lady McAthelyre, with whom Fanny lived before she went to the Countess of Cœurdesart's (Lady McA. was a terrible old lady, not unsuspected of a penchant for shoplifting and drinking *eau de cologne* grog), used to cut up all her old dresses for aprons, and the fingers off her gloves for mittens, and was the sort of old lady altogether who might reasonably be expected to skin a flea for the hide and tallow thereof.

Mrs. Colonel Scraw, Fanny's mistress after Lady Cœurde-sart, made her old clothes her own peculiar perquisites, and sold them herself. But such exceptions are rare, and Fanny has had, on the whole, no great reason to complain. Perhaps you will, therefore, at some future time, meet with her under the name of Whatnext, or Jellytin, or Figgles, or Seakale, in a snug, well-to-do West-End business, grown into a portly matron (with ringlets yet; for they are vital to the lady's-maid through life), with two little girls tripping home from Miss Weazel's dancing academy. I hope so, with all my heart.

There is a custom common among the English nobility, and yet peculiar to that privileged class, to get the best of everything. Consequently, whenever they find foreign cooks and foreign musicians more skilful than native talent, it is matter of noble usance to refect upon foreign dishes; to prefer the performances of foreign minstrels and players; to cover the head, or hands, or feet, with coverings made by foreign artisans; and, even in the ordinary conversation of life, to pepper discourse with foreign words, as you would a sheep's kidney with cayenne. So my lord duke entertains in his great mansion a French cook, a Swiss confectioner, an Italian house steward, a French valet, German and French governesses, a German under-nurse or *bonne* (that his children may imbibe fragments of foreign language with their pap), besides a host of non-resident foreign artists and professors gathered from almost every nation under the sun. It is, therefore, but reasonable that her grace the duchess should have a foreign attendant—a French, or Swiss, or German lady's-maid. I will take Mademoiselle Batiste, warranted from Paris, as a sample.

When I say warranted from Paris, I mean what the word
" warranted " is generally found to mean—not at all like
what it professes to be. Mademoiselle Batiste says she is
from Paris; but she does not bear the slightest resemblance
to the pert, sprightly, coquettish, tasteful, merry creation in
a cunning cap, a dress closed to the neck, a plaited silk
apron and shiny shoes, that a Parisian lady's maid generally
is. My private impression is that she is a native of some
distressingly lugubrious provincial town in the *midi* of France
—Aigues-Mortes, perchance—whence she has been sent, for
our sins, to England, to make us mournful. She is a most
dolorous Abigail; a lachrymose, grumbling, doleant, miserable waiting woman. When she is old (she is in the
thirties, now,) she will take snuff and keep a poodle on
some fifth floor in the Marais. Whether she has been disappointed in love, or her relations were guillotined during
the great revolution; whether she was born on the eve of
St. Swithin, or like Apollodorus, nourishes scorpions in her
breast, I know not, but she is a very grievous woman—a
female knight of the rueful countenance. If you fail to
please her she grumbles; if you remonstrate with her, she
cries. What are you to do with a woman, whose clouds
always end in rain, unless you have Patience for an umbrella?
In person, Mademoiselle Batiste is tall; in compass wofully
lean and attenuated; her face is of the hatchet cast, and she
has protruding teeth, long dark eyebrows, stony eyes, and
heavy eye-lashes. A sick monkey is not a very enlivening
sight; a black man with chilblains and a fit of the ague is
not calculated to provoke cheerfulness, and there are spectacles more cheerful than a workhouse funeral on a wet day;

but all these are positively carnivals of joviality compared to Mademoiselle Batiste wailing over her lady's wardrobe, her own wrongs, and her unhappy destiny generally. The climate, the food, the lodging, the raiment, the tyranny of superiors, and the insolence of inferiors; all these find a place in the category of this gruesome lady's unhappiness. She prophecies the decadence of England with far more fervour than M. Ledru Rollin. She will impress herself to leave this detestable land; without sun, without manners, without knowledge of living. Somehow she does not quit this detestable land. She is like (without disrespect) that animal of delusive promise, the conjuror's donkey, which is always going for to go, but seldom does really go, up the ladder. Mademoiselle Batiste weeps and moans, and grumbles, and changes her situation innumerable times, and packs up her "effects" for the continent once a week or so; but stays in England after all. When she has saved enough money, she may perhaps revisit the land of the Gaul, and relate to her compatriots the affliction sore which long time she bore among *ces barbares*.

In reality, Mademoiselle Batiste is an excellent servant; she is not only apt but erudite in all the cunning of her craft. M. Anatole, of Regent Street, might take lessons in hair-dressing from her. She far surpasses Miss Tarlatan in dress-making; although she disdains to include that accomplishment in the curriculum of her duties. But her principal skill lies in *putting on a dress*, in imparting to her mistress when dressed an air, a grace, a *tournure*, which any but a French hand must ever despair of accomplishing. Yet she grumbles meanwhile; and when she has made a peri of a peeress, sighs dolefully and maintains that an English-woman does not know how to wear a robe. This skill it is that makes her fretfulness and melancholial distemper borne with by rank and fashion. She has, besides, a pedigree of former engagements of such magnitude and grandeur, that rank and fashion are fain to bow to her caprices. The beauteous Duchesse de Faribole in Paris, and the Marquise de Lysbrisée (very poor, very Legitimist, but intensely fashionable); the famous Princess Cabbagioso at Florence, Countess Moskamujikoff at St. Petersburgh, the Duchess of Champignon, the Marchioness of Truffleton and Lady Frances Frongus in England—all these high-born ladies has she delighted with her skill, awed with her aristocratic antecedents, and annoyed with her melancholia. Although so highly skilled in dress-making she pays but little regard to costume herself. Her figure is straight all the way down, on all sides. She wears a long pendent shawl, a dreary bonnet with trailing ribbons; and carries, when abroad, a long, melancholy, attenuated umbrella, like a parasol that had outgrown itself, and was wasting away in despair. These, with the long dull gold drops to her ear-rings; two flat thin smooth bands of hair flattened upon her forehead; long listless fingers, and long feet encased in French boots of lustreless kid, give her an unspeakably mournful, trailing appearance. She seems to have fallen altogether into the "portion of weeds and outgrown faces." Her voice is melancholy and tristfully surgant, like an Æolian harp; her delivery is reminiscent of the Dead March in Saul;—a few wailing, lingering notes, closed with a melancholy boom at the end of the strophe. Adieu, Mademoiselle Batiste.

H

There are many more lady's-maids who want places ; and, taking into consideration the increased facilities offered by the abolition of the duty on advertisements, I sincerely hope they may all be suited satisfactorily. But I cannot tarry to discuss all their several qualifications. Although I can conscientiously recommend " Wilkins" (Christian name unknown), the lady's-maid of middle age, and domesticated habits, who was with Mrs. Colonel Stodger during the whole of the Sutlej campaign ; who is not too proud to teach the cook how to make curries ; is reported to have ridden (with her mistress) in man's saddle five hundred miles on camel's back in India, and to have done something considerable to-wards shooting a plundering native discovered in Mrs. Stodger's tent. Nor would I have you overlook the claims of Martha Stirpenny, who is a "young lady's-maid," and is not above plain needlework ; or of Miss Catchpole, the maid, nurse, companion, amanuensis, everything, for so many years to the late Miss Plough, of Maunday Terrace, Bayswater, who ungratefully left all her vast wealth in Bank and India stock to the " Total Abstinence from Suttee Hindoo Widow's Society," offices Great St. Helens, secretary, G. F. L. B. Stoneybatter, Esq. ; and bequeathed to her faithful Catchpole, after twenty years' service, only a silver teapot and a neatly-bound set of the Rev. Doctor Duffaboxe's sermons. All these domestics want places, and all letters to them must be post-paid.

A S COOK (Professed) a Person who fully understands her business. Address L., Pattypan Place, Great Brazier Street.

There is something honest, outspoken, fearless, in this brief advertisement. L. does not condescend to hint about the length and quality of her character, or the distinguished nature of the family she wishes to enter. " Here I am," she seems to say ; " a professed cook. If you are the sort of person knowing what a professed cook is, and how to use her, try me. Good cooks are not so plentiful that they need shout for custom. Good wine needs no bush. I stand upon my cooking, and if you suit me as I suit you, nothing but a spoilt dinner shall part us two." L., whom we will incarnate for the nonce as Mrs. Lambswool, widow, is fat and forty, but not fair. The fires of innumerable kitchen ranges have swarthed her ruddy countenance to an almost salamandrine hue. · And she is a salamander in temper too, is Mrs. Lambswool, for all her innocent name. Lambswool, deceased (formerly clerk of the kitchen to the Dawdle club), knew it to his cost, poor man ; and for many a kept back dinner and unpraised made dish did he suffer in his time.

If Fate could bring together (and how seldom Fate *does* bring together things and persons suited for one another), Mrs. Lambswool and Sir Chyle Turrener, how excellently they would agree! Sir Chyle—who dwells in Bangmarry Crescent, Hordover Square, and whose house as you pass it smells all day like a cook-shop—made his handsome competence in the war time by contracts for mess-beef as execrable, and mess-biscuits as weevily, as ever her Majesty's service, by sea or land, spoilt their digestion and their teeth with. He is, in these piping times of peace, renowned as the most accomplished epicure in the dining world. He does not dine often at his club, the Gigot (although that establishment boasts of great gastronomic fame, and entertains a head man cook at a salary of two hundred and fifty pounds a year); he accused M. Relevay, the *chef* in question, of paying more attention to the greasing and adornment of his hair, and the composition of his bills of fare in ornamental penmanship, than to the culinary wants of the members ; he will not have a man cook himself; "the fellows," he says, "are as conceited as peacocks and as extravagant as Cleopatra." Give him a woman cook—a professed cook, who knows her business, and does it : and the best of wages and the best of places are hers, at 35, Bangmarry Crescent.

Let us figure him and Mrs. Lambswool together. Sir Chyle—a little apple-faced old gentleman with a white head, and as fiery in temper as his cook—looks on Mrs. Lambswool as, next to the dinners she cooks and the government annuity in which (with a sagacious view towards checking the prodigality of his nephew and expectant heir) he has sunk his savings, the most important element in his existence. He places her in importance and consideration far beyond the elderly female attached to [his household in the capacity of wife—used by him chiefly in forming a hand at whist and in helping soup (catch Sir Chyle trusting her with fish !) and by him abused at every convenient opportunity. He absolutely forbids any interference on her part with the culinary economy and discipline. "Blow up the maids as much as you like, Ma'am," he considerately says, "but don't meddle with my cook." Mrs. L. crows over her mistress accordingly, and if she were to tell her that pea soup was best made with bilberries, the poor lady would, I dare say, take the dictum for granted. Sir Chyle Turrener is exceedingly liberal in all matters of his own housekeeping—although he once wrote a letter to the *Times* virulently denouncing soup-kitchens. When a dinner of a superlative nature has issued from his kitchen, he not unfrequently, in the warmth of his admiration, presents Mrs. Lambswool with gratuities in money; candidly admitting that he gives them now, because he does not intend to leave his cook a penny when he dies, seeing that she can dress no more dinners for him after his decease. On grand occasions she is summoned to the dining room, at the conclusion of the repast, and he compliments her formally on this or that culinary triumph. He lauds her to his friends Tom Aitchbone, of the Beefsteak club, Common Councillor Podge, Sergeant Buffalo, of the Southdown circuit, and old Sir Thomas Marrowfat, who was a prothonotary to something, somewhere, some time—no matter when or where—and can nose a dinner in the lobby (the poor old fellow can hardly hold his knife and fork for the palsy, and his napkin tucked under his wagging old chin looks like a grave-cloth) with as much felicity as Hamlet stated that the remains of King Claudius's chamberlain might have been discovered. It is a strong point in the Turrener and Lamswool creed and practice to hold all cookery-books—for any practical purposes beyond casual reference—in great indifference, not to say contempt. Sir Chyle has Glasse and Kitchener, Austin, and Ude, Francatelli, and Soyer, besides the Almanack des Gourmands, and the Cuisinier Royal in his library, gorgeously bound. He glances at them occasionally as Bentley, the critic, might have glanced at a dictionary or a lexicon; but he does not tie himself nor does he bind his cook to blind adherence to their rules. True cookery, in his opinion, should rest mainly on tradition, on experience, and pre-eminently, in the inborn genius of a cook. Mrs. Lambswool holds the same opinion, although she may express it in different language. She may never have heard of the axiom, "One becomes a cook, but one is born a roaster;" but she will tell you in her own homely language that "roasting and biling comes nateral, and some is good at it, and some isn't." Her master has told her the story of Vatel and his fish martyrdom, but she holds his suicide to have been rank cowardice. "If there was'nt no fish," she, remarks, "and it wasn't his fault, why couldn't he have served up something neat in the made-dish way, with a bit of a speech about being drove up into a corner?" But she hints darkly as to what she would have done to the fishmonger. Transfixure on a spit, would have been too good for *him*, a wretch.

Through long years of choice feeding might this pair roll on, till the great epicure, Death, pounces on Sir Chyle Turrener to garnish *his* sideboard. · If dainty pasture can improve meat, he will be a succulent morsel. He has fed on many things animate and inanimate: Nature will return the compliment then. For all here below is vanity, and even good dinners and professed cooks cannot last for ever. The fishes have had their share of Lucullus, and Apicius has helped to grow mustard and cress these thousand years. So *might* the knight and the cook roll on, I say; but a hundred to one if they ever come in contact. The world is very wide; and, although the heiress with twenty thousand pounds, who has fallen in love with us, lives over the way, we marry the housemaid, and our heads grow grey, and we die, and we never reck of the heiress. Sir Chyle Turrener may, at this moment, be groaning in exasperation at an unskilful cook, who puts too much pepper in his soup and boils his fish to flakes; and Mrs. Lambswool's next place may be with a north country squire with no more palate than a boa-constrictor, who delights in nothing half so much as a half-raw beefsteak, or a pie with a crust as thick as the walls of the model prison, and calls made dishes "kickshaws."

"As Good Cook in a private family," &c., &c., &c.,—the usual formula, with a hint as to irreproachable character, and a published want of objection to the country. The Good Cook does not pretend to the higher mysteries or the 'professed.' I doubt if she knows what a *bain marie* pan is, or what *Mayonnaises, Salmis, Sautés, Fricandeaux, Gratins,* or *Soufflés* are. Her French is not even of the school of "Stratford-atte-Bow,' and she does not understand what a *met* can mean. Her stock made dishes are veal cutlets, haricot mutton, stewed eels, and Irish stew. She makes all these well; and very good things they are in their way. She is capital at a hand of pork and pea soup; at pigeon pies; at roasting, boiling, frying, stewing, and baking. She is great at pies and puddings, and has a non-transcribed receipt for plum pudding, which she would not part with for a year's wages. She can cook as succulent, wholesome, cleanly a dinner as any Christian man need wish to set down to; but she is not an artist. Her dinners are not in the "first style." She may do for Bloomsbury, but not for Belgravia.

HOUSEMAID (where a footman is kept), a respectable young woman, with three years' good character. Address L. B., Gamms Court, Lamb's Conduit Street.

Letitia Brownjohn, who wishes to be a housemaid, who has three years' good character (by her pronounced "krakter") is two-and-twenty years of age. Her father is a smith, or a pianoforte maker, or a leather dresser, stifling with a large family in Gamms Court. Her mother has been out at service in her time, and Letitia is in the transition state now— in the chrysalis formation of domestic drudgery ; which she hopes to exchange some day for the full-blown butterflyhood of a home, a husband, a family, and domestic drudgery of her own. Ah, Letitia, for all that you are worried now by captious mistresses, the time may come when, in some stifling Gamms Court of your own, steaming over a washtub, with a drunken husband and a brood of ragged children, you may sigh for your quiet kitchen, the cat, the ticking clock, the workbox in the area window, and your cousin (in the Guards) softly whispering and whistling outside the area railings.

Letitia Brownjohn, like most other young ladies of the housemaid calling, has had an university education. Not, I need scarcely tell, at theological Oxford, or logarithmical Cambridge ; nor at the Silent Sister's, who would not suit Letitia by any means ; nor at Durham, famous for its mustard and its mines ; nor at any one of those naughty colleges in Ireland which the Pope is so angry with ; nor even at any one of the colleges recently instituted in this country "for ladies only," as the railway carriages have it— yet in an university. Letitia, as most of the university-educated do, went in the first instance to a public school ; that founded by Lady Honoria Woggs (wife of King William the Third's Archbishop Woggs), where intellectual training was an object of less solicitude by the committee of management than the attainment of a strong nasal style of vocal elocution, as applied to the sacred lyrics of Messrs. Sternhold and Hopkins, and the wearing a peculiarly hideous costume, accurately copied and followed from the painted wooden statuette of one of Lady Wogg's girls, in Lady Wogg's own time, placed in a niche over the porch of the dingy brick building containing Lady Wogg's school, and flanked in another niche by another statuette of a young gentleman in a muffin cap and leathers, representing one of Lady Woggs's boys.

From this establishment our Letitia passed, being some nine or ten years of age, to the university; and there she matriculated, and there she graduated. Do you know that university to which three-fourths—nay, nineteen-twentieths—of our London-bred children " go up ? " Its halls and colleges are the pavement and the gutter ; its lecture-theatre the doorstep and the post at the corner; its schools of philosophy are the chandler's shop, the cobbler's stall, and the public-house ; of which the landlord is the chancellor; its proctor and bull-dogs are the police-sergeant and his men ; its public orators, the ballad-singers and last-dying-speech criers ; its lecturers are scolding women. The weekly wages of its occupants form its university chest. Commemoration takes place every Saturday night, with grand musical performances from the harp, guitar, and violin, opposite the "Admiral Keppel," The graduates are mechanics and small tradesmen and their wives. The undergraduates are Letitias and Tommies. The University is the Street.

Right in its centre stands the Tree of Knowledge of good and evil. And all day long children come and pluck the fruit and eat it ; and some choose ripe and wholesome fruit, the pleasant savour of which shall not depart out of their mouths readily ; but some elect bad and rotten apples,

which they fall upon and devour gluttonously, so that the
fruit disagrees with them very much indeed, and causes them
to break all out in such eruptions of vicious humours, as
their very children's children's blood shall be empoisoned
with, years hence.   And some, being young and foolish and
ignorant, take and eat indiscriminately of the good and of
the bad fruit, and are sick and sorry or healthful and glad
alternately ; but might fare badly and be lost in the long
run did not Wisdom and Love (come from making of rain-
bows and quelling of storms, perhaps a million miles away,
to consider of the sparrows and take stock of the flies in the
back street university) appear betimes among these young undergraduates gathered under the branches, and teach their hearts
how to direct their hands to pluck good sustenance from that
tree. I never go down a back street and look on the multitude of
children (I don't mean ragged, Bedouin children, but decently
attired young people, of poor but honest parents, living hard
by, who have no better playing-ground for them), and hear
them singing their street songs, and see them playing street
games, and making street friendships, and caballing on doorsteps, or conspiring by posts, or newsmongering on kerb-
stones, or trotting along with jugs and halfpence for the
beer, or listening open-mouthed to the street orators and
musicians, or watching Punch and the acrobats, or forming
a ring at a street fight, or gathered round a drunken man, or
running to a fire, or running from a bull, or pressing' round
about an accident, bonnetless and capless, but evidently
native to this place—·without these thoughts of the university
and the tree coming into my head.   You who may have been
expensively educated and cared for, and have had a gymna-

sium for exercise, covered playing courts, class-rooms, cricket-fields, ushers to attend you in the hours of recreations ; who have gone from school and college into the world, well recommended and with a golden passport, should think more, and considerately too, of what a hazardous, critical, dangerous nature this street culture is. With what small book-learning these poor young undergraduates get, or that their parents can afford to provide them with, is mixed simultaneously the strangest course of tuition in the ethics of the pawn-broker's shop, the philosophy of the public-house, the rhetoric of drunken men and shrewish women, the logic of bad associations, and bad examples, and bad language.

Our Letitia graduated in due course of girlhood, becoming a mistress of such household arts as a London-bred girl can hope to acquire at the age of fourteen or fifteen. Well, you know what sort of a creature the lodging-house maid-of-all-work is, and what sort of a life she leads. You have seen her; her pattens and dishevelled cap, her black stockings and battered.tin candlestick. We have all known Letitia Brownjohns—oft-times comely, neat-handed Phillises enough — oft-times desperately slatternly and untidy — in almost every case wofully over-worked and as wofully underpaid. Letitia must be up early and late. With the exception of the short intermission of sleep doled forth to her, her work is ceaseless. She ascends and descends every step of every flight of stairs in the house hundreds of times in the course of the day ; she.is the slave of the ringing both of the door bell and the lodgers. She must be little more than an animated appendage to the knocker—a jack in the box, to be produced by a double rap. She is cook, house-

maid, lady's-maid, scullery maid, housekeeper, all in one;
and for what? For some hundred and fifty shillings every
year, and some—few and far between—coppers and sixpences,
doled out to her in gratuities by the lodgers in consideration
of her Briarean handiwork. Her holidays are very, very few.
Almost her only intercourse with the outer world takes place
when she runs to the public-house at the corner for the dinner
or supper beer, or to a neighbouring fishmonger for oysters.

A rigid supervision is kept over her conduct. She is expected to have neither friends, acquaintances, relations, nor
sweethearts. "No followers," is the Median and Persian
law continually paraded before her; a law unchangeable, and
broken only under the most ruinous penalties. When you
and I grumble at our lot, repine at some petty reverse, fret
and fume over the curtailment of some indulgence, the depri-
vation of some luxury, we little know what infinite gradations
of privation and suffering exist; and what admirable and exemplary contentment and cheerfulness are often to be found among
those whose standing is on the lowest rounds of the ladder.

But Letitia is emancipated from the maid-of-all-work
thraldrom now, and aspires to be a "Housemaid where a
footman is kept," yet not without considerable difficulty, and
after years of arduous 'apprenticeship and servitude. With
the maid-of-all-work, as she begins, so 'tis ten to one that as
such she ends. I have known grey-headed maids-of-all-
work; and from these—with a sprinkling of insolvent laun-
dresses and widows who have had their mangles seized for
rent—is recruited, and indeed, organised, the numerous and
influential class of "charwomen" who do household work
for eighteenpence a day and a glass of spirits.

But Letitia Brownjohn has been more fortunate. Some lady lodger, perchance, in some house in which he has been a servitor, has taken a fancy to her ; and such lodger, taking in due course of human eventuality a house for herself, has taken Letitia to be her own private housemaid. And she has lived with City families, and tradesmen's families, and in boarding-schools, and she has grown from the untidy " gal " in the black stockings, and the mob cap, to be a natty young person in a smart cap and ribands, aspiring to a situation where a footman is kept. That she may speedily obtain such an appointment; that the footman may be worthy of his companion in service ; that they may please each other (in due course of time), even to the extent of the asking of banns and the solemnisation of a certain service, I very cheerfully and sincerely wish.

VIII.

OLD LADIES.

ARE there any old ladies left, now-a-days ? The question may at first appear absurd; for, by the returns of the last census we find that seven per cent. of the whole female population were, four years since, widows :* and that, at the same period, there were in Great Britain three hundred and fifty-nine thousand nine hundred and sixty-nine " old maids " above the age of forty. Yet I repeat my question, and am prepared to abide by the consequences : Are there any old ladies left, now-a-days ?

Statistically, of course, substantially even, old ladies are as plentiful as of yore ; but I seek in vain for the old lady types of my youth ; the feminine antiquities that furnished forth my juvenile British Museum. Every omnibus-conductor has his old lady passenger—pattens, big basket, umbrella. The cabman knows the old lady well—her accurate measurement of mileage, her multitudinous packages, for which she resists extra payment ; her objections to the uncleanliness of the straw and the dampness of the cushion ; her incessant use of the checkstring and frequent employment of a parasol handle, or, a key, dug into the small of the driver's back as a

* Written A.D. 1855.

means of attracting his attention; her elaborate but contra-
dictory directions as to where she wishes to be set down;
and, finally, her awful threats of fine, imprisonment, and
treadmill should that much-ill-used Ixion-at-sixpence-a-mile
offend her. No railway train starts without an old lady, who
screams whenever the whistle is sounded; groans in the tunnels; is sure there is something the matter with the engine;
smuggles surreptitious poodles into the carriage; calls for tea
at stations where there are no refreshment-rooms; summons
the guard to the door at odd times during the journey, and
tells him he ought to be ashamed of himself, because the train
is seven minutes behind time; insists upon having the window
up or down at precisely the wrong periods; scrunches the
boots of her opposite neighbour, or makes short lunges into
his waistcoat during intempestive naps, and, should he remonstrate, indulges in muttered soliloquies, ending with, "One
doesn't know who one is travelling with, now-a-days;" and
carries a basket of provisions, from which crumbs disseminate
themselves unpleasantly on all surrounding laps and knees,
and from which the neck of a small black bottle *will* peep:
the cork being always mislaid in the carriage, and causing
unspeakable agonies to the other passengers in the efforts for
its recovery. There are old ladies at every theatre, who
scream hysterically when guns are discharged; who, when the
Blaze of Bliss in the Realms of Dioramic Delight takes place,
seem on the point of crying "Fire!" and who persist in sitting before you in huge bonnets, apparently designed expressly
to shut out the dangerous seductions of the ballet. Churches
teem with old ladies—from the old ladies in the pews who
knock down the prayer-books during the "I publish the

banns," and turn over the mouldy hassocks, blinding you with a cloud of dust and straw-chips, — to the old ladies, mouldier and dustier than the hassocks, who open the pews, cough for sixpences, and curtsey for shillings; and the very old ladies who sit in the free seats, have fits during the sermon, and paralysis all through the service. There are old ladies in ships upon the high seas who *will* speak to the man at the wheel; in bad weather, moaningly request to be thrown overboard, and block up the companion-ladder—mere senseless bundles of sea-sick old-ladyism. There is never a crowd without an old lady in it. The old lady is at almost every butcher's shop, at almost every grocer's retail establishment, on Saturday nights. Every housemaid knows an old lady who objected to ribands, counted the hearthstones, denounced the "fellows" (comprising the police, the household troops, and the assistants of the butcher and grocer aforesaid), and denied that the cat broke all the crockery at her (the housemaid's) last place. Every cook has been worretted dreadfully, by the old lady; every country parson knows her and dreads her, for she interferes with the discipline of the village school, and questions the orthodoxy of his sermons. Every country doctor is aware of, and is wroth with her; for there is either always something the matter with her, or else she persists in dosing, pilling, and plaistering other old ladies who have something the matter with them, to the stultification of the doctor's prescriptions, and the confusion of science. The missionaries would have little to eat, and nobody to eat them up in the South Seas, were it not for the old ladies. Exeter Hall in May would be a howling wilderness, but for the old ladies in the front seats, their umbrellas, and white pocket-handkerchiefs. And what Professor Methusaleh and his pills, Professor Swallow with his ointment, Doctor Bumble-puppy with his pitch-plaisters, and Mr. Spools, M.R.C.S., with his galvano-therapeutic blisters, would do without old ladies I'm sure I don't know. Yea, and the poor-boxes of the police-courts for their Christmas five-pound notes, the desti-tute for their coals and blankets, the bed-ridden old women for their flannel petticoats would often be in sorry plight but for the aid of the old ladies, bless them! At every birth and at every death there is an old lady. I have heard that old ladies are sometimes seen at courts. It is whispered that old ladies have from time to time been found in camps. Nay, irre-verent youth, hot-headed, inconsiderate youngsters, doubtless —bits of boys—have sometimes the assurance to hint that old ladies have, within these last thousand years, been known to sit the councils of royalty, and direct the movement of armies, the intricacies of diplomacy, and the operations of commerce.

But these are not *my* old ladies. Search the wide world through, and bring before me legions of old ladies, and I shall still be asking my old question.

No. I will be positive and give my self-asked question a negative, once for all. There are *no* old ladies now-a-days. You know as well as I do that there are no children now; no tender rump-steaks; no good-fellows; no good books; no chest-tenors; no clever actors; no good tragedies, and no old port wine. The old ladies have followed all these vanished good things. If they exist at all, they exist only to that young generation which is treading on our corns and pushing us from our stools, which laughs in its sleeve at us, and calls us old fogies behind our backs; to that generation which

I

yet believes in the whisperings of fancy, the phantoms of hope, and the performance, by age, of the promises of youth. The old women have even disappeared. Women there are, and old, but no old women. The old woman of Berkeley; the old woman of Tutbury, who so marvellously supported herself by suction from her pocket-handkerchief; the aërostatic old woman who effected an ascent so many times higher than the moon; the old woman who lived in a shoe, and frugally nurtured her numerous offspring upon broth without bread; the delightful old woman, and member of the society for the prevention of cruelty to animals—Mother Hubbard—who so tenderly entertained that famous dog, though, poor soul, she was often put to it, to find him a bone in her cupboard; the eccentric old woman who, is it possible to imagine it, lived upon nothing but victuals and drink, and yet would never be quiet (she vanished from my youthful ken at about the same time as the old man of Tobago—who lived on rice, sugar, and sago); the terrible old French woman La Mère Croquemitaine who went about France with a birch and a basket, wherewith to whip and carry away naughty little girls and boys, and who has now been driven away herself by the principals of genteel seminaries in the Champs Elysées; the marvellous, fearsome old women of witchcraft, with brooms, hell-broths, spells, and incantations; the good and wicked old women of the Arabian Nights and the Child's Own Book; fairy godmothers; hump-backed old women sitting by wellsides; cross old women gifted with magic powers, who were inadvertently left out of christening invitations, and wove dreadful spells in consequence; good women in the wood;

old women who had grandchildren wearing little Redriding-hoods and meeting (to their sorrow) wolves; Mother Goose, Mother Redcap, even Mother Damnable (I beg your pardon) —all this goodly band of old women have been swept away. There are no types of feminine age left to me now. All the picturesque types of life besides seem melting away. It is all coming to a dead level: a single line of rails, with signals, stations, points, and turntables; and the Cradle Train starts at one fifteen, and the Coffin Train is due at twelve forty-five. —An iron world.

Somewhere in the dusty room, of which the door has been locked for years, I have a cupboard. There, among the old letters—how yellow and faded the many scored expressions of affection have grown! the locks of hair; the bygone washing-bills—" one pare sox, one frunt;" the handsome bill of costs (folio, foolscap, stitched with green ferret) that came up as a rider to that small legacy that was spent so quickly; the miniature of the lady in the leg of mutton sleeves; the por-traits of Self and Schoolfriend—Self in a frilled collar, grin-ning; Schoolfriend in a lay-down collar, also grinning; the rusted pens; the squeezed-out-tubes of colour; the memo-randa to be sure to do goodness knows what for goodness knows whom; the books begun; the checkbooks ended; the torn envelopes; the wedding cards with true lovers' knots dimmed and tarnished; the addresses of people who are dead; the keys of watches that are sold; the old passports, old hotel bills, dinner tickets, and theatrical checks; the multifarious odds and ends that will accumulate in cupboards, be your periodical burnings ever so frequent, or your waste paper basket system ever so rigorous; among all these it may be that I can find a portfolio—shadowy or substantial matters little—wherein lie nestled, all torn, blotted, faded, mildewed, crumpled, stained, and moth-eaten, some portraits of the old ladies I should like to find now-a-days.

Yes; here is one: The Pretty Old Lady. She must have been very, very beautiful when young; for, in my childish eyes she had scarcely any imperfections, and we all know what acute and unmerciful critics children are. Her hair was quite white; not silvery nor powdery, but pure glossy white, resembling spun glass. I have never been able to make my mind up whether she wore a cap, a hood, or one of those silken head-coverings of the last century called a calash. Whatever she wore, it became her infinitely. I incline, on second thoughts, more to the calash, and think she wore it in lieu of a bonnet, when she went abroad; which was but seldom. The portrait I have of the old lady is, indeed, blurred and dimmed by the lapse of many winters, and some tears. Her title of the "pretty old lady" was not given to her lightly. It was bruited many years ago—when ladies of fashion were drunk to, in public, and gentlemen of fashion were drunk too in public—that the pretty old lady had been a "reigning toast."

A certain gray silk dress which, as it had always square creases in it, I conjectured to be always new, decorated the person of the pretty old lady. She wore a profusion of black lace, which must have been priceless, for it was continually being mended, and its reversion was much coveted by the old lady's female friends. My aunt Jane, who was tremendously old, and was a Lady; but whose faculties decayed somewhat towards the close of her life, was never so coherent (save on the subject of May-day and the sweeps) as when she speculated as to "who was to have the lace" after the old lady's demise. But my aunt Jane died first, and her doubts were never solved. More than this, I can remember a fat-faced old gold watch which the pretty old lady wore at her waist; a plethoric mass of gold, like an oyster grown rich and knowing the time of day. Attached to this she wore some trinkets — not the nonsensical charms that young ladies wear at their girdles now, but sensible, substantial ornaments—a signet-ring of her grandfather's; a smelling-bottle covered with silver filagree; and a little golden box in the form of a book with clasps, which we waggish youngsters declared to be the old lady's snuff-box, but which, I believe, now, to have been a pouncet-box— the same perhaps, which the lord, who was perfumed like a milliner, held 'twixt his finger and his thumb upon the battle-field, and which, ever and anon, he gave his nose.

I trust I am not treading upon dangerous ground, when I say, that two of the chief prettinesses of the pretty old lady were her feet and their covering. "To ladies' eyes a round, boys!" Certainly, Mr. Moore, we can't refuse ; but to ladies' feet, a round boys, also, if you please. Now the pretty old lady had the prettiest of feet, with the most delicate of gray silk stockings, the understandings of the finest, softest, most lustrous leather that ever came from innocent kid. I will back those feet (to use the parlance of this horse-racing age) and those shoes and stockings against any in the known world, in ancient or modern history or romance : against Dorathea's tiny feet dabbling in the stream; agains Musidora's paddling in the cool brook ; against Sara la

Baigneuse swinging in her silken hammock; against De Gram-
mont's Miss Howard's green stockings ; against Madame de
Pompadour's golden clocks and red-heeled *mules ;* against No-
blet, Taglioni, Cerito's ; against Madame Vestris's, as modelled
in wax by Signor N. N. There are no such feet as the pretty
old lady's now ; or, if any such exist, their possessors don't
know how to treat them. The French ladies are rapidly
losing the art of putting on shoes and stocking with taste ;
and I deliberately declare, in the face of Europe, that I have
not seen, within the last three months in Paris—from the
Boulevard des Italiens to the Ball of the Prefect of the Seine
—twenty pairs of irreproachable feet. The systematically
arched instep, the geometrical ankle, the gentle curves and
undulations, the delicate advancement and retrogression of
the foot of beauty, are all things falling into oblivion. The
American overshoes, the machine-made hosiery, and the
trailing draperies, are completing the ruin of shoes and
stockings.

The pretty old lady had never been married. Her father
had been a man of fashion—a gay man—a first-rate buck, a
sparkling rake ; he had known lords, he had driven curricles,
he had worn the finest of fine linen, the most resplendent of
shoe-buckles ; he had once come into the possession of five
thousand pounds sterling, upon which capital—quite casting
the grovelling doctrine of interest to the winds—he had determined to try the fascinating experiment of living at the
rate of five thousand a-year. In this experiment he succeeded
to his heart's content for the exact period of one year and
one day, after which he had lived (at the same rate) on credit ;
after that on the credit of his credit ; after that on his wits ;

after that in the rules of the King's Bench ; after that on the
certainty of making so many tricks, nightly at whist ; and,
finally upon his daughter. For the pretty old lady, with
admirable self-abnegation, had seen her two ugly sisters
married ; had, with some natural tears, refused Captain Cutts,
of the line, whom she loved (but who had nothing but his
pay) and had contentedly accepted the office of a governess ;
whence, after much self-denial, study, striving, pinching, and
saving (how many times her little cobwebs of economy were
ruthlessly swept away by her gay father's turn for whist and
hazard — cobwebs that took years to reconstruct !), she had
promoted herself to the dignity of a schoolmistress ; governing
in that capacity that fine old red-brick ladies' seminary at
Paddington,—pulled down for the railway now—Porchester
House.

'Twas there I first saw the pretty old lady : for I had a
cousin receiving her " finishing " at Porchester House, and
'twas there—being at the time some eight years of age—
that I first fell in love with an astonishingly beautiful creature, with raven hair and gazelle-like eyes, who was about
seventeen, and the oldest girl in the school. When I paid
my cousin a visit I was occasionally admitted—being of a
mild and watery disposition, and a very little boy of my age
—to the honours of the tea table. I used to sit opposite to
this black-eyed Juno, and be fed by her with slices of those
curious open-work cross-barred jam tarts, which are so frequently met with at genteel tea-tables. I loved her fondly,
wildly : but she dashed my spirits to the ground one day,
by telling me not to make faces. I wonder whether she
married a duke !

The pretty old lady kept school at Porchester House for many, many years, supporting and comforting that fashionable fellow, her father. She had sacrificed her youth, the firstlings of her beauty, her love, her hopes, everything. The gay fellow had grown a little paralytic at last; and, becoming very old and imbecile and harmless, had been relegated to an upper apartment in Porchester House. Here, for several years, he had vegetated in a sort of semi-fabulous existence as the " old gentlemen ; " very many of the younger ladies being absolutely unaware of him; till, one evening, a neat coffin with plated nails and handles, arrived at Porchester House, for somebody aged seventy-three, and the cook remarked to the grocer's young man that the " old gentleman " had died that morning.

The pretty old lady continued the education of generations of black-eyed Junos, in French, geography, the use of the globes, and the usual branches of a polite education, long after her father's death. Habit is habit ; Lieutenant-Colonel Cutts had died of a fever in the Walcheren expedition—so the pretty old lady kept school at Porchester House until she was very, very old. When she retired, she devised all her savings to her ugly sisters' children ; and calmly, cheerfully, placidly prepared to lie herself down in her grave. Hers had been a long journey and a sore servitude ; but, perhaps, something was said to her at the End, about being a good and faithful servant, and that it was well done.

Such is the dim outline which the picture in my portfolio presents to me of the pretty old lady. Sharpened as her pretty features were by age, the gentle touch of years of peace—of an equable mind and calm desires, had passed

lovingly over the acuities of her face, and softened them.
Wrinkles she must have had, for the stern usurer Time will
have his bond; but she had smiled her wrinkles away, or had
laughed them into dimples. Our just, though severe mother,
Nature, had rewarded her for having worn no rouge in her
youth, no artificial flowers in her spring ; and gave her
blooming roses in her December. Although the sunset of
her eyes was come and they could not burn you up, or melt
you as in the noontide, the sky was yet pure, and the lumi-
nary sank to rest in a bright halo : the shadows that it cast
were long, but sweet and peaceful,—not murky and terrible.
The night was coming ; but it was to be a night starlit with
faith and hope, and not a season of black storms.

It was for this reason, I think, that being old, feeling old,
looking old, proud of being old, and yet remaining handsome,
the pretty old lady was so beloved by all the pretty girls. They
adored her. They called her " a dear old thing." They insisted
upon trying their new bonnets, shawls, scarfs, and similar feminine fallals, upon her. They made her the fashion, and dressed
up to her. They never made her spiteful presents of fleecy
hosiery, to guard against a rheumatism with which she was
not afflicted ; or entreated her to tie her face up when she
had no toothache ; or bawled in her ear on the erroneous
assumption that she was deaf,—as girls will do, in pure
malice, when age forgets its privileges, and apes the levity
and sprightliness of youth. Above all, they trusted her with
love-secrets (I must mention, that though a spinster, the
pretty old lady was always addressed as Mistress). She was
great in love matters,—a complete letter-writer, without its
verbosity : as prudent as Pamela, as tender as Amelia, as

judicious as Hooker, as dignified as Sir Charles Grandison. She could scent a Lovelace at an immense distance, bid Tom Jones mend his ways, reward the constancy of an Uncle Toby, and reform a Captain Booth. I warrant the perverse widow and Sir Roger de Coverley would have been brought together, had the pretty old lady known the parties and been consulted. She was conscientious and severe, but not intolerant and implacable. She did not consider every man in love a "wretch," or every woman in love a "silly thing." She was pitiful to love, for she had known it. She could tell a tale of love as moving as any told to her. Its hero died at Walcheren.

Where shall I find pretty old ladies now-a-days? Where are they gone,—those gentle, kindly, yet dignified, antiquated dames, married and single?

My young friend Sprigly comes and tells me that I am wrong, and that there are many good old ladies now as of yore. It may be so; it may be, that we think those pleasant companionships lost because the years are gone in which we enjoyed them; and that we imagine there are no more old ladies, because those we loved are dead.

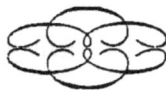

IX

LITTLE CHILDREN.

" NO man can tell," wrote that good Bishop of Down, Connor, and Dromore, whose elevation to the mitre in an unbelieving and profligate age makes at least one jewel of pure water in the besmirched diadem of Charles the Second, " No man can tell," wrote Jeremy Taylor, " but he who loves his children, how many delicious accents makes a man's heart dance in the pretty conversation of those dear pledges. Their childishness, their stammering, their little angers, their innocence, their imperfections, their necessities, are so many little emanations of joy and comfort to him that delights in their persons and society." With all due respect and reverence to my beloved author of the " Golden Grove," the " warbler of poetic prose," I must dissent from his first proposition. A man who loves children *can* tell, without necessarily having any of his own, how delightful is their society, how delicious are their accents, their persons, their little ways. It may be that I write these lines in a cheerless garret, my only friends my books, the only other thing beside me that has life, my lamp ; yet do you not think that I can sympathise with, without envying, the merry party at the merry house over the way ?

—the house with all the windows lighted up, the broughams and hack cabs at the door; the prim, white neckclothed visitors taking off their paletôts in the passage; the smiling, ringleted, rosy cheeked, rosy ribboned young person who attends to the ladies' bonnets and the tea and coffee; the jangling of Collard and Collard's piano; the tinkling of Erard's harp; the oscillations in their upstairs passage of the negus glasses, the singing, the dancing, the flirtation, and the supper. Yet, I know nothing about Mrs. Saint-Baffin and her evening party. She never invited me to it: she does not know, very probably, of my existence; but I am sure I wish most sincerely that her "at home" may be perfectly satisfactory and successful; that every body may get as much as he wants to eat and drink at supper; that the supply of lobster salad and iced champagne may not run short; that Miss Strumminson's "Cossacco della Volga" may be sung by that young lady amid general applause; that all General Fogey's stories may tell, and that none of young Miller's jokes may have been heard before; that the right men may secure their right hats and right wrappers; that all the young ladies may depart duly shawled and bonnetted, to the defiance and confusion of the demon cold; that all mammas may be placable; all true lovers satisfied with their innocent flirtations; all stolen camellias, scraps of riband, and odd gloves warmly prized; that years to come there may be little children laughing and playing round papa and mamma, all unconscious that papa and mamma first thought of love and courtship and matrimony over lobster salad, iced champagne, or the *valse à deux temps* at Mrs. Saint-Baffin's "at home."

Come! Though I am not bidden to the banquet—though there be no cover laid for me at the table matrimonial—may I not feast (though in no ogre fashion) upon little children? Some day perhaps Hymen's table may lack guests; and, messengers being sent out into the highways in quest of the lame, the halt, and the blind, I may have a chance.

I might speculate upon little children in a purely negative fashion for some time. For instance: as regards the child being father to the man: of men being but children of a larger growth. These are both very easy things to say; and we get them by heart pat, and somewhat in the parrot manner; and we go on repeating our pet phrase, over and over, backwards and forwards, time after time, till we firmly believe it to be true; and, if any one presume to argue or dissent, we grow indignant, and cry "turn him out;" as the member of the Peace Society did the other day, when an opinionated person happened to dissent from the whole hog proposition that the world was to be pacificated, and universal fraternity established, by the lambs shearing the wool off their backs, and taking it to the wolves in a neat parcel, with a speech about arbitration.

Now at the risk of being turned out myself, I must venture to dissent from the axiom that the child is father to the man. I say that he is not. Can you persist in telling me that this fair-haired innocent—this little sportive, prattling, loveable child, with dimpled, dumpling hands that almost fold themselves spontaneously into the attitude of supplication and prayer; with cherry lip—" some bee has stung it newly " lisping thanksgiving and love; with arms that long to em-

brace; with eyes beaming confidence, joy, pity, tenderness:
—am I to be told that this infant is father to yon hulking,
sodden, sallow-faced, blue-gilled, crop-haired, leaden-eyed,
livid-lipped, bow-shouldered, shrunken-legged, swollen-handed
convict in a hideous grey uniform branded with the broad
arrow; with ribbed worsted hose and fetters at his ancles,
sullenly skulking through his drudgery under the rattan of an
overseer and the bayonet of a marine in Woolwich dockyard?
Is the child whom I love and in whom I hope, father to yon
wretch with a neck already half-dislocated with fear, with
limbs half-dead, with heart wholly so, who droops on his
miserable pallet in Newgate cell, his chin on his breast, his
hands between his knees, his legs shambling; the stony walls
around him; the taciturn gaolers watching him; a Bible by
his side, in whose pages, when he tries to read, the letters
slide and fall away from under his eye? Is this the father to
—can *this* ever become *that?*

Not only in your world-verbiage must the child be father
to the man, but the man is merely a child of a larger growth.
I deny it. Some boys are tyrants, bullies, hypocrites, and
liars for fear of punishment; thieves alas, through ill-example,
oftimes. Some girls are tell-tales, jealous, spiteful, slanderous,
vain and giddy, I grant. If you were to tell me that bad boys
and girls often grow up to be bad men and women, I should
agree with you. The evil example of you bad men and women
begins to corrupt boys and girls early enough, Heaven knows;
but do not brand the child—you know when infancy begins
and childhood terminates—with being but your own wickedness seen through the small end of the glass. The man a
child of larger growth? Did you ever know a man of smaller

growth—a child—to discount bills at forty per cent., and
offer you for the balance half cash, and the rest poison (put
down in the bill as "wine") and opera stalls! Did you ever
know a child to pawn his sister's play-things, or rob his
playmate of his pocket money to gamble, and to cheat while
gambling, and to go hang or drown himself when he had lost
his winnings and his stolen capital? Could you ever discern
a hankering in a child to accumulate dollars by trading in the
flesh and blood of his fellow-creatures? Did you ever know
a child to hoard halfpence in a rag or a teapot, to store rinds
of mouldy cheese in secret, or to grow rich in rotten apple
parings? Did you ever hear a child express an opinion that
his friend Tommy must eternally be burnt, for not holding
exactly the same religious opinions as he, Billy, did? Are
children false swearers for hire, liars for gain, parasites for
profit? Do they begin to throw mud with their earliest pot-
hooks and hangers: do they libel their nurse and vilify the
doctor? Men have their playthings, it is true, and somewhat
resemble overgrown children in their puerile eagerness for a
blue ribbon, an embroidered garter, a silver cross dangling to
a morsel of red silk, or a gilt walking stick. But will the
child crawl in the gutter for the blue ribbon, or walk barefoot
over broken bottles for the garter, or wallow in the mire for
the gilt walking stick? I think not. Give him a string of
red beads, a penny trumpet, or a stick of barley sugar, and he
will let the ribbons and garters go hang. Try to persuade,
with your larger growth theory, one of your smaller men to
walk backwards down a staircase before the King of Lilliput.
Persuade Colonel Fitz Tommy, aged four, to stand for five
hours on one leg behind the King of Lilliput's chair in his

box at the Marionette Theatre. Try to induce little Lady Totsey, aged three, to accede to the proposal of being maid of honour to her doll. Tommy and Totsey leave such tomfooleries to be monopolised by the larger children.

We have another school of axiomatic philosophers; who, abandoning the theorem that manhood is but the enlarged identity of infancy, maintain that the child is an intellectual negation—nothing at all physically or mentally. The enlightened M. Fourier has denied children the possession of sex, calling them Neuters; and numbers of philosophers, with their attendant schools of disciples, have pleased themselves by comparing the child's mind to a blank sheet of paper; innocent, but capable of receiving moral caligraphy, good or bad. The mind of a child like a blank sheet of Bath post!' The sheet is fair, hot-pressed, undefiled by blot or erasure if you will, but not a blank. In legible ineffaceable characters thereupon, you may read Faith and strong belief. The child believes without mental reservation; he does not require to be convinced; and if even, now and then, some little struggling dawn of argumentative scepticism leads him to doubt faintly, and to ask how bogey can always manage to live in the cellar among the coals; how the black dog can be on his shoulder, when he sees no dog there; why little boys should not ask questions, and why the doctor should have brought baby with him under his cloak—he is easily silenced by the reply that good children always believe what is told them; and that he must believe; so he *does* believe. His faith was but shaken for a moment. Belief was written too strongly in his little heart to be eradicated by any little logic. Would that when he comes to be a child of larger growth, forsooth, no subtle powers of reasoning should prompt him to dissect and anatomise his body of belief, till nothing but dry bones remain, and it fall into a pit of indifference and scepticism!

That child has a maimed child-mind who does not believe implicitly in all the fairy tales—in the existence of ogres, fairies, giants, and dwarfs. I dare say thousands will read this who have lain a-bed as children, awake, and quaking lest Hurlothrumbo, or the dread Giant Bolivorax, or the wolf that devoured little Red Riding Hood should enter unto them and devour them. How many do I address who have cherished one especial beanstalk in the back garden as the very identical beanstalk up which Jack clomb; and, in the slightness of their childish vision, deemed that the stalk grew up and up till it reached the wondrous land of faëry—who, also, have firmly believed that the huge pack the old Jew pedlar carried on his back was full of naughty children; and that from parsley-beds, by means of silver spades, fruits—of whose species Mr. Darwin is aware—were procured. I remember having when a very little child two strong levers of belief. One was a very bright fire-place with a very bright fender, very bright fire irons, and a very bright coloured rug before it. I can see them now, all polished steel, brass and gay worsted work—and all of which I saw strictly forbidden to touch. The other was a certain steel engraving in an album: a landscape with a lake, and swans, and ladies with parasols. I know the fire-place now to have been a mere register stove with proper appurtenances, and the picture an engraving of the Park of St. Cloud after Turner; but I declare that I firmly, heartily, uncompromisingly believed then, that angels' trumpets were like those

K

fire-irons, and that the gay rug, and the pretty landscape was an accurate view if not an actual peep into Fairyland itself. A little dead sister of mine used to draw what we called fairyland on her slate. 'Twas after all, I dare say, but a vile childish scrawl, done over a half smeared-out game of oughts and crosses, with a morsel of slate pencil, two sticks a half-penny. Yet I and she and all of us believed in the fairyland she drew. We could pluck the golden fruit on the boughs, and hear the silver-voiced birds, and see the fairy elves with their queen (drawn very possibly with a head like a deformed oyster) dancing beneath the big round moon upon the yellow sands. I am sure my sister believed her doll was alive and peculiarly susceptible to catching cold from draughts. I am certain that I never questioned the animated nature of the eight-day clock on the staircase that ticked so awfully in the hot silent summer nights, and gnashed its teeth so feroci-ously when his weights were moved. My aunt promised everything when her ship came home; and I believed in the ship that was always coming and never did come, without one spark of scepticism. I believed in, and shuddered at, all the stories about that famous juvenile (always held up to us as a warning and example, and alluded to as " there was once a little boy who ") who was always doing the things he ought not to have done; and was, in consequence, so per-petually being whipped, caught in door jambs and suspended in the air by meat-hooks, eaten up alive by wild beasts, burnt to death in consequence of playing " with Tommy at lighting straws," that I have often wondered, so many have been his perils, by flood and field, that there should be any of that little boy left. He is alive though, nevertheless, and still firmly believed in. I was under the necessity the other day of relating a horrible misadventure of his to a little nephew of mine own, showing how the little boy reached over a dining table to put his fingers into a sugar dish, and came to signal shame by knocking over a tumbler and cutting his fingers therewith; and I am happy to state that my anecdote was not only received as genuine, but met with the additional criticism from my small nephew (his own digits still sticky with the sugar) that it " served the little boy right." Faith and strong belief! When children play at King or Queen, or Castles or Schools, they believe that they are in verity the persons they enact. We children of a larger growth yawn through our parts, requiring a great deal of prompting, and waiting, now and again, for the applause; or, if we be of the audience, applaud listlessly, knowing the play to be a deception.

Faith and strong belief! How is the child to distinguish between the Witch of Endor and the Witch of Edmonton; between Goliah that David slew, and the Giant that Jack killed? Let him believe it all in his happy faithful childhood, I say. Do not think I wish to propagate or encourage error. But that young flowret is too tender yet to bear the crude blast of uncompromising Fact. And battle with error in the child's mind as you will, feed him with diagrams and clothe him with Euclid's Elements before he is breeched as you may, the innate Belief that is in him, even though draped in imaginations and harmless fictions, will beat your logic and philosophy hollow.

On that blank sheet of paper to which you compare a child's mind, I find yet more words written that all may read. I find Truth. Prone to believe the most extravagant fictions, because his belief is indiscriminating through innocence, he is yet essentially and legibly a truthteller and is logically true. If he objects to you or me he tells us candidly, "I don't like you." If asked to assign a reason for his dislike, he answers as candidly: "Because you are old—because you are ugly—because you smell of snuff." If he likes his old nurse better than his new nurse he tells her so plainly. Herein is no cogging, no qualifying, no constructive lying. When he demands a present or *backsheesh*, he employs no bowing or scraping; no beating about the bush to effect his purpose. He says simply, " Give Doddy a sugar-plum," and holds out his hand. Years to come he will learn to cringe and fawn, and write begging letters, and attribute his want of sugarplums to the hardness of the times, or to his having to "take up a little bill." So blunt is his truthfulness that it frequently becomes inconvenient and embarrassing. He makes the most alarming revelations, in all innocence and unconsciousness, respecting the malpractices of the servants, and the criticisms passed by his relatives upon the appearance and manners of their friends and acquaintances. He suffers in the flesh for this, and is a martyr to his truthfulness. Not strong enough in purpose to hate, he is yet afraid and ashamed to lie. He blushes and stammers over an untruth. 'Tis practice makes the liar perfect. The infant knows the truth and its seat, for it is in his heart, and he has no need to go wandering about the earth in search of it, like that mad fellow who, hearing that Truth lay at the bottom of a well, jumped into a well and was drowned ; finding indeed Truth at the bottom—for he found Death. You, foolish, cockering mothers, teach your children to lie, when you aid them in denying or concealing their faults from those who would be stern with them. You, unreasoning, impetuous parents, nourish lying scorpions in your bosom, when you · beat your children savagely for an involuntary accident, for a broken vase, or a torn frock. You give the child a motive for concealment; you sow lying seed that will bear black fruit; you make truth to mean punishment, and falsehood impunity.

In letters as large and bold, as beautiful and clear to view, is written on the sheet of paper you are pleased to call blank in little children's minds the word Charity. Large-hearted, open-handed, self-denying charity. Unreasoning, indiscreet, indiscriminate, perchance, but still charity of the Christian sort, which, done in secret shall be rewarded openly. I am compelled to admit that little children know nothing about the Mendicity Society and the indefatigable Mr. Horsford; that they have never perused the terrific leaders in the *Times* against street mendicancy, and the sin of indiscriminate almsgiving; that they would, if they could read bad writing, become an easy prey to begging letter impostors; and would never be able to steel their hearts against the appeals to the benevolent in the newspapers. I must own, too, that their charity does not stop at humanity but extends itself to the animal creation. I never saw a child feed a donkey with macaroons; but I have seen one little girl press pound-cake · upon a Shetland pony, and another little girl give half of her bread and butter to a four-footed acquaintance of the Newfoundland breed. I have watched the charitable instincts of children from babyhood to school-hood, when hopes and cankering

fears, desire of praise, solicitude for favour and lust of gain
begin, shutting up charity in an iron-bound strong box of
small-worldliness. Children love to give. Is it to feed the
ducks in the park, or slide warm pennies into the palsied
hands of cripples, or drop them into the trays of blind men's
dogs, or pop them, smiling, into slits of money-boxes, or
administer eleemosynary sustenance to Bunny and Tiny the
rabbits, or give the pig a "poon"—to give it is indeed their
delight. They want no tuition in charity: it is in them,
God-sent. Yonder little chubby "sheet of blank stationery"
who is mumbling a piece of parliament in his nurse's arms,
has scarcely consciousness of muscular power sufficient to
teach him to hold the sweetmeat fast; yet, if I ask baby half
by word half by gesture to give me a bit, this young short-
coated Samaritan—who not long since began to "take notice,"
and can only just ejaculate da-da, ma-ma—will gravely
remove the parliament from his own lips and offer it to mine.
Were he a very few months older he would clutch it tighter
in his tiny hand, and break a piece off, and give it me. Is
not this charity? He does not know, this young neophyte,
that the parliament is moist and sticky with much sucking
and mumbling; that I am too big to eat parliament; and
that it is mean and paltry in me, a great, hulking, able-
bodied, working man, to beg cates of him, a helpless infant.
But he knows in his instinctive sapience that he cannot fill
my belly with wise saws, or with precepts of political economy. He cannot quote Adam Smith, Ricardo, or S. G. O.
to me; he administers, in his instinctive charity, corporeal
sustenance to my corporeal necessity. The avaricious infant
is a monster.

What word is that that shines so brightly—whose letters dance and glitter like precious gems on the so-called blank scroll? Love. Instinct of instincts, inborn of all innate things, little children begin to love as soon as they begin to live. When mere flaccid helpless babes their tiny faces mantle with smiles—ah! so full of love and tenderness—in their sleep. The first use they make of their arms is to clasp them round the neck of those they love. And whom will they not love? If the witch Sycorax had nursed Miranda, and Caliban had been her foster-brother, the little monster and the little maiden would have loved each other, and Prospero's little child would have kissed and fondled her hideous nurse. The first words children utter are words of love. And these are not necessarily taught them; for their very inarticulate ejaculations are full of love. They love all things. The parrot, though he bites them; the cat, though she scratches; the great bushy blundering house-dog; the poultry in the yard; the wooden-legged, one-eyed negro who brings the beer; the country lout with clouted shoon who smells so terribly of the stable; the red-faced cook, the grubby little knife-boy, the foolish fat scullion, the cross nurse. They love all these; together with horses, trees, gardens, and toys, and break their little hearts (easily mended again, thank Heaven), if they are obliged to part from them. And, chiefer, still, they love that large man with the gruff voice, the blue rough chin, the large eyes, whose knees comprise such an inexhaustible supply of cock-horses always standing at livery, yet always ready to ride post-haste to Coventry: they love papa. And, chiefest of all, they love her of the soft voice, the smiles, the tears, the hopes, the cares, the tenderness—who is all in all, the first, the last to them, in their tender, fragile, happy childhood.

Mamma is the centre of love. Papa was an after acquaintance. He improves upon acquaintance, too; but mamma was always with them to love, to soothe, to caress, to care for, to watch over. When a child wakes up hot and feverish from some night dream, it is upon his mother he calls. Each childish pain, each childish grief, each childish difficulty is to be soothed, assuaged, explained by her. The pair have no secrets; they understand each other. The child clings to her. The little boy in the Greek epigram that was creeping down a precipice was invited to his safety, when nothing else could induce him to return, by the sight of his mother's breast.

You who have little children and love them—you will have borne patiently with me, I know, through all these trivialities. And you, strong-minded philosophers who "celibate, sit like a fly in the heart of an apple," and dwell indeed in perpetual sweetness, but sit alone and are confined and die in singularity, excuse my puerility, my little theme, my smaller argument, my smallest conclusions. Remember the Master suffered little children to come unto him; and that, strong-minded philosophers as we are, we were all of us, once, but little helpless innocents.

X.

THE CONVERSION OF COLONEL QUAGG.

SOME of our religions in the States are not over well paid.
Down Punkington way, now, they have a religion with a
chandelier; at least the chapel in which Reverend Rufus
P. Pillsbury officiates has one. That religion has a bell, and
a weathercock, and a flight of steps of General Buffum's
patent scagliola adamant, and columns with Corinthian fixings
outside—bright and handsome. There's another religion in
those parts though, that has no better chapel than a loft,
formerly used for warehousing dry goods; and our citizens
have to go to worship up a ladder, and through a trap-door.
Elder Peabody Eagle proposed that they should have a crane
outside the building, as was the case in Baggby Brothers',
the former proprietors' time, and so hoist the congregation up
like cotton or molasses; but the proposition, though practical, was thought irreverent, and came to nothing. Reverend
Doctor Nathan Flower, who officiated over the dry goods,
was very poorly off. Indeed, people said that he had nothing
under his black doctor of divinity's gown but a shirt and
pants, and that his whole income did not amount to two
hundred dolls. a-year; whereas Reverend Rufus P. Pillsbury

had a clear seven or eight hundred; besides a store of silk gowns as stiff as boards and that rustled beautifully; white cambric handkerchiefs by the whole dozen; a real diamond ring; starched collars and bands by scores; and better than all, the run of all his congregation's sympathies and houses,. which was worth I don't know how many corncakes and cups of tea every day; besides comforters, over-shoes, umbrellas, gold watches, silver teapots, self-acting coffee-biggins, and select libraries of theology, given or sent to him in the way of testimonials in the course of the year, without end.   Folks do say, too, that when Reverend Rufus was in the ministry down South, before he came to Punkington, he was even still richer in worldly goods, for that he owned something mentionable in niggers.   But you know how folks will talk.

Punkington is in Buffum county, Mass.   There are a good many religions there.   They don't quite hate each other; strive, speechify, write and talk against each other, as seems to be indispensable with orthodoxy and heterodoxy in Britain. Each religion gets along pretty well as it can : some grandly, some poorly, from Reverend Rufus P. Pillsbury with his chandelier, stiff silk gown and diamond ring, down to Reverend Lovejoy Snowdrop, who is quite black, and preaches to the coloured people (they can sing, some—coloured people can) down in a little crazy affair sot up with planks and sailcloth close to the wharf, and which is more like a wash-house than a chapel.

It may be ten years ago that there was a religion in rather a small way in Punkington, called the Grace-Walking Brethren.   They had originally been called the Punkington Seceders; but, coalescing with Reverend Pygrave Clapp—

who had just sloped from Coonopolis, Ga., where he had had
a slight difficulty with the citizens on the Freesoil (whole
ticket) question, which ended by his being ridden on
a rail out of the state, and a report being spread abroad that
the darkness of his complexion came from his having been
tarred; and that under his clothes he was feathered like a
bird—coalescing with this persecuted Testifier, the amalgamated ticket was thenceforward known as Grace-Walking.
They encountered some little opposition at first. The Baal-
Peor congregation (brass band connection) felt it incumbent
upon them to denounce and repudiate the Grace-Walkers as
Erastians, Ebionites, Arminians, Socinians, nigger-saviours,
shoulder-hitters, money-diggers, and traders in shin-plaisters,
Reverend Lysander Sphoon published a card in the Punkington Sphynx and Commercial Advertiser, in which he accused
Reverend Barkley Baggs of the Grace-Walkers of whittling in
the pulpit, chewing in the vestry, and having a bust of Tom
Paine over his bookcase. Reverend B. B. retorted by another
card in the Punkington Sibyl and North-and-South Buffum
Oracle, in which he alluded to the well-known story of Reverend L. Sphoon having been in early life in Sing-Sing penitentiary for picking up things on the wharf; adding some
little anecdotes concerning what he had done subsequently in
the wooden nutmeg trade, the clocks-that-wouldn't-figure
trade, the school-teaching trade, the spirit-rapping trade, the
tarred-oakum-imitation-India-rubber trade, the temperance
lecturing trade, and the whiskey selling trade. He regretted
that his sacerdotal character precluded him from cowhiding
Reverend L. Sphoon the first time he met him in town; but
offered to match any one of his lay-elders against his oppo-

nent's deacons, and to forfeit fifty dolls. if the former left
a strip of skin broader than a finger on the body of the
latter after half-an-hour's "licking."

This was the only feud of any consequence in which the
Grace-Walking Brethren were concerned. They were peaceful,
decent, harmless bodies enough, minding their own business,
not interfering with that of anybody else, and our citizens
took to them kindly. Their congregations soon began to
multiply in number, and they had chapels at Marathon,
Squashborough, Lower Whittle, Thermopylæ, Jeffersonville,
and East Halleluia. Within a year from their establishment
they had five circuits within a fifty miles circle of Punkington.

Now a circuit, you must understand, may comprehend
five, ten, fifteen, twenty congregations ; and, the religion not
being quite rich enough to entertain a minister for each
separate congregation, there are so many circuits—religious
"beats," in fact—each of which is assigned to a different
clergyman, who goes the round thereof in turn. Punkington
circuit, including as it did the townships of Eggnogville,
Bunkum, and Beersheba, together with Rapparoarer city and
the villages of Snakesby, Fiscopolis, New Marseilles, Globbs,
and Ephesus, was a very popular circuit indeed. There were
always dreadful handsome girls at preachings and camp
meetings, and plenty of comfortable farm-houses where the
ministers were entertained with such delicacies in the way of
pork fixings, mush, hominy, johnnycakes, canvas-backed
ducks, pumpkin pies, squash, whitepot, curds, molasses,
turkeys, hams, and apple pasties ; with elder wine, and perhaps a small drop of peach brandy or Monongahela whiskey,
that would have brought water into the mouth of a London

alderman all cloyed and soggy from a tortoise dinner at Guildhall, or a proud British nobleman surfeited with the luxuries of a regal banquet at the court of St. James's. The country around Punkington was pretty and picturesome; and the brethren walked in grace with meekness and devoutness. There was but one thing wanting to make the whole circuit · one real land of milk and honey; or, rather, there was one thing that turned it into a land of gall and wormwood—of soreness of flesh and bitterness of spirit; and that thing was an individual; and that individual was Colonel Quagg.

A dreadful man, a skeery man, a man to waken snakes and rile monkies was Colonel Quagg. Goliah Washington Quagg was his name; and two and a half miles from Punkington did he locate, on the main road to Rapparoarer city. He was six foot three without his stockings, which would have made him, in jack-boots screeching tall to look at. He had a bushy beard and whiskers, and the integument that covered his bones was hard and horny as a crab-shell. The hair of his head was like a primeval forest, for it looked as though it had never been lopped, combed, weeded, or trimmed. His eyes were fearful to look upon when they flashed, and they flashed almost always. He ate so much that people said he was hollow all through—legs, arms, and all—and packed his food from the feet upwards. Some people compared him to a locomotive, for he was always smoking, drinking, roaring, and coming into collision with other folks. He compared himself to a Mississippi steamboat with the safety-valves tied down with rope-yarn. "Rosin me up, and stand on my boilers," he used to cry. "Give me goss and let me rip. Strangers pay your bills, and liquor up once more before you die, for I must lick every 'coon of you or bust." He was always licking 'coons. He licked a backwoodsman; four "Bowery bhoys" from New York, one after the other; an Irish hod-carrier (with one hand), and an English prize-fighter. They sot a giant out of a menagerie at him once, and the giant closed with him, and was heard, soon afterwards to crack like a nut. The giant said (after he was cracked), that it was a darned, tarnation, everlasting shame it was; for he had gone in to whip a man, not a grisly bear.

Colonel Quagg was a blacksmith. He was not by any means the sort of blacksmith that Professor Longfellow has described. He had no boys to sit in the church among, no little daughter to hear singing in the choir. He was not the sort of blacksmith *I* saw once, during my travels in Europe, in a little village in the south of France, and who, on a broiling July day, was hammering away at his anvil with might and main,—in his shirt, and with his hair in curl papers; for it was Sunday, and there was to be a fête in the village in the evening. No. Colonel Quagg was a very different kind of Mulciber: not a harmonious blacksmith or a learned blacksmith; but a roaring, rampagious, coaly, knotty, sooty Vulcan of a man. To hear him shout out hoarsely to 'Zeek, his long, lank, bellows-blower: to see him whirl his tremendous hammer above his head as though it had been a feather, and bring it down upon the iron on his anvil with such a monstrous clang that the sparks flew about, and the flames leaped up the chimney and tripped up the heels of the smoke, as if they were frightened out of their wits. This was a sight—grand if you like—but fearful.

The colonelcy of Goliah Quagg arose from his command of the Rapparoarer Tigers. These redoubtable volunteers were (of course) the ægis of the Union, and the terror of Buffum County. On fourth of July day they fired off so many rounds of musketry that their eventually blowing themselves up with gunpowder was thought to be by no means a matter of extreme improbability. The Rapparoarer Screamer newspaper teemed with cards headed "Rapparoarer Tigers, attention!" and commanding the attendance of the corps at reviews, burials or weddings of members, or political meetings. Colonel Quagg, in his Tiger uniform, at the head of his corps, vowing vengeance against the Punkington National Guards, the Lower Whittle Fire Corps; the Squashborough Invincibles; the Bunkum Defenders; the East Halleluia Hussars (between which last-named volunteers and the Tigers there had occurred a deadly fray at the corners of Seventh Street and Slog Avenue, Punkington: the Hussars being at last obliged to take refuge in a liquor-store in the next block, and two eyes and unnumbered double teeth being left on the field): Colonel Quagg brandishing his sabre and threatening gouging, cowhiding, and etarnal chawing up to creation in general and rival militia and fire-corps in particular, was a great and glorious sight to see once, perhaps twice, but not oftener; for the sun at noon-day dazzles, and distance lends enchantment to the voice of a powder magazine, or Vesuvius, or a mad dog.

Colonel Quagg had neither wife nor relations, chick nor child. He lived behind the smithy, in a grim cabin; where, for aught anybody knew he slept on the bones of his enemies, or kept bears and wolves, or burned brimstone and Bengal

lights iu his stove.   Where he was raised was uot certain.
What he did on Sundays (for he never went to church or
meetings, and could not, in deference to our citizens, work in
his smithy on the Sabbath) was not known.   There were but
two things about him on which arguments could be, with
tolerable certainty, held.   That he liked rum—raw— which
he drank in vast quantities without ever winking, or being
intoxicated; and that he hated the Grace-Walking Brethren.

What these, or any other brethren had ever done to incur
his dislike was not stated; but it was clear and certain that
he hated them fiercely and implacably.   He declaimed against
them in drinking bars; he called them opprobrious names in
the street; and, which was particularly disagreeable to the
brethren themselves, he made a point of giving every minister
who passed his smithy—on horse or on foot, on business or
pleasure—a sound and particularly humiliating beating.

Colonel Quagg's method was this.   'Zeek, the long,
lanky assistant would, as he blew the bellows, keep a sharp
look out through a little round hole in the smithy wall.
When, on the crest of the little hill in the valley beneath
which the smithy lay (the bridge over the Danube, leading to
Punkington, was in the other direction), there appeared the
devoted figure of a Grace-Walking clergyman, 'Zeek would
call out, "one o' 'em, Colonel!"   Whereupon the blacksmith would lay down his hammer, and say grimly, 'Zeek,
'ile.'"

The "ile," or oil, being brought, the Colonel would
therewith anoint a tremendous leather strap, in size and
appearance between the trace for a cart-horse and the lathe
for a steam-engine.   Then would he sally forth, tug the

luckless preacher by one leg off his horse—if he happened to be riding — or grapple him by the collar of his coat if he were a-foot, and thrash him with the strap—not till he howled for mercy; for the victim always did *that* at the very first stroke of the terrible leather; but till his own brawny arm could no longer hold the mighty weapon. All this was accompanied by a flood of abuse on the part of the Colonel: the minister, his congregation, sect, person, and presumed character, were all animadverted upon ; and, after having been treated with brutality, he was dismissed with scorn, with a sardonic recommendation to send as many more of his brethren that way as he could, to be served in the same way. Then, execution being done, and the miserable victim of his ferocity gone on his bruised way towards Punkington, the Colonel would stride into Silas B. Powkey's tavern over the hill, hot, perspiring, and fatigued; and, throwing his strap on the bar, and seating himself on a puncheon, would throw his legs aloft, half in weariness half in triumph, even till they reached the altitude of the mantel-piece ; would there rest them ; and, ejecting a mighty stream of tobacco juice, cry :

" Squire, strapped another Grace-Walker: Rum."

Now this, as in the celebrated Frog and Boy case (*vide* spelling-book reports), albeit excellent sport to one party . concerned, was death to the other. Martyrdom had not exactly been contracted for when the Grace-Walking Brethren entered the ministry; and without martyrdom there was no riding the Punkington circuit. There was no avoiding the colonel and his awful strap. There was no going round another way. There was no mollifying, persuading, or infusing soft pity into the colonel's breast. "I licks ye," he was wont to reply when interceded with, "because I kin, and because I like, and because ye'se critters that licks is good for. Skins ye have on and skins I'll have off; hard or soft, wet or dry, spring or fall. Walk in grace if ye like till pumpkins is peaches; but licked ye must be till your toe-nails drop off and your noses bleed blue ink." And licked they were accordingly.

What was to be done with such a man—a man with this dreadful fixed idea of strapping clergymen—a man with an indomitable will, a strong arm, and an abusive tongue. Warrants, summonses, exigents, and actions for battery, the colonel laughed to scorn. "As much law as you like," he said, "but not one lick will that save you." The female members of the Grace-Walking congregation were fain to write anonymous letters to him, exhorting him to repentance. Reverend Joash M'Tear wrote to Lucretia Z. Tackeboguey of Grimgribberopelis, Va., the celebrated table-turner and spirit-rapper, and begged her to consult a four-legged mahogany of extraordinary talent and penetration with reference to Colonel Quagg's persecution of the saints. He received in reply a highly-flattering and interesting communication from the spirits of Cleopatra and Johanna Southcote, in which it was confidently predicted that shortly after the passing of the Maine liquor law in Holland, and the adoption of Bloomerism at the British court, Colonel Quagg would be bound in leathern straps for five hundred years: which, all things taken into consideration, was not a very encouraging look-out for the Grace-Walkers. Then they took to holding public meetings, mass meetings, indignation meetings, against him; then to praying for him; then to praying to be delivered from him as from a serpent or fiery dragon. One bright spirit of the sect suggested bribery, either directly, by the enclosure of dollar-notes, or indirectly, by the encouragement of the colonel's trade in having horses shod at his smithy. But both artifices failed. The colonel took the first ten-dollar bill that was offered him, and administered a more unmerciful thrashing than ordinary to the giver—as a receipt, he said. The next victim happened to have a horse that opportunely cast both his fore-shoes in front of the colonel's residence. The enemy of Grace-Walkers shod the beast; but the only benefit that its proprietor derived from giving Quagg his custom was the privilege of being strapped inside the smithy instead of out of it, and the threat that the next time he presumed to come that way he should be laid on the anvil and beaten as flat as a wheel-tire with a red-hot crowbar.

This state of things was growing intolerable. The more the brethren went on preaching the more the colonel went on licking. The more they beat the—

> " Pulpit drum ecclesiastic
> With fist instead of *a* stick,"

the more Colonel Quagg proved his doctrine orthodox—

> " By apostolic blows and knocks."

The Punkington circuit began to lack ministers. Clergymen were not forthcoming. The pulpits were deserted. The congregations began to cry out. No wonder. Devotion, meekness, self-abnegation are all admirable qualities in their way, but human nature, after all, is not cast iron. It will, wrestle with wild beasts at Ephesus, but it does not exactly love to wrestle when the wild beasts are twisting the bars of their cage, and have not had a shin-bone to feed on for three weeks. To put one's head into the lion's mouth is good once in a way; but it is hardly prudent to do so when the lion's tail begins to wag, and his mane to bristle, and his eyes to flash fire and fury.

There was a meeting held at Punkington to decide upon what ministers should go the ensuing Spring circuit; just as, in Europe, the Judges meet to arrange among themselves who shall go a-hanging, and where. The question of Colonel Quagg was debated in solemn conclave : for, though all the other places in the circuit found ready volunteers, not one clergyman could be found to offer to adminster to the spiritual necessities of the Rapparoarer brethren. Brother M'Tear had a bad cold; brother Brownjohn would rather not; brother Knash had a powerful call down Weepingwail way; brother Bobberlink would next time — perhaps. Brother Slocum gave a more decided reason than any one of his brother ministers. He said that he would be etarnally licked if he'd go, because he'd be sure to be considerably licked if he went.

A brother who, up to that time, had said little or nothing —a long, thin, loose-limbered brother, with a face very like a quince more than three parts withered—who sat in the corner of the room during the debate, with his legs curled up very much in the fashion of a dog :—a brother, to say the truth, of whose abilities a somewhat mean opinion was entertained, for he was given to stammering, blushing, hemming, hawing, scraping with his feet, and seemed to possess no peculiar accomplishment save the questionable one of shutting one eye when he expectorated—this brother, by name Zephaniah Sockdolloger, here addressed himself modestly to speech :—

"Thorns," he said, "is'nt good eating ; stinging-nettles isn't pleasant handling, without gloves; nor is thistles comfortable, worn next to the skin. Corns is painful. Man's skin was not made to be flayed off him like unto the hide of a wild cat. But vocation is vocation, and dooty, dooty—some. I, Zephaniah Sockdolloger, will go on the Rapparoarer location, and if Brother Brownjohn will lone me his hoss I will confront the man—even Goliah Quagg." After which the devoted brother shut one eye and expectorated.

The meeting turned their quids and expectorated too ; but without shutting their eyes. They adopted the long brother's disinterested proposition, *nem. con.* But Brother Bobberlink whispered to Brother Slocum that he had allers thought Zephaniah Sockdolloger considerable of a fool, and that now he know'd it—that was a fact.

The fire roared, the sparks flew up the chimney, and the bellows blew fiercely one April evening ; and Colonel Quagg and his anvil were in fierce dispute about a red hot horseshoe. The Colonel had the advantage of a hammer that Tubal Cain might have wielded when he fashioned the first ploughshare ; but the anvil was used to hard knocks, and stood out against the blacksmith bravely. Indeed, if a certain metallic vibration was to be taken into account, the anvil had the best of it; for it had the last word. Only the unfortunate horseshoe came to grief ; and, like the man between two stools who came to the ground, was battered into all sorts of shapes between the two disputants. Suddenly, 'Zeek, the bellows-blower, ceased for a moment in his occupation, and remarked :

"One 'o them. colonel, top o' the hill. On a hoss. Legs as long as a coulter."

"Twankeydillo! twankeydillo!"* sung out Colonel Quagg in great exultation. "Ile, 'Zeek, and plenty of it for Jack Strap, the crittur, is getting tarnation rusty."

The fatal strap being "iled" rather more liberally than usual, the colonel grasped it in his mighty hand, and passed out of the smithy door.

He saw, coming towards him down the hill, a long-legged, yellow-faced man in black, with a white neckcloth and a broad brimmed hat. He bestrode a solemn-looking, white horse with a long tail. He had but one spur (the rider) but it was a very long and rusty spur. In his hand he carried a little dog's-eared book; but, as he rode, he sung quite softly a little hymn that ran something like unto the following:—

> "We are marching through the gracious ground,
> We soon shall hear the trumpet sound;
> And then we shall in glory reign,
> And never, never, part again.
>> What, never part again?
>> No, never part again.
>> No never, never, never, &c.
> And then we shall, &c."

Colonel Quagg waited till the verse of the hymn was quite finished, and the horseman had got to within a couple of yards of his door, when he called out in a terrible voice,

"Hold hard!"

"Brother," said the man on the horse, "good evening and peace."

* Twankeydillo is the burden of an old country blacksmith's song.

"For the matter of that," responded Colonel Quagg, "rot! Hold hard, and git out of that hoss."

"Brother?" the other interrogated, as if not quite understanding the command.

"Git out, I tell you," cried the blacksmith. "Legs and feet. Git out, you long-tailed blackbird. Git out, for I'm riz, and snakes will wake! I want to talk to you."

The long man slid rather than got off his horse. It was indeed, Brother Zephaniah Slockdolloger; for his face was quincier than ever, and, as he descended from his steed, he shut one eye and expectorated.

"Now," said the blacksmith, seating himself on the horse block in front of his dwelling, and giving a blow on the ground with his strap that made the pebbles dance. "Where do you hail from?"

"From Punkington city, brother," answered the reverend Zephaniah.

"And whar are you a goin' tu?"

"To Rapparoarer city."

"And what may you be goin' for to du in that location?"

"Goin' on circuit."

"What?"

"Lord's business, brother."

Colonel Quagg shook out the strap to its full length, and passed it through his horny hand.

"There was a brother of yours," he said sententiously, "that went to Rapparoarer city on Lord's business last fall. He passed this edifice he did. He met this strap close by here. And this strap made him see comets, and dance like a shaking Quaker, and feel uncommon like a bob-tailed bull in fly-time."

There was something so dreadfully suggestive in the position of a bob-tailed bull in fly-time (the insects frequently kill cattle with their stings) that brother Sockdolloger wriggled uneasily.

"And I *du* hope," the colonel continued, "that you, brother, aren't of the same religion as this babe of grace was as met the strap as he was riding. That religion was the Grace-Walking religion, and that religion I always lick."

"Lick brother?"

"Lick. With the strap. Dreadful."

"Colonel Goliah Quagg," said the minister, "for such, I know, is your name in the flesh, I *am* a preacher of the Grace-Walking connection. Humble, but faithful, I hope."

"Then," returned Colonel Quagg, making an ironical bow, "this *is* the strap with which I am going to lick you into sarse."

"Brother, brother," the other cried, shaking his head, "cast that cruel strap from out of thine hand. Close thine hand, if thou wilt, upon the hammer of thy trade, the coulter of thy plough, upon a pen, the rudder of a ship, the handle of a lantern to light men to peace and love and goodwill; but close it not upon sword of iron, or bludgeon of wood, or strap of leathern hide. For, from the uplifting and downfalling of those wicked instruments came never good; but rather boiling tears, and bruises and blood, and misery, and death."

"Now look you here," the blacksmith cried, impatiently. "Talk as long as you like; but talk while I am a-licking of you. For time is precious, and must not be thrown away nohow. Lick you I must, and lick you I will. Hard."

" But, brother—but, colonel——"

" Rot ! " exclaimed the colonel. " Straps is waiting. Stubs and fences ! I'll knock you into horseshoes and then into horsenails, if you keep me waiting."

" Have you no merciful feelings ? " asked Zephaniah, as if sorely troubled.

" Not a cent of 'em ' Air you ready ! Will you take it fighting, or will you take it lying down ! Some takes it fighting; some takes it like lambs, lying down. Only make haste."

" Goliah Quagg," the minister responded, " I am a man of peace, and not one that goes about raging with sword and buckler, like unto Apollyon, or a corporal of the Boston Tigers ; and I would rather not take it at all."

" You must," the colonel roared, now fairly infuriated. " Pickled alligators ! you must. Hold hard, you coon ! Hold hard ! for I'm a goin' to begin. Now, once more; is it fighting, or is it quiet, you mean for to take it ? "

" Well," said brother Zephaniah, " you are hard upon me, Colonel, and that's true. It's fighting or lying down, is'nt it ? "

" Aye," returned the colonel, brandishing his strap.

" *Then I'll take it fighting*," the man of peace said quietly.

Colonel Quagg halted for a moment, as if amazed at the audacity of the Grace-Walker. Then, with a wild halloo, he rushed upon him very much as a bob-tailed bull does rush about under the aggravating influence of flies. His hand was upon the minister's collar ; the strap that had done so much execution in its time was swinging high in the air, when—

Stay. Can you imagine the rage, astonishment, and despair of a schoolmaster caned by his pupil; of the Emperor of China sentenced to be bambooed by a Hong Kong coolie; of the beadle of the Burlington Arcade expulsed therefrom by a boy with a basket: of a butler kicked by a footpage; of a Southern planter cowhided by one of his own niggers; of a Broadway dandy jostled by a newly landed Irish emigrant; of a policeman ordered to move on by an apple-woman; of the Commander-in-chief of the army desired to stand at ease by a drummer; of the Pope of Rome blessed with two fingers by a chorister boy? If you can imagine anything of that sort,—but only if you can,—you may be able to form some idea of how Colonel Quagg felt when a storm of blows, hard, well-directed, and incessant, began to fall on his head, on his breast, on his face, on his shoulders, on his arms, on his legs—all over his body, so rapidly that he felt as if he was being hit everywhere at once,—when he found his strap would hit nowhere on the body of his opponent, but that he himself was hit everywhere.

Sledgehammers! Sledgehammers were nothing to the fists of the Grace-Walking brother. A bob-tailed bull in fly time was an animal to be envied in comparison to the colonel. He danced with all the vigour of a nigger toeing and healing a hornpipe. He saw more comets than Tycho Brahe or Erra Pater ever dreamed of. He felt that he was all nose, and that a horribly swollen one. Then that he had swallowed all his teeth. Then that he had five hundred eyes, and then none at all. Then that his ribs went in and his blood came

out. Then his legs failed under him, and he fell down all of
a heap; or perhaps, to speak classically and pugilistically, he
hit out wildly, felt groggy, and went down at the ropes. The
tall brother went down atop of him, and continued pounding
away at his body—not perhaps as hard as he could, but
decidedly much harder than the colonel liked—singing all
the while the little hymn beginning

"We are marching through the gracious ground."
quite softly to himself.

"Hold hard!" gasped the colonel at last, faintly. "You
don't mean murder, do you? You won't hit a man when
he's down, much more, will you, brother?"

"By no means," answered Zephaniah, bringing down his
fist nevertheless with a tremendous "bash" upon the colonel's nose, as if there were a fly there, and he wanted to kill
it. "But you've took it fighting, colonel, and you may as
well now take it like a lamb, lying down."

"But I'm broke, I tell you,'" groaned the vanquished
blacksmith. "I can't do no more. You air so mighty hard,
you *are*."

"Oh! you give in, then?"

"Aye," murmured Colonel Quagg, "I cave in."

"Speak louder, I'm hard of hearing."

"Yes!" repeated the colonel, with a groan. "I du cave
in. For I'm beat; whittled clean away to the small end o'
nothing—chawed up—cornered."

"You must promise me one little thing, Colonel Goliah
Quagg," said the reverend Sockdolloger, without however
removing his knees from the colonel's chest. "You must
promise before I leave off hammering of your body, never

for to ill-treat by word or deed any of our people—ministers, elders, deacons, or brethren."

" I'll promise," replied the colonel; " only let me up. You're choking me."

" Not to rile, lick, or molest any other peaceable critturs as are coming or going past your way upon Lord's business."

" I promise," muttered the colonel who was now becoming purple in the face.

" Likewise," concluded Zephaniah, playfully knocking away one of his adversary's loose teeth, so as to make his mouth neat and tidy, " you must promise to give up drinking of rum; which is a delusion and a snare, and bad for the innards, besides being on the trunk-line to perdition. And finally, you must promise to come to our next camp meeting, clean shaved, and with a contrite heart."

" No," cried the almost-expiring colonel, " I won't, not for all the toebacco in Virginny! Nor yet for Martin Van Buren, or Dan'el Webster! Nor yet for to be postmaster!"

" You won't, brother?" asked Zephaniah, persuasively raising his fist.

" No, I'm darned if I do."

" Then," said the Grace-Walker, meekly, " I must sing you another little hymn."

Immediately afterwards Colonel Quagg's tortures recommenced. He struggled, he roared, he entreated, but in vain. All he could see were the long man's arms whirling about like the sails of windmills. All he could feel was the deadly pain of the blows on his already hideously bruised face and body. All he could hear was the snuffling voice of his tormentor singing, with an occasional stammer, a verse of a little hymn, commencing

> "I'm going home to bliss above—
> Will you go, will you go ?
> To live in mercy, peace, and love—
> Will you go, will you go ?
> My old companions fare you well,
> A brighter fate has me befel,
> I mean up in the skies to dwell,
> Will you go, will you go ?"

He could stand it no longer. He threw out his arms, and groaned, " Spare my life, and I'll promise anything."

"Happy to hear it, colonel," answered brother Sockdolloger, helping his adversary to rise, and then coolly settling his own white neckcloth and broadbrimmed hat. " Perhaps you'll be good enough to look after my hoss a bit. He cast a shoe just after I left Punkington."

Colonel Quagg, quite humiliated and crestfallen, proceeded to shoe the horse, which had been quietly cropping the stunted herbage while the colonel was being licked. The operation finished, as well as Quagg's bruised arms would permit, the Grace-Walker gravely handed him a coin, which the black-smith as gravely took; then mounted his steed, and rode away. As for 'Zeek he had been hiding away somewhere during the combat. But he now appeared ; and, to judge by the energetic manner in which he blew the bellows, and a certain grin overspreading his swarthy countenance, he seemed not altogether displeased at the discomfiture of his master.

Colonel Quagg had never read Shakespeare, but he had

unconsciously acted the part of Ancient Pistol. He had been compelled to eat the leek which he had mocked. He had been a woodmonger, and bought nothing of brother Sockdolloger but cudgels. He had taken a groat, too, to heal his pate. Let us hope, with Fluellen, that it was good for his wounded sconce.

There is a seat at religious camp meetings in America called the "anxious seat." A camp meeting is not unlike a fair—a very pious one, of course; and the anxious seat is one on which sit the neophytes, or newly-entered—those who have anything to confess, anything to complain of, anything to disclose, or to tell, or to ask.

Upon the anxious seat at the next camp meeting near Rapparoarer city of the Grace-Walking Brethren sat Colonel Goliah Quagg. Amid a breathless silence, he frankly avowed his former evil course of life, narrated the events of his conversion by brother Sockdolloger, and promised amendment for the future. A brother, who had been reposing on a bench, with his limbs curled up after the manner of a dog—a long, yellow-faced, brother, who had a curious habit of shutting one eye when he expectorated—rose to speak when the colonel sat down. He expressed how happy he was to have been the instrument of Colonel Quagg's conversion, and that the means he had employed, though somewhat rough, had been effectual. With much modesty, also, he alluded to his own conversion. It was not such a long time ago, he said, that he himself had been but as one of the wicked. He owned it with shame that he had at one time been one of the abandoned men called prizefighters—a pugilist to be backed and betted on for hire and gain; and that he had beaten Dan Grummles, surnamed the Brooklyn Pet, in a stand up fight for two hundred dolls: a side.

Colonel Quagg has kept his promise. He left off rum and parson licking. He resigned the command of the Tigers, and is now, as Elder Quagg, one of the burning and shining lights among the Grace-Walking Brethren.

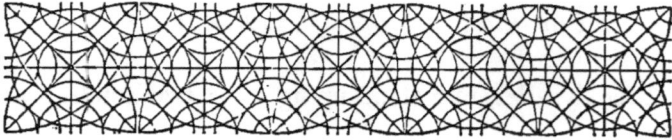

XI.

DEMETRIUS THE DIVER.

THERE are no bygones that have greater need to be by-gones than those of wickedness, violence, and cruelty. The blood and dust that besmear some pages of history might glue the leaves together for ever. Yet from time to time necessities will occur that leave us no choice but to open the old grave; to turn to the old dark register; to unlock the old dark, grim skeleton closet; to turn the retro-spective glass towards the bad, bold days that are gone.

We are at present the allies*—and worthily so—of the Turks. A brave people, patient, high-minded, slow to anger, terrible yet magnanimous in their wrath. Yet, while we ac-knowledge and respect all the good qualities possessed by this valiant nation, it is impossible to forget that the Turk has not always been the complacent Pacha in an European frock-coat and a sealing-wax cap with a blue tassel, who writes sensible, straightforward state papers, reviews Euro-pean troops, does not object to a quiet glass of champagne, and regales English newspaper correspondents with coffee, and pipes. Nor is he always the sententious, phlegmatic,

* 1854.

taciturn, apathetic Osmanli, who, shawled and turbaned, sits cross-legged upon the divan of meditation, smoking the pipe of reflection; who counts his beads and says his prayers five times a-day, and enjoys his *kef;* and who, as to wars and rumours of wars, fire, famine, pestilence, and slaughter, says but: "Allah akbar"—God is great.

There are men in London whom we may meet and converse with in our daily walks, who can remember the horrible massacre of Scio, in the year eighteen hundred and twenty-two. We had just begun then, through the edifying cobweb-spinning of diplomacy, the passionate poetry of Lord Byron and the crude intelligence of the English press, to understand that there was something on hand between the Greeks and the Turks in the Morea and the Archipelago, and that the former were not, on the whole, quite rightly used. We were just going to see about forming an opinion on these and other matters when the news of the massacre of Scio burst upon us like a thunder-clap. Gloomily and succinctly the frightful news was told us how the terrible Kara Ali—or the Black—Pacha had appeared with a fleet and an army in the harbour of Scio, then one of the fairest, peacefullest, most prosperous, most densely-populated islands in the Græco-Turkish Archipelago, and that all and everything—peaceful rayahs, gold and purple harvest, university, commerce, wealth —had in three days disappeared. The story of the massacre of Scio has never been fully told in England; and only in so far as it effects my story am I called upon to advert to it here. Besides, no tongue could tell, no pen could describe, in household language, a tithe of the atrocities perpetrated in the defenceless island by order of the Black Pacha. Suffice

M

it to say that for three days Scio was drenched in blood; that the dwellings of the European consuls were no asylums; that the swords of the infuriated Osmanlis murdered alike the whiteheaded patriarch, the priest of the family, the nursing mother, the bride of yesterday, the bride of that to-morrow which was never to come to her, the tender suckling, and the child that was unborn. Upwards of eighteen thousands persons were massacred in cold blood; and the blackened ruins of Scio became a habitation for bats and dragons, howling dogs, and wheeling birds of prey.

Some few miserable souls escaped the vengeance of the Black Pacha. There was a Greek ecclesiastic lately in London, who was hidden by his mother in a cave during the massacre, and brought away unhurt. When the fury of the invaders began, through lassitude, to cool, they selected such boys and young girls as they could find alive, and sent them to be sold in the slave market at Constantinople. Then, when they had left the wretched island to itself, half-famished wretches began to crawl out of holes and thickets and ditches, where they had hidden themselves. They saw the charred and smouldering remnants of what had once been Scio; but they abode not by them. In an agony of fear lest the murderers should return, they made the best of their way across the seas to other islands, or to inaccessible haunts on the mainland. Those who had the means took refuge on the French and Italian shores of the Mediterranean.

There is a sultry city which, if you were minded to go to it over land, you could have reached in those days by diligence, as you can reach it in these, by a commodious railway from Paris; but, to attain which by sea you must cross the stormy Bay of Biscay and pass the rocky straits of Gibraltar, and coast along the tideless sea almost in sight of the shores of Africa. To this great mart of southern commerce, with its deep blue sky, its slackbaked houses, its Cannébiere, its orange groves, its black-eyed, brown-skinned children, its Quai de la Joliette, and crowded port, where floats the strangest medley of ships, and on the wharves of which walk the most astonishing variety of costumes that ever you saw—to the city of Marseilles in France, came many of these refugee Greeks, some from Scio, some from the Morea, some from Candia, many from the Fanal or Fanar of Constantinople—which had also had its massacre—some from the interior of Bulgaria and Roumelia. There were Greek gentlemen with their families who could never congratulate themselves sufficiently on having saved their heads and their piastres; there were merchants quite stripped and bankrupt, who nevertheless, in the true Grecian manner began afresh, trading and making money with admirable assiduity and perseverance. And above all there were poor rayahs, who had been *caikjees*, coffee-house waiters, *portefaix*, at home—who had lost their little all, and had nothing but their manual labour to depend upon, and who were glad to carry burdens, and run messages, and help to load and unload the ships in the port of Marseilles.

Among these, was one Demetrius or Dmitri Omeros. Nobody knew much about him, save that he was a Sciote, and had escaped after the massacre; that he was quite alone, and very poor. He was fortunate enough to possess a somewhat rare accomplishment, which made his earnings although precarious, considerably more remunerative than those of his fellow-countrymen occupying the station to which he appeared to belong. Demetrius was a most expert swimmer and diver. Had Demetrius Omeros lived in our days he would have been a Professor to a certainty; the walls would have been covered with posting bills and woodcuts pourtraying his achievements; and he would have had a convenient exhibition-room, and a sliding-scale of prices for his Entertainment. In eighteen twenty-three he contented himself with the exhibition of his talents in the open port of Marseilles, and was satisfied with the stray francs, half-francs, copper sous, and liards, flung to him when he emerged from the water, all soaked and dripping, like a Newfoundland dog. He thus managed to lead a sufficiently easy, lounging, idle life; splashing, swimming, and diving sometimes for sheer amusement; at others, basking in the genial sun with such profound indolence that had you not known him to be a Sciote you would have taken him for a genuine lazzarone of the Quai Santa Lucia. Demetrius was some thirty years old, tall, magnificently proportioned, with a bronzed countenance, wavy black hair, and sparkling black eyes. His attire was exceedingly simple, being ordinarily limited to a shirt, red and white striped trowsers secured round the waist by a silken sash, and a small Greek tarbouch on his head, ornamented with a tarnished gold tassel. Shoes and stockings he despised as effeminate luxuries. He was perfectly contented with his modest fare of grapes, melons, brown bread, garlic, and sour wine. House rent cost him nothing, as one of the Greek merchants settled at Marseilles allowed him to sleep in his warehouse, as a species of watch-dog. When the weather was fine, he swam and dived and dried himself in

the sun : when it was foul, he coiled himself into a ball and
went to sleep.

In the year eighteen hundred and twenty-four it occurred
to the Turkish government considerably to strengthen its
navy. There was an arsenal and dockyard at Constantinople
then, as there is now ; but the Ottomans did not know much
about ship-building, and in the absence of any material
guarantee for the safety of their heads, European artizans
were rather chary of enlisting in the service of the Padishah.
So, as the shipwrights would'nt go to Sultan Mahmoud,
Sultan Mahmoud condescended to go to the shipwrights;
that is to say he sent an Effendi attached to the department
of Marine, to Marseilles, with full powers to cause to be
constructed four frigates by the shipbuilders of that port.
As the French government had not then begun to interest
itself openly one way or other in the Eastern question, and as
the shipbuilders of Marseilles did not care one copper cent
whether the Turks beat the Greeks or the Greeks the Turks,
and, more than all this, as the Effendi from Stamboul had
carte-blanche in the monetary department, and paid for each
frigate in advance, the Marseillais set about building the four
frigate with a hearty good will, and by the spring of eighteen
hundred and twenty-five, two of them were ready for launching.

It was observed by the French workmen that Demetrius
the Diver appeared to take very great interest in the process
of shipbuilding. Day after day he would come into the slip
where the frigates were being constructed, and, sitting upon
a pile of planks, would remain there for hours. Other Greeks
would come occasionally, and launch forth into fierce invec-
tives against the Turks, and against the French too, for

lending their hand for the fabrication of ships which were to
be employed by infidels against Christians.   In these tirades
Demetrius the Diver seldom, if ever, joined.   He was a man
of few words, and he sat upon the planks, and looked at the
workmen, their tools, and their work.   Nobody took much
notice of him, except to throw him a few sous occasionally,
or to say what a lazy, skulking fellow he was.

At length the day arrived which was fixed for the launch
of the first frigate, the " Sultani Bahri."   Half Marseilles
was preŝent.   The sub-prefect was there—not officially, but
officiously (whatever that subtle distinction may be).   Crowds
of beautiful ladies, as beautifully dressed, were on the raised
seats fitted round the sides of the slip ; the " Sultana Bahri "
was dressed out with flags, and aboard her were the great
Effendi himself, with his secretary, his interpreter, his pipe-
bearer, and the shipbuilder.

The sight of a ship-launch is to the full as exciting as
any race.   The heart beats time to the clinking of the ham-
mers that are knocking the last impediments away, and when
the mighty mass begins to move, the spectator is in a tremour
of doubt, and hope, and fear.   When the ship rights herself,
and indeed walks the waters like a thing of life, the excitement is tremendous.   He who sees the gallant sight *must* shout,
he *must* congratulate himself, his next neighbour,—everybody in short, upon the successful completion of the Work.

Now, everything had been looked to, thought of, prepared
for the triumphant launch of the " Sultani Bahri."   The only
obstacles between her and the waters were certain pieces of
wood technically called in England (I know not what their
French name may be) " dogshores," and these were being

knocked away by the master shipwright. This operation, I may remark, was formerly considered so dangerous that in the royal dockyards it was undertaken by convicts, who obtained their liberty if they accomplished the task without accident. Just as the first stroke of the hammer became audible, Demetrius the Diver, who had hitherto been concealed among the crowd, plunged into the water, and swam right across the track that the frigate would probably take on her release from the slip. A cry of horror burst from the crowd as he swam directly towards the ship's stem : for the vessel had begun to move, and every one expected the rash diver to be crushed or drowned. But, when he was within a few feet of the frigate, Demetrius the Diver threw up his arms, held them aloft for a moment in a menacing manner, then quietly subsided on to his back, and floated away. The "Sultani Bahri" slid down her ways to a considerable extent, she was even partially in the water; but she walked it by no means like a thing of life, for her stern began to settle down, and, if the truth must be told, the new frigate of his Imperial Highness the Sultan—stuck in the mud !

They tried to screw her off, to weight her off, to float her off, but in vain, When a ship sticks in launching, there is frequently no resource but to pull her to pieces where she sticks, and this seemed to be the most probable fate in store for the "Sultani Bahri." The Effendi was in a fury. The ship-builder was " desolated ;" but the Frenchman only ascribed the misadventure to the clumsiness of his launching-hands, whereas the Moslem, superstitious like the majority of his co-religionists, vowed that the failure was solely owing to the evil eye of the Giaour diver, Demetrius Omeros. Had the

Effandi been in his own land, a very short and summary process would have preserved all future ship-launches from the troublesome presence of Demetrius Omeros and his evil eye; but at Marseilles, in the department of the Bouches du Rhône, the decapitation, bowstringing, or drowning, of even a rayah, was not to be thought of. So, the Effendi was obliged to be satisfied with giving the strictest orders for Demetrius's exclusion from the shipbuilder's yard in future; and after a delay of some months, the second frigate (the first was rotting in the mud) was ready for launching.

Anxiety was depicted on the Effendi's face as he broke a bottle of sherbet over the bows of the frigate and named her the " Achmedié." Immediately afterwards a cry burst from the crowd of " Demetrius! Demetrius the Diver!" and, rushing along the platform which ran round the vessel, the Effendi could descry the accursed diver holding up his arms as before, and doubtless blighting the onward progress of the " Achmedié " with his evil eye.

Evil or not, a precisely similar disaster overtook the second frigate, and the launch was a lamentable failure. The shipbuilder was in despair. The Effendi went home to his hotel, cursing, and was about administering the bastinado to his whole household as a relief to his feelings, when his interpreter, a shrewd Greek, one Yanni, ventured to pour the balm of advice into the ear of indignation.

" Effendi," he said, "this rayah who dives is doubtless a cunning man, a magician, and by his spells and incantations has arrested the ships of my lord the Padishah, whom Allah preserve, in their progress! But he is a rayah and a Greek, and a rogue of course. Let my lord the Effendi bribe him, and he will remove his spells."

"You are all dogs, and sons of dogs," answered the Effendi, graciously, "but out of your mouth devoted to the slipper, O Yanni, comes much wisdom. Send for this issue of a mangy pig, this diver with the evil eye."

Demetrius was sent for, and in due time made his appearance, not so much as salaaming to the Effendi, or even removing his cap. The envoy of the Sultan was sorely tempted to begin the interview by addressing himself through the intermediary of a bamboo to the soles of the diver's feet; but, fear of the sub-prefect and his gendarmes, and, indeed, of the magical powers of the diver himself, prevented him.

"Dog and slave!" said he, politely, "dog, that would eat garbage out of the shop of a Jew butcher, wherefore hast thou bewitched the ships of our lord and Caliph the Sultan Mahmoud?"

"I am not come here to swallow dirt," answered the diver, coolly, "and if your words are for dogs, open the window and throw them out. If you want anything with a man who, in Frangistan, is as good as a Bey Oglou, state your wishes."

"The ships, slave, the ships!"

"The first two stuck in the mud," said the Greek; "and the third, with the blessing of Heaven and St. George of Cappadocia, will no more float than a cannon-ball!"

"You lie, you dog, you lie!" said the Effendi.

"'Tis you who lie, Effendi," answered Demetrius the Diver; "and, moreover, if you give me the lie again—by St. Luke I will break your unbelieving jaw."

As the Effendi happened to be alone with Demetrius (for he had dismissed his interpreter), and as there was somewhat exceedingly menacing in the stalwart frame and clenched teeth of the Greek, his interlocutor judged it expedient to lower his tone.

"Can you remove the spells you have laid on the ships?" he asked.

"Those that are launched are past praying for."

"Will the next float?"

"If I choose."

"And the next?"

"If I choose."

"Name your own reward, then," said the Effendi, immensely relieved. "How many piastres do you require? Will ten thousand do?"

"I want much more than that," replied Demetrius the Diver, with a grim smile.

"More! What rogues you Greeks are! How much more?"

"I want," pursued the Diver, "my wife Katinka back from Stamboul. She was torn away from Scio, and is in the harem of the Capitan-Pacha. I want my three children, my boy Andon, my boy Yorghi, and my girl Eudocia. When I have all these, here at Massalian (Marseilles), and twenty thousand piastres to boot, your frigates shall be launched in safety."

"All well and good," said the Effendi; "I will write to Stamboul to-night, and you shall have all your brood and the piastres as well within two months. But what security have I that you will perform your part of the contract? The word of a Greek is not worth a para."

"You shall have a bond for double the amount which you

will hand over to me, from two merchants of Marseilles. You cannot give me *all* I should like," concluded the Diver, with a revengeful frown. " You cannot give me back my aged father's life, my sister's, my youngest child's ; you cannot give me the heart's blood of the Albanian wolf who slew them."

Within a quarter of a year, Demetrius the Diver was restored to his family. He insisted upon receiving the stipulated reward in advance, probably holding as poor an opinion of the word of a Turk as the Effendi did of the word of a Greek. The momentous day arrived when the third frigate was to be launched ; and a larger crowd than ever was collected. Everybody was on the tiptoe of expectation. Demetrius the Diver, who, during the past three months had had free access to the ship-builders' yard, was on board. The dogshores were knocked away, the frigate slid down her ways, and took the water in splendid style. The launch was completely successful. The Effendi was in raptures, and believed more firmly in the power of the evil eye than ever. A few days afterwards the fourth frigate was launched with equal success.

" Marvellous man ! " cried the envoy of the Sublime Porte ; " by what potent spells wert thou enabled to bewitch the first two frigates ? "

" Simply by these," answered Demetrius the Diver, in presence of a large company assembled at a banquet held in honour of the two successful launches. " Five years ago, my father was one of the most extensive shipbuilders at Scio, and I was bred to the business from my youth. We were rich, we were prosperous, until we were ruined by the Turkish atrocities at Scio. I arrived in Marseilles, alone, beggared, my father murdered, my wife and children in captivity. How I lived, you all know. While the first two frigates were being built, I watched every stage of their construction. I detected several points of detail which I felt certain would prevent their being successfully launched. When, however, I had entered into my contract with this noble Effendi, I conferred with the shipwrights; I pointed out to them what was wrong; I convinced them, by argument and illustration, of what was necessary to be done. They did it. They altered, they improved. Behold, the ships are launched, and the evil eye had no more to do with the matter than the amber mouthpiece of his excellency the Effendi's chibouque! I have spoken."

The Effendi, it is said, looked rather foolish at the conclusion of this explanation, and waddled away, muttering that all Greeks were thieves. Demetrius, however, kept his piastres, gave up diving as a means of a livelihood, and, commencing business on his account as a boat-builder, prospered exceedingly with Katinka his wife, and Andon, Yorghi, and Eudocia, his children. As to the two frigates, they were equipped for sea in good time, and were, I believe, knocked to pieces by the allied fleets at the battle of Navarino.

XII.

NOT many miles from Kendal, in Westmorcland, there is a little town which I will call Bridgemoor. Bridgemoor has a long, scattered, straggling street of houses built in the "any how" style of architecture. The market-place in Bridgemoor has a circular flight of steps in the midst, surmounted by a jagged stone stump—the pedestal, in old Catholic times, of Bridgemoor market-cross. There is a market-house, within whose cloister is a statue of Sir Gervase Gabion, Knight, of Gabion Place, hard by; who barricaded, loopholed, casemated, and held out the market-house, against Colonel Barzillai Thwaites, commanding a troop of horse and two companies of the Carlisle Godly train-bands, in the Cavalier and Roundhead days. The loyal baronet is represented in full Roman costume, including, of course, the voluminous periwig essential to strict classicality in those days. He stands in a commanding attitude, irremediably crushing with his left sandal a hideous stone griffin, supposed to be an effigy of anarchy, or Cromwellism, embodied in the person of Colonel Barzillai Thwaites aforesaid. The baronet's right hand holds an elongated cylinder of stone, which may be assumed to mean

a bâton, a telescope, or a roll of paper, exactly as the spectator chooses, and with which he points in the direction of
his ancestral mansion, Gabion Place, nearly half of which
mansion he had the patriotism to blow up with gunpowder
about the ears of the Godly trainbands; in consideration of
which eminent, loyal, and patriotic service, the inhabitants
of Bridgemoor caused this statue to be erected to him in the
market-house cloister; and King Charles the Second, on His
Majesty's happy restoration, did him the honour of playing
basset with him twice in the gallery at Whitehall, being
actually, in addition, condescending enough to win two score
pieces of him and to make two jokes on the fashion of his
periwig;—which was all he ever did for him.

Bridgemoor has, besides the architectural embellishments
I have noticed, the usual complement of decent, or genteel,
or stylish houses, being the residences of its clergyman,
lawyer, doctor, and other local big-wigs. It has a quiet,
humdrum, harmless population; and manners quite as harmless, as quiet, and as humdrum; but, amidst its general
tranquillity, it possesses so great a warmth of feeling on a
certain subject, that if a Certain Personage were to come
over from foreign parts and set up, aggressively and defiantly,
his Toe to be kissed in Bridgemoor market-place, he would
be told something from Bridgemoor folk that would, I warrant, astonish him.

Such is Bridgemoor, and such it was, with few exceptions, some one hundred and sixteen years ago, about
which time the story I have to tell had action. The same
street, market-place, market-house, quiet humdrum people,
and manners existed then as now; but, in 1746, the men

wore cocked hats, and square cut coats; the ladies coifs, pinners, and quilted petticoats. The Bridgemoor ladies now ride in railway carriages from the Bridgemoor station along the railway to Kendal; in 1746 they rode on a pillion behind John the servant-man. In 1746 the market-place could boast of two time-honoured monuments or institutions, called stocks and a whipping-post; at which latter institution very many vagrants, male and female, were salutarily scourged by the parish constable, according to the letter of the humane statute of Elizabeth in the case of vagrancy made and provided. Both of these institutions, together with a cheerful-looking gibbet on an adjacent moor, on which the bones of shackled corpses swung in the northern blast, and which was the chief lounge for the Bridgemoor crows, ravens and starlings, and the terror of vinous farmers returning from fair or market, have long since disappeared. So have some score cottages which tumbled down from time to time through rottenness, and were rebuilt in a more modern style. So has Gabion Place, the ancient mansion of the Gabion family which (house and family both), were demolished at the time, and in the manner I am going to tell you of.

In the fatal Forty-five, as all men know, Charles Edward Stuart came from France into Scotland, and from thence as far as Derby in England to fight for what he conceived to be his own. There were many widows and orphans made in England and Scotland, many tears of blood shed through his bootless quarrel for the crown with George of Hanover. In the more fatal Forty-six, after Culloden, there was martial law in the highlands of both countries. Dragoons scoured as the country side in search of fugitive Jacobite officers, of Jesuits, of papal emissaries, and of disaffected persons of every degree. Gentlemen's mansions were broken into, wainscoting was torn down, flooring wrenched up, pictures were pierced for the discovery of the "priest's hole;" farmhouses were ransacked, barns .searched, hay and straw turned up with swords and bayonets lest Jacobite refugees should be concealed beneath. In every ditch, there was a corpse; in every rivulet, blood; in every farm field, a smouldering hay-stack, or a shattered plough; in every house, fear and horror and trembling cheek by jowl with savage brutality and drunken exultation. On every hearth where the red stream of Civil War had flowed to quench the fire of love and house-hold hope, there were the ashes of desolation. Women and young children slaughtered or outraged; men shot and hanged without trial or shrift or hearing; goods and chattels wantonly destroyed; crops burnt, homesteads razed;—such was martial law in Northern Scotland. In England and at Bridgemoor, its aspect, though less sanguinary, was as gloomy. One hideous uniform system of military terrorism was in force; and though—from the number of persons resident in the northern counties who were attached to the existing Government, and had never taken any part with the adherents of the Pretender—there did not exist the same pretence for the wholesale plunder, spoliation, and blood-shedding with which Scotland was ravaged, still an un-ceasing round of domiciliary visits was made, and in almost every house military were quartered.

Of the many families directly or indirectly compromised by the political events of the foregoing, none were so seriously implicated as that represented at Bridgemoor by the Lady Earnest Gabion, who resided at Gabion Place, and superintended for her son the management of the vast estates he owned. The lady's husband, Gervase Gabion, Lord of the Manor of Bridgemoor, died in 1725, leaving issue one son, Gervase Earnest, now twenty-two years of age. The family were rigid Catholics, and as rigid partisans of the House of Stuart. The last Squire Gabion had been intimately mixed up with the Earl of Mar's rash outbreak in 1715. In the course of a long sojourn in France before he could make his peace with the Government, he married, in 1720, the Lady Earnest Augusta Mary, sole daughter and orphan of Earnest, Baron Brierscourt, of Brierscourt, in the Kingdom of Ireland, who was attainted for his share in Sir John Fenwick's conspiracy; but escaped, went abroad, and —bidding adieu to the pomps and vanities of the world, political and social—took the cowl, and died in the famous Monastery of La Trappe. The Lady Earnest would probably have imitated his example, and have been received as a nun in the convent where she was already a boarder, had she not been, at the passionate instance of her brother, the titular Lord Brierscourt (who, under the name of the Baron de Bricourt, had taken service in the French king's Grey Musketeers), eventually persuaded to accept the hand of Mr. Gervase Gabion. They lived together very happily, as the story-books say, till the demise of the squire, who died in his bed, and in decent odour with Sir Robert Walpole, leaving an infant, as I have told you, who at two years of age became sole lord of Bridgemoor Manor and of a rent-roll of twenty thousand pounds a year.

N

As the little lad grew he imbibed, together with a doting affection for his mother, and a bigoted attachment to his Church, an attachment quite as doting, as bigoted, as self-denying, as irrational it may be to the princes and politics of that ill-fated, false, and faithless house, which never brought anything but misery and ruin upon the lands they ruled over. Everything around him conspired to confirm him in his love for the house of Stuart. The mother he idolised valued a golden crucifix which her father had received from James the Second, at Saint Germain's, next to the relics of the saints. His nurse was never tired of telling him of the great and good Earl of Derwentwater; of how he fought and bled for James the Third; of how the Whigs slew him on Tower Hill, in London, and of the brave words he spake to the people there; of how his body was brought home to the Lakes in earl's state and splendour, travelling only by night, and resting in Catholic places of worship during the day; of how she dressed him in a laced shroud and helped to sew his severed head on when he came home. The peasants in the neighbourhood were for ever telling him that, when he was a man, he was to bring the rightful King home; his tutor, an Irish priest, mixed up Jacobitism and the Delphin Classics for him, and instilled the divine right of kings into his accidence. Is it to be wondered at, therefore, that at eighteen years of age Gervase Gabion was compelled to leave even orthodox and Jacobitical Oxford, for openly expressed and obstinately maintained anti-Hanoverian principles; that at twenty-one he raised, equipped, and commanded as fierce a troop of Westmoreland troopers as you could find now in the Life Guards— that he went in, over head and ears for Charles Edward Stuart?

When Culloden had been fought, and the Prince was hiding, and the proscription came, a troop of Morrish's regiment of dragoons (the yellow horse) came to Bridgemoor. The name and character of the widow of Squire Gabion stood so high, she was so beloved far and near for meekness and goodness, that her house, until the date of the commencement of this story, had been left sacred. But a strict watch was kept on her and hers.

The Lady Earnest had been, for nearly a score of years, in the habit of receiving, in the great oak parlour of Gabion Place, every night in the week save Sunday, the principal inhabitants of Bridgemoor. They ate and drank nothing, save on stated occasions, for which special invitations were issued ; but the ladies brought their needlework, and the men played at a very solemn and intricate game called Trictrac. Two circumstances may have induced the Lady Earnest to hold these very frequent *réunions*. In the first place, there was no family in Bridgemoor of sufficient rank to admit of her visiting them ; in the next, she had been educated abroad, where it is the custom for the principal lady in a provincial town to "receive" six times a week. · So, night after night, winter and summer, there assembled in the great oak parlour Doctor Boyfus the Æsculapius of Bridgemoor, (sometimes Mrs. Boyfus,) and Mr. Tappan the solicitor; the three Miss Tappans, his elderly sisters (very assiduous in their attendance), old Captain Limberup, who had been with the Duke at the battle of Hochstedt ; one Mr. Paul, who had formerly dealt in druggets at Leeds, and was, consequently, somewhat looked down upon ; but who was so devout a Catholic, so warm a Jacobite, and so good a man, that he had been admitted on a sort of good-humoured sufferance for full ten years as an honorary member of the Gabion coterie. The venerable Mrs. Vanderpant, whose husband, a Dutch sea captain, had been summarily shot, in by-gone days, by William the Third for tampering with the adherents of the Pretender, closed the list of the regular frequenters of the oak parlour. The rector of the parish, Dr. Small, came but seldom; he was a Low Churchman, who had for the greater part of his life been very much occupied with the composition of a folio refutation or Bentley's "Phalaris." A non-juring archdeacon of the Protestant persuasion (very much put to his shifts, and forced to earn his bread as a travelling tutor) dropped in occasionally; but he talked too much about Doctor Sacherverell, all of whose sermons he had by heart, and quarrelled too, with Father Maziere, the Irish Benedictine chaplain and tutor, whom I have not mentioned hitherto as one of the circle, he being as much an article of household furniture, as the great, long-backed armchairs or the trictrac board. Many a summer and winter's day had past and gone since young Squire Gervase had put his foot across his own threshold. In his place there came another visitor, unwelcome, though not unbidden; dreaded, yet nightly expected; courted, but hated and feared. This was Captain Seagreest, the commander of the troop of horse stationed at Bridgemoor. He was the Fate of the town, he held the strings of life and death; he could hang all Bridgemoor, so they said, as high as Haman, if he chose, in half an hour.

On a certain cold Thursday evening in November, 1746, Lady Gabion had determined to close her doors to her entire circle of visitors, as she had closed them on the preceding Tuesday and Wednesday. The existence, almost cloistral, led by those who dwell in small towns, creates in them a species of habit of analysing and explaining—to their own satisfaction at least—the minutest actions of ther neighbours. All Bridgemoor was agog for the two days, and for a considerable portion of the two nights, to find a solution for Lady Gabion's seemingly inexplicable conduct.

On Thursday morning, after the reception by old Mr. Paul of a missive from the Lady Gabion, intimating her renewed inability to receive that evening, and begging him to communicate her apologies to her visitors in collective, public curiosity reached the boiling point, and well nigh boiled over. With this curiosity began to be mingled alarm, not for the health of Lady Gabion, but for her life. At twelve o'clock in the forenoon, old Mr. Paul, walking on the High Street, was smartly tapped on the shoulder by a tall man with a black campaigning wig, a scarlet coat, a grizzled moustache, an evil-minded cocked hat, cruel eyes, a great gash across the left cheek, a trailing sabre, and jack-boots with long brass spurs. Mr. Paul, a venerable man, of full seventy years, with flowing white hair and an infirm gait, trembled violently when he felt the hand of captain Seagreest on his shoulder, and when, turning round, he found himself face to face with that horrible trooper.

" I know what's going on up yonder," was the greeting of the dragoon.

" Know, captain ? " faltered out Paul.

" Ay," responded his interlocutor, with an oath, " and so do you, you infernal Jacobitical old rag pedlar. *I've* watched the crew at the Place. I know their game, and I'll spoil it too. The old Cumberland witch, Bridget," he continued, "was in the market almost before daylight this morning, and bought eggs: the Gabion woman never eats eggs. She bought fowls: the Gabion woman never eats poultry. As I passed this morning after parade, I found the second window on the first floor of the left wing had been cleaned, and fresh curtained. I know who sleeps there when he is at home; and you know, too, you whining Popish hunks."

He struck the old man, sportively it may be, a blow on the cheek as he spoke, with his soiled gauntlet. Sportively, I hope, but rudely enough to bring a blush to the pale cheek, and a clench to the palsied hand, that, twenty years ago, would have been as good as a knock down blow to the ruffian soldado.

Look you here, Master Teazel and Wool," he went on, gripping the retired cloth-merchant by the arm. "You are hand and glove with this Babylon baron's daughter; you mumble out of the same mass-book, and plot against His sacred Majesty together. Now mark! go you up, and tell my Lady this,—she expects her son to-night. Don't lie, old Judas, and say she doesn't. In this pocket," and the captain slapped his thigh, "I have the proclamation for the taking of Gervase Gabion of Gabion, dead or alive, with two hundred pounds reward. I come to Gabion Place to-night. Either I go away the accepted suitor and affianced husband of my Lady Gabion, or I go away, to-morrow morning, with a serjeant and a squad behind me. I'll ride my horse Turenne, d'ye hear; but I'll have the bridle of another horse in my hand, and as I go away on that horse shall be her dainty master Gervase Gabion, gagged, handcuffed, and with his legs tied together underneath the horse's belly."

"Captain, captain!" faltered Paul.

"Tell her that!" concluded the captain triumphantly, snapping the fingers of the soiled gauntlet. "Tell her that her pet boy shall swing at Carlisle within a fortnight; that he shall be hanged, drawn, and quartered according to law, like a traitor as he is. Tell her *that*, and that I'll marry her afterwards into the bargain, if she isn't civil."

And with these words swaggered away, with much jingling of spurs and clanging of the sabre, Captain Jesse Seagreest of Morrish's regiment of horse. He was as great a bully, ruffian, and gamester, as ever was permitted, in those somewhat free and easy Horse Guard days, to disgrace His Majesty's service.

The cloth-merchant hurried away as fast as his tottering limbs would permit him, in the direction of Gabion Place. He was panting and trembling with exhaustion and excitement when he reached the quaint iron gate, which gave entrance by a sinuous carriage drive to the picturesque old mansion. The old porter was not so deaf and stupid, but he sufficiently comprehended the importance of the occasion, when Mr. Paul pencilled hastily on one of his tablets a passionate request to the Lady Gabion, to let him have one minute's interview with her. Simon Candy, the lodge-keeper, was as devout a Catholic, and as staunch a vassal of the houses of Stuart and Gabion as can well be imagined, and he had no sooner read the words held before his eyes by the cloth-merchant, than with a nod of acquiescence, he admitted him within the gate, and bidding him wait an instant before the lodge door, hurried away towards the house.

He returned almost immediately.

· "My lady 'll see thee," he said. "Gang thee ways oup yander, lad : thee know'st t' way." The lad of eighty, having indicated to the lad of seventy the route he was to take, retired into his lodge.

Slowly and sadly—a contrast to the hurried eagerness with which he had approached the house—the ancient man proceeded upon his mission. Now that he was so near upon its completion, an unaccountable reluctance seemed to take possession of him in unfolding its purpose. He trod laggingly through a trim, prim, square-cut garden, arranged in that Helvetico-Italian style of which Lenôtre was the inventor and prime professor. By hedges cropped like horsehair cushions, through quaint triumphal arches of herbage, under trees cut into fantastic shapes, by zig-zag flower-pots he went, the gravel rasping discordantly under his feet, the leaves of the evergreens soughing piteously. So, on till he came to a glass grape-house, where was a large grape-vine, near which, in a rustic chair, was a lady of noble presence, with a pale face and great brown eyes, a white hand, a supple yet commanding form, and fair hair. Some forty years had passed their hands across her features, but they had dealt with her lightly, and had left few scars behind. If her face had not been so deathly pale, and her eyes so sorrowful, she would have been beautiful.

The cloth-merchant was a plain man, and told what he had to say as plainly and succinctly as he could. "Dear lady," he said in conclusion, "if what this murthering trooper says be true, tell us at least if he has reason for his suspicion. Let us see what we can do to hide the truth, to save our boy. There is not a soul in Bridgemoor, I will be sworn, but would go through fire and water to serve you—the swashbuckler dragoons excepted. Joe Limberup (the captain) is in the commission of the peace. *He* might help us."

For reply she took him by the hand, and pulled him rather than led him into a little shed, outside, in which the gardener kept his tools. She closed the ricketty door, she hung her mantle over the latch, she looked around so scared and bewildered, as if she feared the sparrows on the window-sill would carry her secret ; then, pulling from her bosom a torn, dirty, crumpled piece of paper, she thrust it into the old man's hand, and bade him read it.

It was a letter from her son, Gervase Gabion. It said that he was in prison, and in peril of his life; but that he had planned an escape. He indicated three days, Tuesday, Wednesday, and Thursday in this same week, on which he might come disguised to Gabion. If he did not come on the third day he was to be considered dead. There was neither place nor date to the hurried scrawl which was as a life or death warrant to two human beings ; but there was a postscript, in which he bade his mother give a munificent reward to the messenger who had brought the letter.

"And this is Thursday," cried the lady. "He will be here to-night, and the red-coats know it, and they will carry him off and hang him ! "

"Trust in me," responded Ezra Paul. "He shall be saved. I will have scouts posted all round the place all night, to watch for him ; but, dear lady, you must disarm suspicion, you must receive your usual visitors to-night."

" But the dragoon—the dragoon ! *He* will be here."

" Hang the dragoon," cried Ezra, in his piping voice, " we will watch him. I'll get .drunk, I'll poison him, I'll kill him."

Passing down the main street, by the threshold of the town-brewery, which had been converted into a temporary barrack, he was hallooed to by Captain Seagreest, who was smoking a pipe and watching one of his troopers clean his famous horse Turenne with a wisp of straw, cursing the man heartily, and kicking him bewhiles.

" You've done your errand I see, old Slyboots," he roared out condescendingly. " See here, what a pretty paper-hanging I mean to cover my barrack-yard with."

Paul looked up. There was a proclamation offering the reward for the apprehension of Gervase Gabion, twenty-two years of age, light curly hair, blue eyes, six feet in height, a scar on the left hand.

The cloth-merchant shuddered, and, in as civil terms as he could command, notified to the dragoon that a slight indisposition, under which the Lady Gabion had been suffering, having yielded to two days' quiet nursing, she was willing to receive as usual that evening, and begged the favour of his company. To his unspeakable joy and relief the captain informed him, with a sarcastic bow, that duty would call him away the whole of that night from Bridgemoor, " and as for the little bit of business I have with my Lady Grandeur," he sneered forth, " that may as well be settled to-morrow evening as this." With this, Paul took leave of him.

"And yet," he said to himself musingly, as he bent his steps towards the abode of Captain Limberup, "there are some devil's thoughts under that campaigning wig of his. Is he going to scour the country with his marauding, tapstering butchers? Yet his plan must evidently be to catch the bird in its nest. To have it taken elsewhere would spoil his plans. Perhaps he is only off on some drinking bout with the other Philistines at Kendal."

The Gabion "Thursday night" was held as usual. The dreary game of trictrac went on as usual. Prodigal Sons, and Sacrifices of Isaacs were worked in parti-coloured silks for chair covers or screens. Snuff was taken, quiet remarks hazarded, half-crowns decorously won and lost. Lady Gabion sat paler than she had been that morning, with forced conventional smiles playing on her wan lips. The ticking of the clock smote on her ear like a hammer on an anvil, the wind outside screamed as in pain, the twisted bell-pulls seemed as hangman's halters, the great oak parlour seemed to her as the Valley of the Shadow of Death. And, though the dreaded Seagreest was not there, his very absence increased instead of allaying her terrors.

Towards eleven of the clock of this same Thursday night, a young man riding a grey horse, with a docked military tail—as troop horses were docked then—and splashed, man and horse, up to the eyes, was making his way from Kendal to Bridgemoor. He seemed to know the country, for he avoided the main route, and came by a devious and circuitous path. For all his caution, though, he was challenged once or twice by horsemen, but a few words, and the sight of a paper he carried in his breast, were a sufficient passport for him. He clattered down the main street of Bridgemoor, as far as the brewery barrack, in front of which stopping boldly and resolutely, he called to the sentry to call the serjeant of the guard.

In a minute or two the officer in question came forth from the guard-house, holding a lantern, and offering; in his unsteady gait, rolling head, and blinking eye, an interesting problem to the philosopher as to whether he were more drunk than sleepy, or more sleepy than drunk.

"I am on the King's business," said the man on horse-back. "I am Corporal Harris of Hawley's dragoons, on my way to Lancaster. Here are my pass, papers, and billet. The mayor of Kendal has given me a billet on one Lady Gabion, of Gabion Place here. Which is the way to it?"

The serjeant held up his lantern to examine the papers which the horseman offered for his inspection.

"Good!" cried the serjeant, lowering his lantern. "Good night, comrade. Jolly good quarters you'll get at the popish woman's. Corporal Foss, tell him the way to Gabion Place!" Upon which the serjeant nodded, and returned, lantern and all, into the guard-house.

Corporal Foss did as he was bidden, and, after watching the retreating figure of the horseman till it disappeared at the curve of the street, returned to the guard-house also.

"Serjeant Scales," he remarked to his superior officer, as the two resumed the consumption of two pipes and two mugs of beer, "wasn't that young fellow very like the chap proclaimed for, dead or alive, with two hundred shiners reward for nailing him?"

" Hang you for a fool, Corporal Foss ! " responded the serjeant. " Didn't I see the Duke of Cumberland's own fist at the bottom of the pass ? We should have more stripes on our backs than on our arms if we had stopped that cull, you whackhead."

As the Lady Earnest Gabion sat trembling in the great oak parlour alone, her guests having left her about half an hour, the ticking of the clock, sharp and distinct as it was, was suddenly rendered partially inaudible by the clattering of distant hoofs. The lady stood up in the middle of the chamber, so that when she heard the hoofs come nearer, nearer, nearer still; when she heard the lodge-gate open, a man dismount, the door-bell ring, the portal open, and the voice of Bridget the old housekeeper cry out below in joyful recognition, " My master—my young master ! " she went down on her knees for joy and thankfulness.

" He is here ! He is here, dear mistress ! " cried the housekeeper, rushing into the room.

" Who is here ? " asked a harsh voice, as a gaunt figure stepped from behind the tapestry on the landing and laid its knotty hand on Lady Gabion's arm. " Who is here ? " asked Captain Seagreest.

" Let me go to my son ! " screamed the lady.

" Hush, for heaven's sake ! hush, my dear mistress," said the housekeeper. " My lady is well-nigh distraught, your honour. The gentleman is one of King George's soldiers quartered here for the night, and here is his paper, sir."

So saying, she held forth to the brutal trooper the BILLET, which the supposed corporal had put into her hand as he entered.

"Bah!" the captain replied with sublime contempt. "Go and see your baby, my lady. Make your most of him for five minutes. After that he belongs to me."

He loosened his hold of the lady, who sprang from his grasp like a bird. She rushed into the wide entrance hall, and folded in her arms the tall young man standing there.

"My own boy!" she cried, sobbing and kissing him passionately. Till, looking up in his face, she gave one loud and awful scream, saying, "*This is* NOT *my son!*" and fell down senseless.

"Goodness forgie us and save us if it is!" cried Bridget in an agony, "and yet how like! The very hair, the very blue een, and wavy hair, and all. Holy mother! the very mark on his hand."

"Not her son!" said Captain Seagreest, stepping unconcernedly over the prostrate form of Lady Gabion, and staring the astonished soldier in the face, "Who are you, in the devil's name?"

"Corporal Harris, Captain Butt's troop, Hawley's dragoons," answered the young soldier drawing himself up, and saluting the uniform of his officer. "On my way to Lancaster with a dispatch to Colonel Tarleton. Here is my pass and papers, there is my billet for the night. God save the King, and confound the Pope, the Devil, and the Pretender."

Lady Gabion died that night of spasms in the heart. It was afterwards known that at the very hour and minute of the arrival of the soldier at Gabion Place her son Gervase, who was being brought under strong escort to London, and had been confined for the night in a barn at Highgate, was shot dead by the guard in an attempt to escape.

XIII.

DOCTOR PANTOLOGOS.

DOCTOR PANTOLOGOS taught school at Accidentium for thirty years. I would rather not reveal where Accidentium is. Let it be in Blankshire. We don't want, down at Accidentium, the Government Commissioner, or any other commissioner or commission whatsoever. If we have grievances, we can suffer and be strong, as Mr. Longfellow says; or, as our homely synonym has it, we can grin and bear it.

Some years ago, indeed, we should have had far greater cause to deprecate the arrival of any strangers among us, or their inquiries into our affairs; for we had one great, patent, notorious, grievance. The school that Doctor Pantologos taught was woefully mismanaged. Not by its master—he was a model of probity, and a monument of learning—but by Somebody, who might as well have been Nobody, for we never saw him or them; and the Free Grammar School at Accidentium went on from year to year becoming more ruinous without, while it decreased in usefulness within. Somebody, who had no right to Anything, received the major portion of the funds, those who ought to have had much got little, and those who were entitled to little got less. There were prebendaries concerned in Accidentium Grammar School, and an Earl of Something, likewise an Act of Parliament, Sythersett's Charity, and sundry charters, which, for anything we ever saw of them, might have furnished the old parchment, crabbed handwriting-filled covers to the school lexicons and dictionaries; but, for all these influential connections, nobody repaired the roof of the school-room, or increased the salary of Doctor Pantologos. Both needed it very much. The vicar talked of looking into it, but he was poor, and half blind besides, and died; and his successor, a vellum complexioned young man, bound in black cloth, white lawn edges, and lettered to a frightful degree of archæological lore, had no leisure for anything out of church time save stone breaking on the road (with a view to geological improvement), and taking rubbings in heelball of the monumental brasses of the church chancel. Moreover, he was supposed to have his own views about a new Grammar School, which he was understood to conceive as a building in the Pointed manner;—the boys to wear cassocks and bands, with crosses on their breasts, like buns; to attend church at eight o'clock every morning, and four times a day afterwards; to learn intoning, and the Gregorian chant generally; and, in the curriculum of their humanities, to study Homer and Virgil far less than Augustine and Jerome. So the Vicar and Doctor Pantologos fell out, as well on this question as on the broad question of surplices, copes, candlesticks, flowers, lecterns, and wax-candles; and the Doctor said he pitied him; while he (his name was Thurifer) wondered whatever would become of an instructor of youth who smoked a pipe, and played at cribbage. Borax, the Radical grocer (we had one grocer, and one Radical in Accidentium), threatened to shew the school up; but he took to drinking shortly afterwards, and ran away with Miss Cowdery, after which he was "buttoned up" (an Accidentium term for financial ruin), and was compelled to fly for shelter to Douglas, Isle of Man.

The little river Dune, which, in the adjoining manufacturing counties of Cardingshire, Rollershire, and Spindleshire, became a broad, sober, gravely flowing, stream, refreshingly dirty (in a commercial sense) at Slubberville, and as black as ink at the great town of Drygoodopolis, was, at Accidentium, a little, sparkling, purling, light-hearted, thread of water; now enlivening the pebbles as a Norman *ménétrier* does the village maidens, making them dance willy nilly; now enticing the rushes into liquor; now condescending to act as a looking-glass for a bridge; now going out, literally, on the loose, of its own accord, by splitting up into little back waters, rivulets, and streamlets, sparkling through the convolvuli to the delight of the wayfarer, and scampering by cottage doors to the glory of the ducks; but everywhere through the valley of the Dune a jovial, hospitable, earnest, little river: the golden cestus of Venus, by day thrown heedlessly athwart the verdant valley, at night shining silver bright—

> "As if Diana in her dreams,
> Had dropped her silver bow,
> Upon the meadows low."

A free hearted river, crying to hot boys, Come bathe! and to the thirsty cows, Drink! and to the maidens of Accidentium, Bring hither your fine linen, and see how white the Dune water will make it!

Close to the river bank (the water was visible through the old latticed windows of the schoolroom; and, suggesting bathing, was a source of grievous disquiet to the boys in summer time) was the Accidentium Grammar School. It was a long, low, old, building, not of bricks, but of stones so old that some said they had once formed part of the ancient abbey of Accidentium, and others that they were more ancient still, and came from the famous wall that the Romans built, to keep out those troublesome Paul Prys who always *would* intrude: the Picts and Scots.

The latticed windows, twinkling through the ivy; the low-browed doorway, with its carved, ironclamped portal; the double-benched porch before it; and sculptured slab overhead, shewing the dim semblance of an esquire's coat-of-arms, and a long, but a most wholly effaced, Latin inscription, setting forth the pious injunctions of Christopher Sythersett, Armiger, relative to the charities he founded—injunctions how observed, oh, ye prebendaries and somebodies! these were the most remarkable features of the exterior of Accidentium Grammar School. There had once been a garden in front, and a pretty garden, too; but the palings were broken down, and the flowers had disappeared long since, and the weeds had it all their own way. Moreover, a considerable number of the latticed panes were broken, there were great gaps in the stone-masonry, the river frequently got into the garden and wouldn't get out again, the thatch was rotten and the belfry nearly tumbling down; but what was that to anybody? Borax said it was a shame; but so is slavery a shame, and war, and poverty, and the streets by night—all of which, we know, nobody is accountable for, or in fault about.

The first thing you heard when you entered the long, low, stone, schoolroom, with its grand carved oak roof all covered with cobwebs, and falling down piecemeal, through neglect, was a din—a dreadful din. Latin was the chiefest thing learnt in Accidentium School, and a Latin noise is considerably more deafening than an English noise. Every boy learnt his lesson out loud—at least, every boy who chose to learn—the rest contenting themselves with shouting out terminations as loud as they could, and rocking themselves backwards and forwards on their forms, after the manner of studious youths, learning very hard indeed. There was a considerable amount of business transacted in the midst of this din, in rabbits, silkworms, hedgehogs, tops, marbles, hardbake, and other toys and luxuries. Autumnal fruits were freely quoted at easy rates between the moods of the verb Amo, and the declensions of nouns and adjectives. One Jack, a killer of giants; and seven shameless, swaggering, fireeating, blades, who called themselves Champions, and of Christendom, forsooth; together with a genteel youth in complete mail, young Valentine indeed, with his brother Orson (not yet accustomed to polite society), were often welcome, though surreptitious, guests at the dog's-eared tables, where nothing but the grim Vocito, the stern Vocitas, and the redoubtable Vocitavi; or, at most, the famous chieftains Mars, Bacchus, and Apollo, should have feasted.

After the din, the next thing that was heard was the voice of Doctor Pantologos. And it *was* a voice. It rolled like the Vesuvian lava—fierce, impetuous, and fiery, at first; and then, still like lava, it grew dry; and then, to say the truth, like lava again, it cracked. Grandiloquent was Doctor Pantologos in diction; redundant in simile, in metaphor, in allegory, irony, diaresis, hyperbole, catechresis, periphrasis, and in all the other figures of rhetoric. Rarely did he deal in comparatives —superlatives were his delight. But, though his voice rolled and thundered—though he predicted the gallows as the ultimate reward of bad scanning, and the hulks as the inevitable termination of a career commenced by inattention to the *As in presenti;* though his expletives were horrible to hear (all in Latin, and ending with *issimus*); though he threatened often, he punished seldom. His voice was *vox et prœterea nihil*—gentle, and kind, and lamblike, for all his loud and fierce talk; and the birchen rod, that lay in the dusty cupboard behind him, might have belonged to Doctor Busby, so long had it been in disuse.

Doctor Pantologos was a very learned man. He could not measure lands, nor presage tides and storms, nor did the rumour run that he could gauge; but he was as full of Latin, Greek, and Hebrew, as an egg is popularly said to be full of meat. He was a walking dictionary. A Thesaurus in rusty black. A Lexicon with a white neckcloth. Bayle, Erasmus, the Scaligers, Bentley, Salmasius, the Scholiast upon Everybody, all rolled up together. The trees, clad with leafy garments to meaner mortals, were to him hung only with neat little discs, bearing derivations of words and tenses. The gnarled oak had no roots to him but Greek roots. He despised the multiplication table, and sighed for the Abacus back again. He thought Buffon and Cuvier, Audubon and Professor Owen infinitely inferior, as natural historians, to Pliny. He had read one novel—the Golden Ass of Apuleius; one cookery book, that of Apicius. Galen, Celsus, Æsculapius, and Hippocrates, were the whole of the Faculty to him. Politics were his abomination; and he deemed but three subjects worthy of argument—the bull of Phalaris, the birth-place of Homer, and the Æolic Digamma.

On this last subject he had written a work—a mighty work, still in manuscript, from which he frequently read extracts, which nobody could understand, and which Borax, the Sceptic, declared the Doctor didn't understand himself. Either, said Borax, the Ironical, the Doctor was mad before he began the work, or he would go mad before he finished it. It was a wondrous book. Written on innumerable fragments of paper, from sheets of foolscap to envelopes of letters and backs of washing bills. The title page, and some half-dozen sheets besides, were fairly copied out and ready for press. "A Treatise on the Origin and History of the Æolic Digamma (with strictures upon the Scholiast upon Every-body, of course), by Thoukydides Pantologos, Head Master of the Free Grammar School at Accidentium." Thus classically did he write his name: he was of the Grotian creed, and scorned the mean, shuffling, evasive, Thucy-dides.

Whenever things went contrarywise with the Doctor, he flew for consolation to the treatise. He made a feint of not employing himself upon it in school hours; but, almost every afternoon, and frequently in the morning, he would cry, after many uneasy pinches of snuff; "Boy! go to my domicile and fetch the leathern satchel that lyeth on the parlour table." Straightway would the boy addressed, start on his errant; for, though the Doctor's cottage was close by, it oft-times happened that the boy managed to find time for the purchase of cakes and apples—nay, for the spinning of tops and tossing of leathern balls, and for unlawful " chivying" round the town pump, a highly ancient and venerable structure of Accidentium. Back would the boy come with the famous leathern satchel gorged with papers. Then Doctor Pantologos would dip his bony arm into it and draw forth a handful of the treatise, and would fall to biting his pen, and clenching his hands, and muttering passages concerning the welfare of the Æolic Digamma, and in a trice he would be happy; forgetting the din and the dust, the ruinous schoolroom, his threadbare coat, the misapplied funds, and his inadequate salary—forgetting, even, the existence of the three great plagues of his life, his sister Volumnia, his sister Volumnia's children, and that boy Quandoquidem.

Volumnia was the widow of a Mr. Corry O'Lanus, an Irishman, and an exciseman who had fallen a victim to his devotion to his official duties, having lost his life in " a difficulty," about an illicit still in the county Tipperary, much whiskey being spilt on the occasion, and some blood. To whom should the widowed Volumnia fly for protection and shelter but to her brother Thoukydides Pantologos? And Thoukydides Pantologos, whose general meekness and lamblikelihood would have prompted him to receive the Megatherium with open arms, and acknowledge the Plesiosaurus as a brother-in-law had he been requested so to do, did not only receive, cherish, aid and abet his sister Volumnia, but likewise her five orphan children—Elagabalus James, Commodus William, Marius Frederick, Drusilla Jane, and Poppæa Caroline. They had all red hair. They all fought, bit, scratched, stole and devoured, like fox-cubs. They tore the Doctor's books; they yelled shrill choruses to distract him as he studied; they made savage forays upon the leathern satchel: they fashioned his pens into pea-shooters, ate his wafers, poured out his ink as libations to the infernal gods. In a word, they played the very dickens with Doctor Pantologos. And Volumnia, whose hair was redder than that of her offspring, and in whose admirable character all the virtues of her children were combined, watched over this young troop with motherly fondness; and very little rest did she let her brother have night or day if the bereaved orphans of Mr. O'Lanus wanted new boots, or socks, or frocks.

Mrs. O'Lanus had no money, no wit, no beauty, no good qualities to speak of, but she had a Temper. By means of this said temper she kept the learned Doctor Pantologos in continual fear and trembling. She raised storms about his ears, she scolded him from doors and objurgated him from windows, she put "ratsbane in his porridge and halters in his pew" (figuratively of course), she trumpeted his mis-doings all over the village, and was much condoled with for her sufferings (a more harmless and inoffensive man than the doctor did not exist); she spent three fourths of his small income upon herself and her red-haired children; yet Thouky-dides Pantologos bore it all with patience, and was willing to believe that Volumnia was a martyr to his interests; that she sacrificed her children to him, and only stayed with him to save him and his house from utter rack and ruin.

Did I ever mention that a great many years before this time, Doctor Pantologos took to himself a wife—a delicate lady who died—called Formosa, and who dying left a little child—a girl, called Pulchrior? I think not,—yet it was so, and at this time this child had grown to be a brown-haired, rosy-cheeked, buxom little lass, some fifteen summers old. It pleased Doctor Pantologos to remark that she was not weak, nor delicate, nor ailing, like the poor lady—her mother—who died, and that still she had her mother's eyes, and hair, and cheery laugh. She was a very merry good little girl this Pulchrior, and I am sure I do not know what the poor Doctor would have done without her. Volumnia hated her, of course. She called her "rubbage," a "faggot" and other unclassical names, which I am ashamed the widow of an O'Lanus should have so far forgotten herself as to make use of; poor Pulchrior had to do the hardest work, and wash and dress the five red-headed children, who always fought, bit, scratched, and yelled, during the operation; she had to run errands for Volumnia, notably, with missives of a tender nature addressed to Mr. O'Bleak, the squinting apothecary at the corner (Volumnia adored Irishmen); she had to bear all Volumnia's abuse, and all the turmoil of the infants with the red heads, but she did not repine. She had a temper, too, had Pulchrior, and that temper happened to be a very good one; and the more Volumnia scolded, and stormed, and abused her, the more Pulchrior sang and smiled, and (when she could get into a quiet corner by herself) danced.

Luckily, indeed, was it for Doctor Pantologos that Volumnia did not deem it expedient that her red-headed children the boys at least, should receive their education, as yet, in the Accidentium Grammar School. The fiery-headed scions of the house of O'Lanus passed the hours of study in simple and pastoral recreations, dabbling in the mud in the verdant

ditches, making dirt-pies, squirting the pellucid waters of the
Dune through syringes at their youthful companions, or casting the genial brickbat at the passing stranger. Ah happy
time ! Ah happy they ! Ah happy, happy Doctor Pantologos !

Happy, at least, in school he might have been, notwithstanding the din, and the boys who could'nt and the boys
who would'nt learn—both very numerous classes of boys in
Accidentum Grammar School—comparatively happy would
the days have passed in the absorption of the treatise upon
the Æolic Digamma but for that worst of boys Quandoquidem. Quandoquidem was a big raw-boned boy of fourteen.
He had an impracticable head, incorrigible hands, and irre-
trievable feet. He was all knuckles—that is, his wrists,
elbows, fingers, knees, toes, shoulders, hips, and feet, all
seemed to possess the property of " knuckling down," and
bending themselves into strange angles. Quandoquidem
was a widow's son, and his mother Venturia, who had some
little property, dwelt in a cottage just opposite the dwelling of Doctor Pantologos, over against the pump. Quandoquidem either could or would not learn. He would
play at all boyish games with infinite skill and readi-
ness, but he could not say his lessons. He could make
pasteboard coaches, and windmills, and models of boats, but
he could not decline *Musa*. He was the bane of the doctor's school life—the plague, the shame, the scandal of the
school. He was the most impudent boy. The rudest boy.
The noisiest boy. He made paper pellets and discharged
them through popguns at the Doctor as he pored over the
treatise, or, as oft-times happened, took a quiet doze. He
shod cats with walnut-shells and caused them to perambulate

the schoolroom.　Doctor Pantologos, mild man, clenched his fist frequently, and looked at him vengefully, muttering something about the proverbs of King Solomon.

I am coming to the catastrophe of Doctor Pantologos. One very hot drowsy summer's afternoon, it so fell out that the boy Quandoquidem, the widow's son, was called upon by Doctor Pantologos to say a certain lesson.　Young Quidvetat, the attorney's son, had just said his as glibly as might be, and he, with Iœ Ægiotat, Tom Delectus, and Bill Spondee, with little Charley Dactyl, his fag and bottle-holder, were all gathered around the doctor's desk, anticipating vast amusement from the performances of the widow's son, who was the acknowledged dunce of the school.　Of course Quandoquidem didn't know his lesson—he never did; but on this summer's afternoon he began to recite it so glibly, and with so much confidence, that his erudite preceptor was about to bestow a large meed of praise upon him, when, his suspicions being roused by a titter he saw spreading amongst the boys on the forms near him, he was induced to look over the brow of his magisterial rostrum or desk.　The incorrigible Quandoquidem had wafered the page of the book containing his lesson against the doctor's desk, and was coolly *reading it.*

Now, it was extremely unlucky for Quandoquidem that the Doctor had been without the treatise all day, and that he had as yet sent no boy for it.　If that famous work upon the Digamma had been at hand, the perusal of the title-page alone would, no doubt, have softened his resentment; but, he was treatiseless and remorseless, and Quandoquidem read in his eyes that the storm was about to burst.

" Varlet," exclaimed the Doctor, in the lava voice, " disgrace to the widow thy mother, and to thy father deceased ! *Oh puer nequissimè, sceleratissimè ;* unworthy art thou of the lenient cane, the innocuous ferula. Let Thomas Quandoquidem be hoisted. Were he to cry *Civis Romanum sum,* he should be scourged ! "

Thus classically did the Doctor announce his dread design. The rod that might have been in the cupboard since Doctor Busby's time, was brought forth ; and Thomas Quandoquidem, the widow's son, suffered in the flesh.

It was a very hot and drowsy summer's afternoon, and the school was dismissed. The afternoon was so hot and drowsy that Doctor Pantologos, who had been hot and drowsy himself since the execution had been done upon Quandoquidem, began to nod in his arm chair, and at length, not having the treatise to divert his attention, fell fast asleep. He was not aware when he did so, that one boy had remained behind, sitting in a corner : or that that boy was Thomas Quandoquidem ! nor was he aware that the widow's son was gazing at him with a flushed face and an evil eye, and that he, from time to time, shook his knuckly fist at him.

When the Doctor was fast asleep, Quandoquidem rose and left the school house as softly as possible. He hastened as fast as he could—not to his mother's home, but to the domicile of Doctor Pantologos.

Volumnia was upstairs writing a tender epistle to Mr. O'Bleak. The red-haired children were all in the back garden, socially employed in torturing a cat. When Quandoquidem lifted the latch and entered the keeping-room, he found no one there but the little lass Pulchrior, who was sitting by the window, mending the Doctor's black cotton stockings.

Now, between Thomas Quandoquidem, the widow's son, and Pulchrior Pantologos, the motherless, there had existed for some period of time, a very curious friendship and alliance. Numberless were the pasteboard coaches, models of boats, and silkworm-boxes he had made her. Passing one day while she was laboriously sweeping out the parlour, what did Quandoquidem do but seize the broom from her hand, sweep the parlour, passage, kitchen, and washhouse, with goblin-like rapidity, dust all the furniture (there was not much to dust, truly), give Pulchrior a kiss, and then dart across the road to his mother, the widow's house, shouting triumphantly? Thus it came about that the little lass, Pulchrior, thought a good deal of Quandoquidem in her girlish way, and did trifles of sewing for him, and blushed very prettily whenever she saw him.

"Miss Pulchrior, please," said Quandoquidem, in a strange hard voice, as he entered the keeping-room, "the Doctor's not coming home yet awhile, and he's sent me for his leathern satchel."

He looked so hot and flushed, his brow was so lowering and ill-boding, that the Doctor's little daughter was frightened. She could not help suspecting, though she knew not what to suspect.

"And did papa send you?" she began, falteringly.

"Miss Pulchrior," interjected Quandoquidem, as if offended, "do you think I would tell you a story?"

Pulchrior slowly advanced to the table, and took up the leathern bag containing the *magnum opus* of her father,

Pantologos, the erudite. She handed it to Quandoquidem, looking timidly in his face, but the eyes of the widow's son were averted. His hand shook as he received the parcel; but he hurriedly thanked her, and, a moment afterwards, was gone. Had Pulchrior followed him to the door, she would have seen that the widow's son did not take the road towards the grammar school; but that, like a fox harbouring evil designs towards a henroost, he slunk furtively round a corner, and, watching his opportunity, crept round the town pump, across the narrow street, and so into his mother's cottage.

Pulchrior was not aware of this, because she did not follow the guilty Thomas: and she did not follow him because it occurred to her to sit down on a lonely stool and have a good cry. She cried she knew not why; only Tom (she called him Tom) was so different from his wonted state, and at the bottom of her heart there was a vague suspicion and terror of she knew not what. But, at the termination of the good cry, she recovered her spirits; and, when the kettle began to sing for tea, she was singing too; albeit the insulting tongue of Volumnia upon the topic of buttered toast was enough to spoil the temper of Robin Goodfellow himself.

Doctor Pantologos slept in the great arm chair so long and so soundly, that the old woman with a broom, who came to give the cobwebs change of air, from the roof to the floor (she would as soon have thought of burning the schoolroom down, as sweeping them away altogether), had to stir him up with the handle of her household implement before she could awaken him. Then Doctor Pantologos arose shaking himself and yawning mightily, and went home to tea.

That repast was not quite ready when he made his appearance; for the red-headed children having tortured the cat until it was mad and they were hungry, had made a raid upon the buttered toast, and had eaten it up. Then Volumnia had to abuse Pulchrior for this, which took some time, and fresh toast had to be made, which took more; so, the Doctor was informed that he would have to wait a quarter of an hour.

" Very well, Sister Volumnia," said the meek Doctor. " I hanker not so much after the fleshpots of Egypt, but that I can wait. *Ad interim*, I will take a pipe of tobacco, and correct my seventy-seventh chapter. Pulchrior, my child, the leathern satchel!"

" The satchel, papa!" cried his daughter; " why, you sent Tom—I mean Master Quandoquidem—for it."

" *I* sent—Satchel—Quandoquidem!" gasped the Doctor.

" Yes, and I gave it him an hour ago."

The Doctor turned with wild eyes to his luckless child. He clasped his forehead with his hands, and staggered towards the door. His hand was on the latch, when a burst of derisive laughter fell upon his ear like red-hot pitch. He looked through the open window of his chamber, through the screen of ivy, and woodbine, and honeysuckle, he could have looked through the town pump, but he looked instead right across the street of Accidentium, and through the open casement of the widow Venturia's cottage; and there he saw a red glare as of fire burning, and the boy Quandoquidem standing beside it with a leathern satchel in his hand, and his form reddened by the reflection like an imp of Hades.

Doctor Pantologos tried to move, but he could not. Atlas was tied to one foot, and Olympus to the other : Pelion sat upon Ossa a-top of his burning head.

The boy Quandoquidem drew a large sheet of paper from the satchel, and brandished it aloft. Had it been a thousand miles off, the Doctor could have read it. It was the title page of his darling treatise. The horrible boy thrust it into the fire, and then another and another sheet, and finally the satchel itself.

" So much for the Digamma, old Pan !" he cried with a ferocious laugh, as he stirred the burning mass with a poker.

" *Dies Iræ !*" said Doctor Pantologos, and he fell down in a dead faint.

Volumnia and Pulchrior came to his assistance; and, while the former severely bade him not to take on about a lot of rubbishing old paper, the latter administered more effectual assistance in the shape of restoratives. The red-headed children made a successful descent upon the fresh buttered toast, and ate it up with astonishing rapidity.

When Doctor Pantologos came to himself he began to weep.

" My treatise ! my treatise !" he cried. " The pride, the hope, the joy, of my life ! My son and my grandson, my mother and my wife ! Poverty I have borne, and scorn, and the ignorance of youth, and the neglect of the wealthy, and the insolence of this woman, and the ferocity of these whelps. Oh, my treatise ! Let me die now, for I have no treatise !"

He could say nothing, poor man, but " treatise," and "Quandoquidem," and "Digamma," weeping pitiably. They were fain to put him to bed; and Volumnia, reserving for a more suitable occasion the expression of her sentiments relative to being called "a woman," and her children "whelps," went for Mr. O'Bleak the apothecary. But, Pulchrior, somewhat mistrusting the skill of that squint-eyed practitioner, sent off for Doctor Integer, who was wont to smoke pipes and play cribbage with her papa.

During the next fortnight Doctor Pantologos drank a great deal of apple tea, and felt very hot, and talked much nonsense. He woke up one morning quite sensible, but with no hair on the top of his head—which was attributable to his having had his head shaved. He was very languid, and they told him he had had a brain fever.

Doctor Integer stood at the bottom of the bed, smiling and snuffing as was his wont. Pulchrior was standing on one side of the bed, smiling and crying at the same time, to see her father so well and so ill. On the opposite side, there stood a lad with a pale face, a guilty face, but a penitent face. He held in his hand a bundle of papers.

"I only burnt the title-page," he said in a low voice. "All the rest is as safe as the Bank."

"He has nursed you all through your illness," faltered Pulchrior.

"He has kept the school together," said Doctor Integer.

"*Tu Marcellus eris!*" said Doctor Pantologos, laying his hand on the head of Quandoquidem.

What they all said was true. Thomas the knuckly, had never intended to destroy the Doctor's treatise, and was grievously shocked and shamed when he saw how well his *ruse* had succeeded. Thomas Quandoquidem was a good lad for all his deficiencies in his accidence, and sedulously endeavoured to repair the evil he had done.

The Vicar, abandoning stone-breaking and heel-balling for a season, had undertaken to teach school during the Doctor's illness; and Quandoquidem, the erst dunce, truant, and idler, had become his active and efficient monitor, awing the little boys, shaming the bigger ones into good order and application, and introducing a state of discipline that Accidentium Grammar School had not known for years. No sooner was school over, every day, than he hastened to the bedside of the sick Doctor. And there was no kinder, patienter, abler, usefuller nurse than Thomas Quandoquidem.

And where was the voluminous Volumnia. Alas! the Doctor's fever was not a week old when she ungratefully abandoned him, and eloped with Mr. O'Bleak—red-haired children and all. Mr. O'Bleak forgot to settle his little debts in Accidentium, and Volumnia remembered to take, but forgot to return, sundry articles of jewellery and clothing belonging to the late Mrs. Pantologos. I said alas! when I chronicled Volumnia's elopement; but I don't think, setting aside the scandal of the thing, that her relatives grieved very much, or that the Doctor was with difficulty consoled, when she and her rubicund progeny took their departure.

Doctor Pantologos is now a white-headed patriarch, very busy still on the treatise, and very happy in the unremitting tenderness and care of his children. I say children, for he has a son and a daughter; the daughter Pulchrior, whom you know; the son, her husband, whom you know, too, though you would scarcely recognise the knuckly boy who could not say his accidence, in Thomas Quandoquidem, Esq.,

B.A., who went to Durham, and distinguished himself there, and was appointed master of the Free Grammar School at Accidentium on the retirement of Doctor Pantologos. Thomas has written no treatises, but he is an excellent master ; and, in addition, he has succeeded in stirring up an earl somewhere, who possessed twenty thousand a year and the gout, who stirred up some prebendary somewhere, who stirred up a chapter somewhere, and they do say that the Free Grammar School at Accidentium has a sound roof now, and that its master has a larger salary, and that the boys are better taught and cared for.

Pleasant fancies ! Thick-coming fancies ! Fancies hallowed by memory which a dog's-eared grammar on a bookstall—the inside of its calf-skin cover scrawled over with schoolboy names and dates—can awaken. But the bookstall keeper is very anxious to know whether I will purchase " that volium," and I am not prepared to purchase it, and the fancies melt into the iron, business day again.

XIV.

TRAVELS IN SEARCH OF BEEF.

IF I have a mission upon this earth (apart from the patent and notable one of being a frightful example to the rising generation of blighted existence and misused energies) —that mission is, I believe, Beef. I am a Cœlebs, not in search of a wife, as in Mrs. Hannah More's white-neck-clothed novel, but in search of beef. I have travelled far and wide to find it—good, tender, nourishing, juicy, succulent; and when I die, I hope that it will be inscribed on my tombstone : " Here lies one who sought for beef. Tread lightly on his grave : *quia multum amavit.*"

Next to the Habeas Corpus and the Freedom of the Press, there are few things that the English people have a greater respect for, and a livelier faith in, than beef. They bear, year after year, with the same interminable unvarying series of woodcuts of fat oxen in the columns of the illustrated newspapers; they are never tired of crowding to the Smithfield Club cattle-show; and I am inclined to think that it is their honest reverence for beef which has induced them to support so long the obstruction and endangerment of the thoroughfares of the metropolis, by oxen driven to slaughter. Beef is a great connecting link and bond of better feeling between the great classes of the commonwealth. Do not dukes hob and nob with top-booted farmers over the respective merits of short-horns and Alderneys? Does not the noble Marquis of Argentfork give an ox to be roasted whole on the village green when his son, the noble Viscount Silvercorrel, comes of age. Beef makes boys. Beef nerves our navvies. The bowmen who won Cressy and Agincourt were beef-fed, and had there been more and better beef in the Crimea some years ago, our soldiers would have borne up better under the horrors of a Tauridan winter. We feast on beef at the great Christian festival. A baron of beef at the same time is enthroned in St. George's Hall, in Windsor's ancient castle, and is borne in by the footmen in scarlet and gold. Charles the Second knighted a loin of beef; and I have a shrewd suspicion that the famous Sir Bevis of Southampton was but an ardent admirer, and doughty knight-errant in the cause of beef. And who does not know the tradition that even as the first words of the new-born Gargantua were "*A boyre! à boyre!*" signifying that he desired a draught of Burgundy wine—so the first intelligible sounds that the infant Guy of Warwick ever spake were, "Beef, beef!"

When the weary pilgrim reaches the beloved shores of England after a long absence, what first does he remark—after the incivility of the custom-house officers—but the great tankard of stout and the noble round of cold beef in the coffee room of the hotel? He does not cry "*Io Bacche! Evöe Bacche!*" because beef is not Bacchus. He does not fall down and kiss his native soil, because the hotel carpet is somewhat dusty, and the action would be, besides, egregious; but he looks at the beef, and his eyes filling with tears, a corresponding humidity takes place in his mouth; he kisses the beef; he is so fond of it that he could eat it all up ; and he does ordinarily devour so much of it to his breakfast, that the thoughtful waiter gazes at him, and murmurs to his napkin, "This man is either a cannibal or a pilgrim grey who has not seen Albion for many years."

By beef I mean, emphatically, the legitimate, unsophisticated article. Give me my beef, hot or cold, roast, boiled, or broiled ; but away with your beef-kickshaws, your beef-stews, your beef-haricos, your corned beef, your hung beef, and your spiced beef! I don't think there is anything so contemptible, fraudulent, adulterine in the whole world (of cookery) as a beef sausage. I have heard that it is a favourite dish with pickpockets at their raffle-suppers. I believe it. There was a boy at school with me in the bygone—a day-boy —who used to bring a clammy brownish powder, in a sandwich box, with him for lunch. He called it powdered beef and he ate this mahogany-sawdust looking mixture between slices of stale bread and butter. He was an ill-conditioned boy who had begun the world in the face-grinding sense much too early. He lent halfpence at usury, and dealt in " sock " (which was our slang for surreptitious sweet-stuff); and I remember with what savage pleasure I fell upon and beat him in the course of a commercial transaction involving a four-bladed penknife he had sold me, and which wouldn't cut—no, not even slate pencil. But the penknife was nothing more than a pretext. I beat him for his beef. It was bruited about afterwards that he was of Jewish parentage; and I heard that when he began life, he turned out badly.

I have merely ventured the above remarks on the bovine topic generally, to preface the experiences I have to record of some recent travels in search of beef I have made in the capital of France. One might employ oneself better, perhaps, than in transcribing the results of a week's hankering after the fleshpots; and surely the journey in search of bread is long and wearisome enough that we might take beef as it comes, and thankfully. But, as I have said, beef is my mission. I am a collector of bovine experiences, as some men collect editions of Horace, and some Raffaelle's Virgins, and some broadsides, and some butterflies. And I know that there are moralities to be found in beef as well as in pre-Adamite zoology and the Vestiges of Creation.

Let me first sum up all the knowledge I have acquired on the subject, by stating my firm conviction that there is no beef in Paris—I mean, no beef fit to be eaten by a philobosopher. Some say that the French cut their meat the wrong way; that they don't hang it properly; that they don't hang it enough; that they beat it; that they overcook it. But I have tasted infinite varieties of French beef, of the first, second, and third categories. I have had it burnt to a cinder, and I have had it very nearly raw. I have eaten it in private English families resident in Paris, and dressed by English cooks. It is a delusion : there is no beef in Lutetia.

The first beef I tried in my last campaign was the evening I dined at His Lordship's. Don't be alarmed, my democratic friend. I am not upon Lord Cowley's visiting list, nor are any coronetted cards ever left at my door on the sixth story.

I did not receive a card from the British Embassy on the occasion of the last ball at the Hôtel de Ville; and I am ashamed to confess that, so anxious was I to partake of the hospitality of the Prefect of the Seine (the toilettes and the iced punch are perfect at his balls), that I was mean enough to foreswear temporarily my nationality, and to avail myself of the card of Colonel Waterton Privilege of Harshellopolis, Ga.; said colonel being at that time, and in all probability exceedingly sick, in his state-room of the United States steamer " Forked Lightning," in the middle of the Atlantic ocean. But, by His Lordship's, I mean an Anglo-French restaurant—named after a defunct English city eating-house —situate near the Place de la Concorde, and where I heard that real English roast beef was to be obtained at all hours in first-rate condition.

Now, there is one thing that I do not like abroad; yea, two, that are utterly distasteful to me. The one thing is my countrymen's usual hotel. This house of refection I have generally found exeeedingly uncomfortable. So I was disposed to look somewhat coldly upon His Lordship's invitation, as printed upon placards, and stencilled on the walls, till I was assured that his beef was really genuine, and that he was an Englishman without guile.

His Lordship's mansion I found unpretending, even to obscurity. There was no *porte-cochère*, no court-yard, no gilt railings, nor green verandahs. His Lordship's hotel was, in fact, only a little slice of a shop, with one dining-room over it; for which, I was told, he paid an enormous rent— some thousands of francs a-year. In his window were displayed certain English viands pleasant to the sight: a mighty beef-steak pie just cut; the kidney end of a loin of veal, with real English stuffing, palpable to sight; some sausages that might have been pork, and of Epping; some potatoes, in their homely brown jackets, just out at elbows, as your well-done potatoes should be, with their flannel under-garments peeping through; and a spherical mass, something of the size and shape of a bombshell, dark in colour, speckled black and white, and which my beating heart told me was a plum-pudding. A prodigious Cheshire cheese, rugged as Helvellyn, craggy as Criffell, filled up the background like a range of yellow mountains. At the base there were dark forests of bottles branded with the names of Allsopp, and Bass, and Guinness, and there were cheering announcements framed and glazed, respecting Pale Ale on draught, L.L. whisky, and Genuine Old Tom.* I rubbed my hands in glee. "Ha! ha!" I said internally. "Nothing like our British aristocracy, after all. The true stock, sir. May His Lordship's shadow never diminish."

His Lordship's down-stairs apartment was somewhat inconveniently crowded with English grooms and French *palefreniers*, and with a lamentable old Frenchman, with a pipe as strong as Samson, a cap, cotton in his ears, and rings in the lobes thereof, who had learnt nothing of English but the oaths, and was cursing some very suspicious-looking meat (not

* Our neighbours have yet much to learn about our English manners and customs. In the Foyer of the Grand Opera, I saw, not very long ago, a tastefully enamelled placard, announcing that "Genuine Old Tom" was to be had at the Buffet. Imagine Sir Harcourt Courtley asking the Countess of Swansdown, in the crush-room of Covent Garden Theatre, if she would take half-a-quartern of gin!

my beef, I hope), most energetically. I have an opinion that stables and the perfume thereof are pretty nearly analogous the old world over; so, at the invitation of a parboiled-look-ing man in a shooting-jacket and a passion (who might have been His Lordship himself for aught I knew), I went up-stairs. There was an outer chamber, with benches covered with red cotton velvet, and cracked marble tables, like an indifferent *café;* where some bearded men were making a horrible rattle with their dominoes, and smoking their abomi-nable cigars (surely a course of French cigars is enough to cure the most inveterate smoker of his love for the weed). This somewhat discomposed me; but I was soon fain to push forward into the next saloon, where the tables were out for dining; and taking my seat, to wait for beef.

There was myself and a black man, and his (white) wife, the Frenchman with the spectacles, and the Frenchman with the bald head (I speak of them generically, for you are sure to meet their fellows at every public dining-table abroad), the poor old Frenchman with the wig, the paralytic head, and the shaking hands that trifle with the knives and forks, as though they were red-hot. There were half-a-dozen other sons of Gaul; who, with their beards, *cache-nez,* and paletôts, all made to pattern, might have been one another's brothers; two ancient maiden ladies, who looked like English gover-nesses, who had passed, probably, some five-and-thirty years in Paris, and had begun to speak a little of the language; a rude young Englishman, who took care to make all the com-pany aware of the locality of his birth-place: an English working engineer, long resident abroad, much travel-worn, and decidedly oily, who had a voice like **a** crank, and might

have been the identical engineer that Mr. Albert Smith met
on the Austrian Lloyd's steamer; and a large-headed little
boy, with a round English jacket, who sat alone, eating
mournfully, and whom I could not help fancying to be some
little friendless scholar in a great French school, whose *jour
de sortie* it was, and who had come here to play at an English
dinner.   The days be short to thee, little boy with the large
head!   May they fly quickly till the welcome holidays, when
thou wilt be forwarded, per rail and boat, to the London
Bridge station of the South Eastern Railway, to be left till
called for.   I know from sad experience, how very weary are
the strange land and the strange bed, the strange lessons and
strange playmates, to thy small English heart!

Now appeared a gaunt, ossified waiter, with blue black hair,
jaws so closely shaven that they gave him an unpleasant resemblance to the grand inquisitor of the Holy Office in disguise
seeking for heretics in a cook-shop, and who was, besides, in
a perpetual cold perspiration of anger against the irate man in
the shooting-jacket below, and carried on fierce verbal warfare
with him down the staircase.   This waiter rose up against
me, rather than addressed me, and charged me with a pike
of bread, cutting the usual immense slice from it.   I mildly
suggested roast beef, wincing, it must be owned, under the
eye of the cadaverous waiter; who looked as if he were accustomed to duplicity, and did not believe a word that I was saying.

"*Ah! rosbif!*" he echoed, *bien saignant n'est ce pas?*"

Now, so far from liking my meat *bien saignant*, I cannot even abide the sight of it rare, and I told him so.   But
he repeated "*bien saignant*," and vanished.

He came again, though; or rather his pallid face

protruded itself over the top of the box where I sat (there were boxes at His Lordship's) and asked :

" Paint portare ? p'lale ? ole' ale ?

I was nettled, and told him sharply that I would try the wine, if he could recommend it. Whereupon there was silence, and then I heard a voice crying down a pipe, " Paint portare ! "

He brought me my dinner, aud I didn't like it. It was *bien saignant*, but it wasn't beef, and it swam in a dead sea of gravy that was not to my taste; fat from strange animals seemed to have been grafted on to the lean. I did not get on better with the potatoes, which were full of promise, like a park hack, and unsatisfactory in the performance. I tried some plum-pudding afterwards ; but, if the proof of the pudding be in the eating, that pudding remains unproved to this day ; for, when I tried to fix my fork in it, it rebounded away across the room, and hit the black man on the leg. I would rather not say anything about the porter, if you please; and perhaps it is well to be brief on the subject of the glass of hot hollands-and-water which I tried afterwards, in a despairing attempt to be convivial ; for it smelt of the midnight-lamp like an erudite book, aud of the midnight oil-can, and had the flavour of the commercial turpentine rather than of the odoriferous juniper. I consoled myself with some Cheshire cheese, and asked the waiter if he had the *Presse*.

" Ze *Time* is 'gage," he answered.

" I did not want the *Times*. I wanted the *Presse*."

" Sare," he repeated wrathfully, " Ze *Time* is 'gage. *Le Journal Anglais* (he accentuated this spitefully) is 'gage."

He would have no further commerce with me after this ; and doubtlessly, thinking that an Englishman who could'nt eat his beef under-done, or indeed at all, and preferred the *Presse* to the *Times* newspaper, was an outcast and a, renegade, abandoned me to my evil devices, and contented himself with crying " *Voila* !" from the murky distance without coming when I called. He even declined to attend to receive payment, and handed me over for that purpose to a long French boy in a blouse, whose feet had evidently not long been emancipated from the pastoral *sabots*, whose hair was cropped close to his head (in the manner suggesting county goal at home, and ignorance of small tooth-combs abroad), and who had quite a flux of French words, and tried to persuade me to eat *civet de lièvre* that was to be served up at half-past seven of the clock.

But I would have borne half a hundred disappointments similar to this dinner for the sake of the black man. Legs and feet! he was a character! He sat opposite to me, calm, contented, magnificent, proud. He was as black as my boot and as shiny. His woolly head, crisped by our bounteous mother Nature, had unmistakably received a recent touch of the barber's tongs. He was perfumed; he was oiled; he had moustachios (as I live!) twisted out into long rat's tails by means of pommade Hongroise. He had a tip. He had a scarlet Turkish cap with a long blue tassel. He had military stripes down his pantaloons. He had patent leather boots. He had shirt-studs of large circumference, pins, gold waistcoat buttons, and a gorgeous watch-chain. I believe he had a crimson under-waistcoat. He had the whitest of cambric handkerchiefs, a ring on his fore-finger, and a stick with an overpowering gold knob. He was the wonderfullest nigger that the eye ever beheld.

He had a pretty little English wife—it is a fact, madam —with long auburn ringlets, who it was plain to see was desperately in love with, and desperately afraid of him. It was marvellous to behold the rapt, fond gaze with which she contemplated him as he leaned back in his chair after dinner and touched up his glistening ivories with a toothpick. Equally marvellous was the condescension with which he permitted her to eat her dinner in his august presence, and suffered her to tie round his neck a great emblazoned shawl like a flag.

Who could he have been? The father of the African twins; the Black Malibran's brother; Baron Pompey; King Mousalakatzic of the Orange River; Prince Bobo; some other sable dignitary of the empire of Hayti; or the renowned Soulouque himself, incognito? Yet, though affable to his spouse, he was a fierce man to the waiter. The old blood of Ashantee, the ancient lineage of Dahomey, could ill brook the shortcomings of that cadaverous servitor. There was an item in the reckoning that displeased him.

" Wass this, sa? " he cried, in a terrible voice, " Wass this, sa? Fesh your mas'r, sa ! "

The waiter cringed and fled, and I laughed.

" Good luck have thou with thine honour: ride on——" honest black man; but oh, human nature, human nature! I would not be your nigger for many dollars. More rib-roasting should I receive, I am afraid, than ever Uncle Tom received from fierce Legree.

I have not dined at His Lordship's since—I would dine there any day to be sure of the company of the black man— but I have more to say about beef.

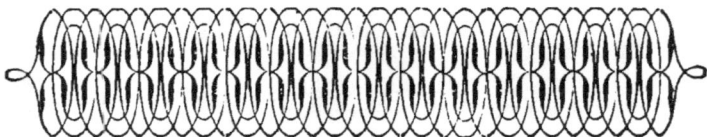

XV.

FURTHER TRAVELS IN SEARCH OF BEEF.

I HAD been recounting my want of success in pursuit of
beef in Paris, and my deplorable break-down at His
Lordship's Larder there, to my friend Lobb (telling him,
too, all about the cadaverous waiter, and the haughty nigger
and his pretty wife); and he, a renowned beefeater, as
well as an able financier, appeared considerably interested
in my narrative.   Lobb is a man of few words, and not
emotional; yet he was good enough to say on this occasion,
that he sympathised with me, and would put me in the way
of procuring good beef shortly.   We were conversing soon
afterwards on the interesting subject of the variation of the
exchanges of Europe; and Lobb was endeavouring to explain
to me by what fortuitous inspiration of rascality the
Neapolitan *cambieri*—those greatest thieves of the world—
charged, during the Russian war, a discount of nineteen per
cent. upon English money, and of no less than thirty-five per
cent. upon their dear friends's, the Austrians's, metallics (which
operation of finance secured my still stronger adherence to
the chorus of a claptrap song current about 'forty-eight, that

I had "rather be an Englishman "). Lobb stopped suddenly, however, in the midst of his exposition of the mysteries of agio and decimals, and, bending his bushy eyebrows upon me, said, " De blace vor de peef is in the Rue Bicdonbin " (meaning the Rue Pictonpin). I bowed my head meekly in acquiescence to the enunciation of this assertion, whereupon he continued concisely, " Vriday, half-bast vive," and thereupon plunged into the history of the *credit foncier*, and the Danish five per cents.

I noticed that Lobb, for the next day or two rather avoided me than otherwise, and that he was studiously chary of any allusion to the Rue Pictonpin ; but, as I knew him, though what is termed a " close customer," to be a man of his word, I kept my appointment on Friday evening. Lobb was to be found at a great banking house in the Rue de la Paix—a suite of palatial apartments, with polished floors, stuccoed ceiling, carpeted and gilt balustraded staircase, walnut-tree desks, velvet *fauteuils*, moderator lamps, a porter's lodge furnished as splendidly as an English stockbroker's parlour; everything, in short, that could conduce to splendour, except money. None of that was to be seen. To one accustomed to the plethoric amount of outward and visible wealth in an English banking house—the heaps of sovereigns, the great scales, the piles of bank notes, the orange-tawny money bags, the shovels dinted in the service of Plutus, the burly porters, the ranges of fire-buckets, (suggestive of the wealth of the Indies to be protected)—the counting-houses of the Parisian banker present but a Barmecide feast of riches. In place, too, of the strong-backed ledgers, the fat cash books, and fatter cashiers, of Messrs. Crœsus and Co., the French seem to keep their

voluminous accounts in meagre little pamphlets like schoolboys's copy books; and the clerks are hungry looking men
with beards.   Fancy Messrs. Crœsus confiding an account to
a clerk with a chin tuft !   As far as I am able to judge, all the
disposable bullion in Paris is displayed in little shop windows
like greengrocers's stalls, for the special admiration of the
Palais Royal loungers, and the accommodation of any Englishman in want of change for a five pound note. At the banking
houses the cash box is like an Eau de Cologne box, and the
principal amount of business transacted seems to consist in
stamping bits of paper, executing elaborate flourishes to
signatures, shifting sand about on wet ink, and asking for
lights for cigars.

I found Lobb, that master of finance, peaceably employed in
his bureau, eating two *sous* worth of hot chesnuts over a bronze
stove of classic design.   Nobody came for any money; and,
peeping into one or two other bureaux, as we left, I caught a
glimpse of another clerk, signing his name all over a sheet of
blotting paper, whistling as he scribbled for want of thought,
and of another absorbed in twisting his moustachios before a
pierglass (A pierglass in a bank !).   Yet banking hours were
not over—they never are in France—and I dare say business
to the amount of some hundred thousand francs was done
before they closed.   A shop boy let us out, a bullet-headed
fellow with a perpetual grin, a blue bib and apron, and who,
Lobb informed me, was even more stupid than he looked.
He was reading a novel.   And of such is a Parisian bank.

It was a pouring wet night—the rain coming down, not
in the sudden, sluicelike, floodgate, English fashion, but in a
concentrated, compact, fine, unceasing, descent, cautiously

and remorselessly, like the sand in an hourglass, or the conversation of a fluent and well-informed bore. The mud had come to stop a long night, and leaped up at you, even to your eyebrows, like a dog glad to recognize a friend. With the rain had come his inseparable French friends, bad odours and biting wind. They had the pavement all to themselves, and tossed the passengers about like ships in the ocean. There were some thousands of ankles abroad, for those who cared to see them; and the tortures of the Inquisition had been revived in the shape of numberless umbrellas, which were probed into your eyes, jambed into your ribs, thrust between your legs, and which gave off cascades, dexterously, down the nape of your neck. Prudent people had all sought safe anchorage in the passages; the wealthy had chartered carriages, and were deciding the knotty point as to which is the pleasanter—to run, or to be run over. I met a lamentable dog in the Rue Montmartre, wet through. He was evidently homeless, and was going towards the Cité, perhaps to sell himself to a *chiffonnier*, probably to drown himself.

I believe that there is no such street in Paris as the Rue Pictonpin, and that Lobb, for some occult reasons of his own, gave me a fabulous address, for I was never able to find out the place afterwards by daylight, nor is it to be discovered in any of the maps of the twelve arrondissements of Paris. We wandered for, it appeared to me, hours; stumbling, splashing, through streets which knew not footpavements which yet boasted the mediæval gutter—a Niagara of mud—which were villainous in aspect, and vile in smell. The lantern of the rag picker crossed our path, like a Will-o'-the-wisp; viragos quarrelled at the doors of charcoal sheds; porters tottered by with gigantic

sacks, like corpses, on their backs ; that novelty in civilized
Paris, a drunken man, staggered out of a wineshop, and asked
us, amid the interruptions of a hiccough, what o'clock it was;
and now and then some great lumbering omnibus with red
eyes, like a bloodshot demon's, swooped by, driving us against
the wall, and casting mud into our teeth. I was just on the
point of revolting, and telling Lobb that I would see his beef
hung before I would go any further, when he stopped (the
cautious man was enveloped in waterproofing, and I had a
great coat like a sponge), and said,

"Dis is de peef shop."

We passed under a scowling archway into a court-yard,
seemingly opening into half-a-dozen others. There was some
gas about ; but the rain must have permeated the pipes, for
the gas blinked and glimmered dubiously, and seemed disposed
to burn blue. Everywhere on the wall, from the basement to
where the hideous height of stone and plaster was lost in darkness, there were stuck those bewildering placards concerning the names and occupations of the tenants of the different
floors, that drive a man mad at Paris, and send him up to the
sixth story in quest of a tailor who lives on the ground floor.
Of course there was a hairdresser in the house; of course
there were "modes" on the second floor; of course there was
a dentist, whose hideous armoury of dead men's fangs and
waxen gums grinned at you from a glass case; of course there
was a professor of photography ; together with the depôt of
some *société génerale* for the sale of medicated chocolate,
camphorated pomatum, hygienic asphalte, Athenian eye-
water, philanthropic corn-plaster, or similar excrescences of
civilization. No French house could be complete without

those branches of industry. But the beef was in the second floor along with the "modes;" at least a hot, unsavoury, meaty smell began in the court-yard and ended there; so I followed it and Lobb, irrigating the stairs involuntarily as I went with the drippings from my garments.

I did not arrive in the most joyous frame of mind; my very appetite was washed out of me. Nor did it increase my merriment of mood, when—pushing aside a green baize-covered door—Lobb preceded me into a bleak ante-chamber, very cold and barren, where there were some bare deal boards on tressels, and a cemetery of empty bottles.

"Sometime dey are zo vull, we dine here," whispered Lobb.

I shuddered. I would as soon have dined in a dead-house. But there was a curtain hanging across a doorway, which he drew aside, and then I entered into the real temple where the beef was to be.

Silence, deep, dead, marrow-freezing silence! From the fifty guests or so, at least; but, from their fifty knives and forks a dull clicking; and, now and then, some smothered sounds of gurgling, with, once in every five minutes on an average, a subdued clatter of plates. But not a word.

There was an outer and an inner saloon, vast, lofty, well-proportioned; but indescribably faded, tarnished. On the old grimy walls, bedewed with the tears of generations of damp, there were here and there painted panels, surrounded by festoons of ghastly flowers; and, in the panels were mildewed Cupids, and cracked shepherds making love to washed-out shepherdesses. There were gilt cornices; and, on the ceiling was painted the apotheosis of somebody, obscured, bleared, almost undiscoverable beneath the smoke of a century, and the fumes of a hecatomb of beef. There was a mirror over one mantelpiece, surrounded by obsolete framework; and, on the shelf, a lugubrious clock, with a heavy mass of carving representing Orestes pursued by the Eumenides, or Clytemnestra inciting Ægisthus to slay Agamemnon, or some equally lively classical episode, ticked dolorously. There were four long tables covered with doubtful table-cloths; three full of guests eating with gloomy avidity, the fourth empty. Dim oil lamps burnt around. Nobody offered us a seat; nobody seemed to acknowledge our presence; no waiter so much as looked at us. One man only, a bald-headed biped in a long coat, who was standing by the funereal clock, took out an ebony snuff-box, just glanced at me, as if to tell me that if I thought he were about to offer me a pinch, I was very much mistaken, took a double pinch himself and sneezed. By Lobb's direction I secured a seat at the vacant table, as near the centre as possible. From minute to minute there dropped in men in cloaks, men in paletôts, men in spencers, men in many-collared carricks. Some were decorated; a few wore moustaches; but the vast majority were old and clean shaven, and looked like men of the first empire. One little old man, with a round scalp polished like a billiard ball, wore a coat-collar of unusual height and stiffness, for the purpose, I believe to this day, of concealing a pigtail, which he persisted in wearing, but was ashamed to show. Nobody took any notice of us; they did not even bring us bread or wine. There were knives and forks and napkins, but one cannot eat these things. This could not be a dining-house. It was the Silent Tomb.

It was, in sober reality, though it looked so much like a

family vault, a *table d'hôte*, at thirty-six *sous*, held in a dilapidated nobleman's mansion, and of the order of cookery known as the *cuisine bourgeoise*. The rule was that, as the tables filled, and not till then, the dinner was served; so that if you arrived a moment after the number of occupants of table number one was completed, you had, very probably, to wait a quarter of an hour before table number two was gladdened with the joyful appearance of the soup.

It seemed to me, on this occasion, as if I should have to wait all night. Lobb relapsed into mental calculations—possibly about Chilian bonds (deferred), and I was left entirely to my own resources. The little man with the supposed pigtail, who was my neighbour, was either hopelessly deaf or obstinately taciturn. To my remarks about the weather he answered not a word. A man opposite me, with a large chest, a flapped waistcoat, and the face of a horse (his wig being brushed up over his eyes like blinkers), leaned over the table, and fixed his gelatinous eyes—not on me—but on the wall behind; till he filled me with a vague terror, and an invincible tendency to picture him changing into the figure-head of a ship bearing down on me to transfix and scuttle me. A palsied dotard, with a head like a pear grown on one side—and yet he was the most brilliant wit of the party—wagged his toothless jaws, and made a chop at me with his knife—so it struck my fancy at least—although, very likely, poor old gentleman, he was only hungry and impatient for his dinner. And the grim silence of the men, and the unholy sounds made by the inanimate objects, and the dreadful ticking of the clock, beating the dead march in Saul on the muffled drum of my ear, so fretted, harried, exasperated, and crazed me, that I would have given a hundred francs for a woman to enter the room; five hundred for permission to bnrst into a howl, to sing, to stamp on someone's toes, to send a bottle flying at the head of the man with the figure-head face,—to do anything to provoke a commotion in this dreadful, dreadful, Silent Tomb.

There were thirteen guests mustered out of the twenty-four, when I thought I must either speak or die. Lobb had slipped out to confer with the landlady (there *was* a landlady), and I had not even the consolation of abusing him for bringing me to such a place. I tried to divert myself by conjuring up images of what the grim *restaurant* had been a hundred years ago. To what Marquis, Fermier Général, or Sous-Intendant the great hotel had belonged; who painted those stained panels, who that misty apotheosis. Of what gay scenes; what nights of revelry, these uncommunicative halls of gloom had been spectators. Some one must have talked there at some time or other; the walls must once have echoed to the laughter · of the marchionesses in brocaded sacks, of marquises with red-heeled shoes,—with the madrigals of enamoured chevaliers in bag-wigs, the gallantries of gay mousquetaires, the pert sayings of spruce little abbés, the epigrams of snuffy wits who drank too much coffee and wrote for the Encyclopedia. Oh for my grandmother's ghost, to revisit, for a moment, the haunts of her contemporaries—if she would but open her mouth and chatter!

At extremest length, when the wheel in the cistern seemed about to make its last revolution, Lobb returned; the last man of the twenty-four indispensable guests took his place, and a solemn lady in black—not my grandmother's ghost—

though she would not have dressed the character badly—
but the mistress of the establishment, glided into the room.
Then a spruce man in raven black, who closely resembled an
undertaker, took his seat by me as president, and proceeded
to ladle the soup out of a huge tureen.

I had grown so accustomed by this time to take the
Silent Tomb for granted, and to consider myself pro-tem. as
a member of a burial-club, that, had a boiled death's head
with parsley and buttter formed the first course, I don't
think I should have evinced much surprise. I contemplated,
too, with a contented sort of stony apathy, four waiters, like
mutes, who came up as I imagined (my retina must have been
affected by this time), perpendicularly, behind as many chairs.
I supposed they placed the array of half-filled bottles of wine
which suddenly appeared on the table, and which were not
there before. I did not care to inquire, neither did it much
matter, whether it were by human agency or not, that a
small clothes-basketful of household bread was passed around.
One thing, however, became manifest. If the guests were
dumb, they were not at least palsied ; for a fiercer or more
active attack upon a bread-basket I never saw. The majority
took two pieces ; and the reputed possessor of the pigtail
carried off a whole armful of the staff of life.

I am bound to admit that the victuals were very good.
The soup was made from meat. Plates of carrots and
turnips were handed round for admixture in the broth, thus
giving us the opportunity of converting it into a Julienne
on a large scale. Then came the old, original, *Cuisine
Bourgeoise, Bouillon Bœuf*—fresh beef, boiled, in large
stringy lumps, with a coronal of fat, like Doctor Sacheverell's

curly wig. With mustard, oil, and pepper, this was not bad.
I could have pronounced it true beef; I could have praised
the roast mutton that followed (a leg cut up in hunks and
handed round), the salad, the haricots, the *compôte* of pears,
and the Roquefort cheese, that concluded this plain, substantial, and, on the whole, cheap meal (for everybody was
helped twice, and there was an indiscreet amount of bread
consumed), if the people would but have spoken. But they
were dumb to the last. One solitary gleam of life (as
connected with Mammon) there was, when the solemn lady
came round after the *bouilli*, and collected our respective thirty-
six sous in a hand-basket. The jingling did me good; but we
soon relapsed into our old Shillibeer joggletrot. There was the
clicking of the knives and forks, and the occasional smothered
rattle of the plates; and the funeral-baked meats did furnish
forth the *table-d'hôte*, and the only thing wanting to complete
this gastronomic Golgotha was the statue of the Com-
mendatore, from Seville, whispering across the table that he
was the father of Donna Elvira, and did you know if Don
Juan were there, because he had an appointment to sup
with him.

The guests were no ghosts, though. Ghosts!—wolves,
rather. I never saw such a set of trenchermen. I am
certain that every man there present must have put under his
waistcoat at least sixty-six sous worth of solid food. The
concern must be a loss. The Silent Tomb can't pay.
Perhaps the proprietress is a widow with large revenues, who
likes to spend it on these taciturn men. Perhaps it is a
tontine, and the surviving members eat up the deceased.
But it is certain—though I should like to renew my acquaint-

ance with the beef—that I can never dine there again. It is not good to eat and say nothing. Even the pig grunts over the trough. Shall we be less sociable than the pig?

By the time wo had finished dinner, and as I turned to give the waiter two sous (who, perceiving my intent, and being plainly a misanthrope, dropped his napkin, and fled into the next room), the table opposite to us had obtained its complement, and an exactly similar dinner was commencing thereat. Do they never stop dining at the Silent Tomb? Is it always turn and turn about? Table full and table empty? Soup and bully, salad and roast? Will it ever be so till Death slips off his waiter's jacket for a shroud, and the beef shall give place to bones?

I dexterously gave Lobb the slip in the court-yard, and there was a coldness between us for some days. I plunged into the noisiest café I could find, where there was a crash o dominoes, a charivari of cups and saucers, violent disputes between Jules and Alphonse over sugar-and-water, and endless shriekings of and for waiters. I went to the Bouffes Parisiennes after that, and was quite delighted with the noisiness of the music and the absurdity of a pantomime: and I walked home singing the Sieur de Framboisy the whole way. But I had the nightmare before the morning.

As already stated, I have never been able to find the Rue Pictonpin since. I do not like to ask Lobb (though we have been reconciled, over kirschwasser), for certain reasons; and were it not that I know him to be a man of mortal mould, and an exemplary clerk in a banking-house, I should be tempted to believe that I had been spirited away to some cave of glamour, and that I had feasted in the Island of Saint Brandon, or spent the evening with Rip van Winkle.

But I was not disheartened. There was more beef, I knew, in Paris than had yet come out of it. I sought a great beef establishment in the narrow street that runs parallel to the east side of the Palais Royal—a time-honoured place of refection by the sign of the "Bœuf à-la-mode." But I found beef no longer in fashion there. The waiter, who was far better dressed than I was, and who was the possessor of a watch-chain I can never hope to have the fellow of, looked down upon me, and thought me a poor-spirited creature—*un homme de rien*—because I would not have oysters and white wine before dinner. To ask for beef at the "Bœuf a-la-monde" was, I found, about the same as asking for a cup of coffee and a thin slice of bread and butter at the London Coffee House. Then I relapsed into the semi-English houses again. At the "John Bull," at the "True Roast Beef," or at the "Renown of Roast Beef." But truth was a fiction and renown a sham. They gave me flaps of flesh that made me ill; they fed me with promises, and the performance was but gravy and sinew. I wandered in a desert of *restaurants*, and came upon no oasis of beef. I began to despond.

But hence, loathed Melancholy—away with thee, Penserosa! See, the Allegro comes tripping soft with sweatest Lyndian measure. Here is Bully Beef in the "Hall of Montesquieu!"

The illustrious author of the "Esprit de Lois" has given his name to, or has had it taken for, a vast saloon on the ground-floor of a street called the Cour des Fontaines, leading from

the Palais Royal to the Galérie Véro-Dodat, where all old
Paris men will remember so well M. Aubert's caricature
shop, and its admiring crowd of loafers and pickpockets,
staring at the inimitable pear-shaped portraits of Louis
Philippe, and the countless Robert Macaires by Daumier.
The Hall of Montesquieu has had its mutabilities. I
remember it as a dancing saloon, well conducted, though the
price of admittance was but fifty centimes. I have seen
there a journeyman butcher in his professional blue frock
dancing the Cellarius with a lady in puce velvet edged with
fur, and a pink bonnet (she was, I declare, my washerwoman),
with a gravity and decorum that showed that he knew his
position, and hers, and respected both. There used to be a
waiter, too—or, rather, an overlooker, a sort of shop-walker,
whose duty it was to pace the galleries moodily, and to cry
out, " *Il faut consommer, messieurs ;* " which signified that, if
the visitors took seats, they must also take refreshment. With
this unchanging, lugubrious speech, he always put me in mind
of the Trappist, crying " Brothers, we must die ! " He never
said anything else; I don't believe he could; but I have an
idea that he had been an idiot from his youth upwards, and
that this one poll-parrot cry had been taught him, and that
this was all he knew. During the short-lived Republic the
hall was one of the fiercest of political clubs ; and I have
no doubt that my friend the butcher, repudiating the pue-
rilities of the Cellarius, spoke out his mind stoutly on the
necessity of proclaiming every master butcher an enemy of
mankind, and of having the professional chopper used on the
heads of the syndics. After the Republic had fallen through,
the hall fell under the dominion of Terpsichore again ; but its

chorographic reputation was gone; and I have often seen the most frenzied mazurkas performed to no better audience than two *sergents de ville*, the *pompier* on duty, a dyspeptic American, and a solemn Englishman. After this, there was a species of assault of arms in the hall, after the fashion of our Saville House. I have not been told whether the Saladin feat, or "the severisation of the quarter of mutton," took place; but there was fencing, and much wrestling, and the exercise of the *savate*, and a series of eccentric gymnastics with gloves, in which paralysis, St. Vitus's dance, the clog hornpipe, mesmeric passes, and the attitudes of Mr. Merryman when he asks you how you are to-morrow, were oddly mingled, and which was called "Le Boxe Anglaise," and was believed by the spectators to be an exact reproduction of an English pugilistic encounter. I sincerely hope that our chivalrous neighbours may never become greater adepts in that brutal and debasing pastime.

Subsequently I lost sight of the "Hall of Montesquieu" for a long time. Hearing, even, that the Docks de la Toilette had been established in the Cour des Fontaines, I concluded that the hall had been pulled down, or converted perhaps into a dry dock for coats, perhaps into a basin for pantaloons. But I suddenly heard that it had been doing a great business in the Beef line, throughout the whole time of the Exhibition of Industry; that it had been dining its two and three thousand a day; and that it was now the "Etablissement du Bouillon-Bœuf," with subordinate establishments in the Rue Coquillière, the Rue de la Monnaie, and the Rue Beauregard.

I was off to the Cour des Fontaines immediately. There

was a great photographic establishment somewhere above the hall, and effigies of scowling captains of dragoons, high-cheekboned ladies, and epileptic children, were hung on the entrance pillars in the usual puzzling manner ; but there was no mistaking the gastronomic character which the place had assumed. A species of triumphal altar had been erected in a niche in front, and on it were piled huge joints of beef, legs and shoulders of mutton, geese, turkeys, fowls, sausages, apples, pears of preternatural size, and real venison, furred, leathern-nosed, and antlered. There was an oyster woman— *a belle écaillière*—before the door (the majority of *belles écaillières* are sixty years of age, and take snuff, even as the most numerous portion of the *vivandières* in the army are wrinkled and ill-favoured). There was a great running in and out of waiters, a great ingress and egress of diners through swing-doors ; the whole place was full of life and movement, and the promise of Beef.

On entering (it was very like entering the Crystal Palace, so great was the throng, so large and lively the vista beyond), a courteous man gave me, with a bow, a *carte* of the viands obtainable, with the day of the month affixed, and blank spaces left for the quantity consumed. Then I passed on into the well-remembered hall ; but, ah ! how changed !

Prettily decorated, brilliantly lighted, crowded as of yore ; but the orchestra and the throng of dancers were replaced by long lanes of marble tables, guiltless of table-cloths, covered with edibles, and at which perhaps four hundred persons were busily dining. In the centre were two immense erections, monuments covered with enamelled plates, and surmounted with pretty *parterres* of flowers. There were some encaustic portraits of waiters flying about with smoking dishes painted on these enamelled plates, giving the erections the appearance of vast mausoleums, erected to the memory of departed *garçons* and cooks who had fallen before too fierce fires, and too hungry customers. But they were not cenotaphs, I discovered afterwards, but merely the cooking apparatus of the Bouillon-Bœuf; for round the base were ledges with the customary furnace holes and stewpans; and round this again, at a distance of a few feet, an oval counter piled with plates, where the waiters gave their orders and received their dishes. In the space between circulated numerous cooks, male and female—the latter mostly very pretty —ah! roguish Bouillon-Bœuf!—all as busy as bees stirring saucepans, dishing up vegetables, ladling out soup, and apportioning modicums of stew. And there was a loud cry afloat of "*Versez;*" for many of the four hundred were taking their coffee after dinner, and waiters scudded, skated rather than walked, from table to table, and from huge coffee-pots frothed up the smoking substitute for mocha. Pour on and be merry; rattle knives and forks; chatter grisettes; hoarsely order "*biftek pour deux,*" oh! waiter; gesticulate, discourse vehemently, oh! moustached men; querulously demand more soup, and drum impatiently on your plates with spoons, oh! little children in bibs, brought to dine at the "Bouillon-Bœuf" by your fond parents; ring out, ye echoes, till the glazed roof vibrates; for here is life, here health, cheerfulness, enjoyment, and be hanged to the Silent Tomb!

As there was rather too much life and merriment below, however, for a man who wished to philosophise upon four

hundred fellow creatures at their meals, I went upstairs into
the gallery, which was partitioned off into boxes, where there
was another kitchen, though on a smaller scale to the one
below, and where there were perhaps a hundred and fifty
diners more. Sitting down at one of the little marble tables
I made the astonishing discovery that Eau de Selz—the
French substitute for soda-water—was laid on to the premises, like gas, or New River water. An Eau de Selz pillar,
neatly surmounted with a blue cut-glass knob, and an Eau
de Selz double-tap, came through the centre of each table;
and on reference to the *carte* I found that for ten *centimes*—
a penny—you might have as much of the Eau de Selz on tap
as ever you liked—and blow yourself up with aërated water,
if you were disposed so to do. Where was the reservoir?
There, yonder, in one of the mausoleums. How was it
made? What was it made of? Aye, there was the rub!
I am no chemist; and lest from one of these metallic taps I
should draw forth a solution of some noxious carbonate,
sulphate, acetate, or phosphate, nauseous to the taste, and
inimical to the coats of the stomach, I refrained from the
Eau de Selz at discretion, at once and for ever.

I must say this for the credit of the "Bouillon-Bœuf,"
that the celerity and agility of its waiters are beyond criticism
and compare. I was no sooner seated than a light-hearted
child of Gaul, with a bright eye, and a chin-tuft, skipped up
to me, brushed the table spotlessly clean (I did not mind his
whisking the crumbs into my eyes), and blithely asked me
what I would have. Soup he had already settled in his mind
I should partake of; and producing a little pencil, attached
by a silken cord to his waistcoat button, had set down a

great black tick against the soup line in my *carte*. *Bouillon* was the word. *Bouilli* afterwards of course. How much wine? half a bottle. Would I have a table-napkin? certainly. Bread? of course (I could have brought both myself). Four more ticks were jotted down on my *carte*, and the jocund youth went skipping off, twiddling his pencil like the dancing Faun his flute.

Perhaps he was one of the departed celebrities of " Montesquieu " when it was a dancing hall. But enough. Before I had well begun to speculate upon him he was back with my soup, my napkin, and my wine. After the discussion of the *potage*, and pending the arrival of the beef, I studied the *carte*, and profited much thereby. I learnt that soup cost twopence, *bouilli* twopence-halfpenny, roast meat and ragouts threepence, vegetables twopence, bread a penny, a napkin a penny, Eau de Selz (as I have already said) a penny, wine fivepence the half-bottle, though half or even a quarter of that quantity was obtainable, and other articles of consumption in reasonable proportion. Not very Sardanapalian, these items, certainly; and yet the company seemed to be not only composed of the pettier middle class, but of very many persons in what may be termed easy circumstances. There were no blouses, but a good number of plain female caps; but there were also a fair sprinkling of red ribbons at buttonholes, and of bonnets with artificial flowers under them. Let me add that in the motley throng, order, good behaviour, and good humour reigned unvaryingly.

I think my dinner cost me elevenpence. I would rather not be questioned about the beef; but what can you expect for five sous? The place was very cheap, and very gay, and exceedingly curious for those who liked to look at men and women in their ways. The waiter's service was gratuitous—ostensibly so at least. You did not pay him the reckoning: but descending to the *contrôle*, you presented your carte to an elegantly dressed lady who added up the items, softly but audibly, and told you the amount. This you paid. Then she stamped the document (oh, nation of stampers!) and delivered your *carte* again to a checktaker. All this light and space, all this life and merriment, all this beef and *bouilli*, all this Selzer water at discretion, all this stamping and restamping, and all for elevenpence!

The next day—a red-letter day—my friend, Bumposiosus, who is wealthy, said, "Come and breakfast." We breakfasted at that Alhambra-like *café*, at the corner of the Chaussée d'Antin, where millionnaires sup, where your cup is filled from silver coffee-pots worth a thousand francs each, and reckonings are paid in bank notes. We had the enlivening wine of Thorins. We had eggs, poached with asparagus tips, we had stewed kidneys, and we had a Chateaubriand—a steak—ah, so tender! ah, so exquisitely done! It was delicious, it was unapproachable, it melted in the mouth; but I still adhere to my former assertion. There is no Beef in Paris. I have not ten thousand a year; Bumposiosus does not ask me to breakfast every morning; and this was not eating beef; it was eating gold.

So I am yet open to continue my travels in search of beef, and expect to be on the move before long. I have been told that in Abyssinia they bring the ox to the door, and that you cut your steak off hot from the living animal, on the cut and come again principle; but apart from the cruelty

R

of the thing, a man cannot be too cautious in receiving statements about Abyssinia. Still, I yearn for beef; and if any gentleman hear of palateable ox-flesh down Otaheite way, I shall be happy to record my notions of a steak in the South Seas.

XVI.

THE METAMORPHOSED PAGODA.

"SEE Naples and then die," is the vain-glorious saying of the Neapolitans. The proverb has been considerably modified in our time. We say : See Naples—that God's own land of beauty and boundless fertility—that golden treasury of God-taught art ; and, also seeing the filthy *lazzaroni*, the swarming *sbirri*, the Ergastolo, the scowling priests, the blood of St. Gennaro, and the million and one rascals who infest this fairest of cities, then see Naples, and die for shame and indignation.*

See Capri, too. There is a page of Roman history that needs no Niebuhr to dispute, no Lewis to examine. Its annals are late enough, accredited enough for us to see, in no shadowy guise, but palpably in the records of the past ; the shrinking, trembling, gloomy, frivolous, yet ferocious tyrant, Tiberius, flying from the world to Capri—striving to shut out the demons his own bad passions had invoked from the choicest fruits and flowers of life, yet forgetting that he had at least a cavity where he had once a heart, and finding, too late, that vacuum-abhorring Nature had filled that cavity with

* Written, *Laus Deo*, before the Great Deliverance by Joseph Garibaldi.

devils. See Capri. The vestiges of the tyrant's palace are there still. There are the same stones that walled in sin and luxury, and that re-echoed to the carousing shouts of decadent Romans and to the cries of tortured slaves.

Not that I ever saw Capri, or Naples either. My Italian travels have been made, hitherto, with my feet on the fender, and my eyes on a book.

But I know of another place which I choose to call Capri. Half a hundred miles from London, on the south-eastern coast of this kingdom, the booth-proprietors of Vanity Fair set up, some half a hundred years ago, a camp that has culminated into the gayest and pleasantest watering-place in the world. I myself have known it intimately full twenty years, and I caught myself, the other day, moralising upon the great palace of Chinese gingerbread that smirks upon—well, I won't be personal—the S. Upon how many thousand work-boxes, toy dioramas, sheets of note paper, Tunbridge-ware tables, pin-cushions, have we seen the counterfeit presentment of this pompous platitude. Where were common sense, taste, fitness, decency, when the thing was done? If George the magnificent had said to Mr. Nash, prince of architects,—" Mr. Nash, will you oblige me by painting your face in parti-coloured streaks, and by walking on your hands into the middle of the S., where one of the lords of my royal bedchamber will provide you with four-and-twenty yards of scarlet riband, which you will be good enough to swallow;"—would Mr. Nash have done this thing, I wonder? Perhaps not. Yet the prince of architects has been guilty of buffooneries quite as gross, in building this pot-bellied palace—this minareted mushroom—this absurdity—this gilded dirt-pie—this congeries of bulbous excrescences, as gaudy and as expensive as Dutch tulips, and as useless.

We are accustomed to see and hear of kings doing extravagant things in the building line. It is their vocation. Cheops had his pyramid, Cleopatra her needle, Nero his golden house, James the First Nonsuch, and Kubla Khan— is it not written :—

> In Xanadu did Kubla Khan
> A stately pleasure dome decree,
> From which a sounding river ran
> Through caverns measureless to man,
> Down to a sunless sea.

William Rufus designed to build a palace so huge, that Westminster Hall, the first instalment thereof, was to be but one of the bed-rooms. Luckily, the state of the civil list, and Sir Walter Tyrrell's pointed behaviour to the king in the New Forest, nipped the grand design in the bud. Louis Quatorze had Versailles, the Abencerrages their Alhambra, the gloomy Philip his palatial gridiron, the Escurial; but we can forgive the first for the Grandes Eaux, the second for the Court of Lions, the third for the pictures of Titian and Velasquez. Frederick had his Sans-Souci, Leo his Loggie and Stanze, Napoleon his dream of a completed Louvre, not realised by him; even our third William took pleasure in enlarging Kensington, and making it square and Dutch, and formal like himself. But there was, it must be owned, something regal, and noble, and dignified in most of these architectural madnesses. When a king raves it should be in his robe and diadem, with gold for straw, and his sceptre for a bauble. But did ever a petty German princelet in his hunt-ing-lodge—did ever a petty Indian nawaub in his zenana—did ever a Dutch burgher in the linsey-woolsey frenzy for a *lusthaus*—did ever an impoverished Italian marquis, in the palazzo he began to build through pride, and left unfinished through bankruptcy—did ever a retired English hatter, going mad, as it is the traditional wont of hatters to do, and running up a brick Folly, in three stories, with a balcony and a belve-dere—did ever any maniac in bricks and mortar perpetrate one tithe of the folly and extravagance that are manifested in every inch of this egregious potato-blight of a building on the S. ?

I mind the time (a child) I used to gaze on the place with reverent curiosity. A king lived there then—a placid, white-headed sovereign, in a blue body-coat with brass buttons, and who had formerly been in the naval service. He played quiet rubbers at whist at night, while his royal partner and the ladies of the household worked in Berlin wool. It was rumoured that he could himself play on the flute, prettily. He had a quiet, decorous court. He used to drive out peace-ably, without any unnecessary fuss, and was not unfrequently to be found on the beach, bargaining with little boys for models of ships, or with mariners for conchological specimens of appalling and weird appearance. He was popular, but suspected by the genteel classes of a tendency to radicalism and economy, which caused him to be slightly depreciated in the higher circles. His name was William. But the great king who dwelt at Capri (and had made it), and who had been dead some years before I came to wot of the palace, was not William. A loftier sounding name had he. He was Georgius Optimus—George the great, the magnificent, the good—who had raised Capri from its mean state as a fishing-village to the exalted rank of the queen of watering-places.

So I moralised at Capri. George had gone the way even that royal venison must go ; William he is dead too ; and we have another sovereign who loves not the wicked gimcrack. She would have pulled the bauble down had not the stout burghers of Capri stept in alarmed, and bought it for fifty thousand pieces of gold. They have turned the place to all manners of wonderful and incongruous uses. They have concerts there, balls where ladies can dance without having first been presented at court, and where lords in blue ribbons are never to be seen. They have exhibitions of pictures and photographs. They have had a circus there ; yes, a circus where spotted horses dance, and M. Desarais' dogs and monkeys bark and chatter, and Mr. Merryman, with his painted face, tumbles in the sawdust ! Pale men in spectacles come from Clapham to Capri to lecture on the Od. Force. I have seen there, myself, exhibiting, two wretched black deformities of children—the Caribbean twins, or some such monstrosities—hawked round the room by a gar-rulous showman. I do not despair of seeing, some day, at the gate of the Pagoda a Beefeater inviting the bystanders to walk in and see the Podasokus, or the " Whiffie Whaffle," or Oozly Bird, which, as is well known, digs a hole in the sand with his beak, and whistles through the nape of his neck. The parochial authorities have offices in the Pagoda, where they give out quartern loaves and orders of relief, and pass destitute hop-pickers to Ireland. The sentry-boxes, in front of which gold-braided hussars used to pace, keeping watch and ward over the sovereign within, are boarded up. Irreverent boys have chalked denunciations of the Pope, and libels on the police authorities, on the boards. They have quartered militiamen in the riding-school—that stately expanse where all the king's satin-skinned horses used to be exercised by all the king's scarlet-coated grooms. They have substituted a railing for the wall that used to veil the mysteries of Capri from the vulgar, and now every flyman on the S. can see the palace in its entirety. They have thrown open the gardens, and the rustic seats are now the resting-places of nursery-maids and valetudinarians, while the wheels of patent perambulators and the heels of the shoes of the plebeian children, craunch the gravel which once resounded with the tread of kings and princes, marchionesses and ministers of state. Placards relative to the concerts and balls, the dogs and monkeys, and the twins, the Courier of St. Petersburg, and the next town-rate of twopence in the pound, flank the portals where yeomen on the guard have stood. They have dismantled the great entrance-gate, and it is as free of ingress to the pauper as all doors are to Death. I remember when I used to regard that gate with awe and wonder, and watch the royal carriage, with its brilliant outriders disappear through it, with bated breath, thinking of the ineffable splendour, the untold gorgeousness, the unimaginable luxuries, that must have their being behind those charmed doors. Now I pass through the gate, whistling. I smoke a cigar, contrary to rule, in the royal gardens. I pay sixpence to see a show in the place where the great kings dwelt : where beauty has languished, and voluptuousness has revelled, and pride has said to itself, " I can never die." I pay sixpence, and sit in my high-lows, in the rooms where investitures have been held, knighthood conferred, treaties concocted, peace and war proclaimed, death-warrants signed. Twenty years ago, how many a millionaire's wife would have given her ears to be invited to the Pagoda ? Now I invite myself, and my wife thinks the room but shabby.

I see breakers a-head that betoken the squall of a sermon. The subject is too enticing. Only this I must say : If any divine wishes to preach a sermon upon vanity and emptiness, and the mutability of earthly things, let him make haste and come here, and take the Pagoda of Capri for a text.

Out on the S., facing the Pagoda, the idol-worshippers erected some years ago a statue of their idol. It was, I believe, originally cast in bronze ; but either neglect or the saline quality of the atmosphere, or some yet more mysterious agent, has converted it into the mournfulest, rustiest, most verdigrised old marine-store you ever saw. This is Georgius— but ah! how changed from him ! The ambrosial wig seems out of curl. The fine features are battered and worn away— the royal nose has especially suffered. The classic drapery hangs in dingy folds, like the garments of a lean and slippered pantaloon. *Fuit, fuit, fuit* is written everywhere. On dark winter's nights, when the sea moans fitfullest, and the wind howls among the Moorish chimney-pots of the Pagoda, and the rain whips the pedestal, I can imagine this statue animated by a ghost, and the ghost wringing its bronzed hands and crying, " Walla ! Walla ! Dogs and monkeys, Caribbean twins and clowns, in the house where I have waltzed with Jersey and gambled with Hertford ; where I have entertained Polignac, and made Platoff tipsy ; where I have suffered princesses to kiss my hand, and said to sheriffs, 'Arise, Sir John ;' where I compounded my inestimable recipe for Champagne-punch ;

mixed my world-famous Regent's-snuff, and cut out my immortal white kid pantaloons!" Alas, poor ghost!

I meet occasionally at the Pagoda Gardens, seldom early
or late, or in doubtful weather, but in the warmest, cheer-
fulest, most genial portion of the day, sundry elderly bucks,
antediluvian dandies, senile old boys, whom I cannot help
fancying to have been *habitués* of the Pagoda in the heyday
of its glory. I meet them, too, on the cliff, and other places
of resort; but the seedy purlieus of this palace out of elbows,
they especially haunt. Seldom do they walk together, or
converse in groups. The Sphinx is solitary. Marius had
no companion when he sat among the ruins of Carthage.
Trotting, or toddling, or creeping, or hobbling, or slinking
along, shall you see these damaged fops, these battered and
bygone beaux. The fur-collar, the hat with raised brim,
and body curved slightly inward, the double eye-glass, the
tightly-strapped trousers, and peaked high-heeled boots, telling of padded calves and bunions; the occasionally braided,
always tightly buttoned surtout, the never-failing umbrella,
the high satin stock, the curly wig, or purple-dyed whiskers,
the thousand crowsfeet on the face, the tired, parboiled eye,
weeping because its owner is too vain to allow it the aid of
spectacles; the mouth, full of evidence of what a capital profession dental surgery must be in Capri; the buck-skin gloves,
the handkerchief peeping from the breast-pocket, the oft-
produced snuffbox, the cough, the scintillating suspicions of
stays, and sciatica, and rheumatism, and paralysis—these
are the most noteworthy exterior characteristics of the old
beau types I meet in the Gardens. They creep about in the
sunshine, tottering over their old shadows, that seem like

guides, showing them the way to the grave. Now I meet them
elbowed by the noisy, healthful, pleasure-seeking throngs by
the sea; now they crouch in the corners of Mr. Thruppell's
subscription reading-rooms; blinking over the newspapers—
during which operation you may hear as many as forty distinct wheezes and coughs in the course of one forenoon.
When it is cold, they come abroad in cloaks and comforters,
but are loath to lose an hour's sunshine. Nobody seems to
invite them to dinner; you do not meet them in society, or
at theatres or concerts. Even in church time on Sunday they
crawl about the shiny streets. They never ride; they never
venture on the beach, or bathe. When they are too old and
feeble to walk, they subside into Bath-chairs, and are dragged
about the Esplanade to pass the time till Mr. Tressel's men
have finished harnessing the black horses to the carriage, and
Doctor Bolus is satisfied that he will get no more fees.
Who are they—these poor old boys? Alas! may they not
have been the strong men who lived before Agamemnon came
into babyhood? These fur-collared spectres lingering about
the scenes of their former triumphs, like a dog about the
grave of his master who is dead: these, O vain and forward
youth, were once the gallant and the gay in that prouder
alcove than Cliefden's—they were the mimic statesmen who
circled the merry king that built Capri. They are old and
broken now; but the days have been when they have seen
the Regent bow, and Fitzherbert smile, and d'Artois dance.
—when they have heard Sheridan laugh, and Brummell jest,
They have seen the tawdy rooms of the Pagoda all blazing
with light, and splendour, and beauty,—upon the orders of
the men, and the jewels of the women. They have seen

Sardanapalus, Tiberius, Heliogabalus, Augustus—which you
will—disporting himself at Capri. They know of the humours
of the wild Prince and Poins. They have heard Captain
Morris sing. They have known George Hanger. Are any
such extant? you ask. I seem to think so when I meet these
ancient dandified men—these crippled invalids from the campaign of vanity, where the only powder was hair-powder, and
the only bullets fancy balls.

But Capri is no longer royal. The old dandies, the metamorphosed Pagoda, and the marine-store statue are the only
relics left to point out that Capri was once the sojourn of
royalty. Stay; there is a Chapel Royal, with the lion and the
unicorn on red velvet within, but it is elbowed by a printing-
office, and stared out of countenance by a boot-shop. I for one
(and I am one, I hope, of many thousands) do not regret the
withdrawal of the Royal patronage. I have an intense dislike
to towns royal or semi-royal. Don't you know how people in
Dublin bore you about "the Kyastle." In Windsor, however
loyal a man may be, he is apt to be driven mad by the interminable recurrence of portraits, not only of the royal family
—Heaven bless them!—but of their dependants, hangers-on,
and Teutonic relatives. The cobbler who vamps your boots,
the chandlery shopkeeper who sells you a ha'porth of twine is
sure to be "purveyor to her Majesty and the Duchess of Kent,"
and you can scarcely take a chop in a coffee-room without a
suspicion that the man in the next box, with the aristocratic
whiskers and heavy gold-chain, may be one of the royal footmen in disguise. Versailles is one of the dreariest, dullest,
dearest, most stuck-up places I know; though it has but the
very shadow of a shade of royalty to dwell upon; Hampton

Court is poor, purse-proud, and conceited; Potsdam, I know, is slow and solemn, ; and Pimlico, I have heard, is proud. The disfranchisement of Capri, as a royal borough, was the making of the place. Dire thoughts of ruin, bankruptcy, grass growing in the streets, or emigration to Dieppe, sacred the inhabitants at first. But they were soon undeceived. The aristocracy continued their presence and patronage. They liked Capri, now royalty was gone, as a breathing-place. Perhaps, too, they liked a little being royalty themselves. The easy middle-classes came down, brought their wives and families with them, and took houses. By and by, a trunk-railway with numerous branches was started, and that wonderful personage Mr. Vox Populi came down, bag and baggage,—Briareus, Argus, Hydra, welded into one. He brought his wife and children with him. Finally, schools multiplied, and doctors disseminated themselves and differed.

Schools! Capri swarms with them. The moral tenets, inculcated there in bygone days, were not precisely of a nature to render their introduction into copybooks, as texts, advisable; but time has purified the naughty place, and the town is now all over targets, at which the young idea is taught to shoot from the quiver of geography, and the use of the globes,— dancing, deportment, and moral culture. There are ladies' schools of the grimmest and most adult status; schools where the elder pupils are considerably bigger than the schoolmistress; which locate in tremendous stucco mansions in the vast squares at the east-end of the town, and which are attended by music-masters with the fiercest of moustachios, and language-masters with long red beards and revolutionary-hats, and dancing-masters who come in broughams, and masters of gymnastics, deportment, and calisthenics, who have been colonels, even generals, in the armies of foreign potentates. To see these schools parade upon the cliff is a grand sight, driving solemn London dandies and dashing Lancer officers to desperation, and moving your humble servant to the commission of perhaps the only folly of which he has not as yet been guilty :—the composition of amatory verses in the *terza rima.* They are too pretty, they are too old to be at school; they ought to be Mrs. Somebodies, and living in a villa at Brompton. Strict discipline is observed in these grown-up schools ; and I have heard that though Signor Papadaggi, the singing-master, and Mr. Stargays, the lecturer on astronomy, must know, necessarily, every pupil they attend, by sight, the young ladies are instructed, whenever' they meet their male instructors in public, by no means to acknowledge their salutations, but to turn their heads— seaward—immediately. This they do simultaneously, as soldiers turn their eyes right, to the great comfort and moral delectation of the schoolmistress, whose axiom it is, that men-folk are of all living things the most to be avoided :— which is sometimes also my opinion, Eugenius.

There are long-tailed ladies' schools, whose pupils average from sixteen to six, blocking up every pathway. You cannot pass down a by-street without hearing pianos industriously thrummed, to the detriment of Messrs. Meyerbeer, Thalberg, and Chopin, but to the ultimate benefit of the music-sellers and the piano-forte manufacturers. Brass plates abound ; and that terrible epidemic, the collegiate system of female education, has declared itself virulently. Saline Parade College for Ladies, Prince Regency Square Ladies' Collegiate

Institute, Hemp Town Academical Gymnasium for Young Ladies, conducted on Collegiate Principles,—what sham next? I marvel what they are like—these ladies' colleges? Have they any affinity to the old young ladies' school?—the Misses Gimp, stiff and starched, the subdued English teacher, the snuffy French governess, the stocks, the backboard, the pinafores, the bread and butter, and the French mark? Or do the young ladies wear trencher caps and black gowns. Do they go to chapel in surplices, and fudge impositions, and have wine parties, and slang bargees, and cap proctors, and sport their oak? Are they rusticated if they are naughty? Are they ever plucked for their little-go? I should like to see a young lady plucked for her little-go.

As for the boys' schools, their name begins with an L and ends with an N. Plenty of colleges of course; Reverend Doctors, M.A.'s, Graduates of the university, willing to take charge of, &c., Gentlemen who have devoted some years to the instruction of, &c., Clergymen most anxious to recommend an, &c., Capri is one huge trap hung with toasted cheese, and the poor little boy-mice are caught in it incessantly. It is good to see the little lads disporting themselves on the beach, or at cricket in the fields, or filing along the cliff, two and two, in every variety of cap and jacket, looking lovingly in at the pastrycooks.' I should like to have boys at school at Capri, that I might come down on Saturday, and tip them, and give them tarts at Button's. Yet there are some boys I see in these scholastic processions, who make me melancholy. Fatherless boys; boys with dark eyes whose parents are far away in burning India, and who have found but a hard step-school-father in Doctor Spanker. They have an ugly habit too, of sending sick boys to school at Capri— poor pale-faced children, who limp wearily on crutches after the healthful crew, or are drawn along in the wake of the young band in invalid-chairs, all muffled up in shawls and bandages, and gaze, ah! so wistfully, at the gambolling children and caracoling horses, and come here to be doctored and taught—to learn their lessons—and die.

The College of Physicians, the Royal College of Surgeons, the Company of Apothecaries, the Faculty of Homœopathists; the confraternity of Hydropathists, the Hygeian heretics, or College of Health-Arians, the great Professorial guild of Pill and Ointment vendors; nay, even the irregular Cossacks of medical science—the Bardolphs, Nyms, and Pistols of Field-Marshal Sangrado's army—rubbers, scrapers, counter-irritators, pitch-plaisters, brandy-and-salt dosers, and similar free lances of physics—known sometimes, I believe, by the generic name of quacks—all these flourish at Capri, a very forest of green bay-trees, and wax exceeding rich. For there are so many really sick people who come to this Capri in search of health, that the convalescent natives, perhaps in deference to their visitors, perhaps by that contagious fancy which leads people to throw themselves off the Monument, and write five-act tragedies, and start newspapers, straightway either imagine that they have something the matter with them, and call in the doctor forthwith, or feel that the mantle of Æsculapius has descended upon their shoulders; and, purchasing a second-hand mortar and half-a-dozen globular bottles, set up as doctors on their own account. To be a doctor, or to be doctored, are the two conditions of existence at Capri. When a man hasn't a bad leg of his own, he bethinks him of his next-door neighbour, who has one of fifteen years' standing, and insists upon curing it. Come to Capri, and you shall at length know who are the purchasers of Professor Swalloway, and Professor Methusaleh, and Doctor Druggem and Widow Wobble's pills; who are the persons that invest capital in old Doctor Isaac Laquedem's Tonic of Timbuctoo, and Messrs. Mullygrubbs' medicated ginger-beer, and Madame de Pompadour's farinaceous food; and how the patentees of those inestimable medicines acquire colossal fortunes. In the stream of equipages in the streets, the doctors' sly brougham spots the gay procession like pips on an ivory domino. Call on your rich aunt; you are almost sure to meet the dentist coming in, or the chiropodist coming out, or Mr. Wollop the great gymnastic doctors' carriage (he makes five thousand a-year by kneading people's joints, and cannot spell) at the door. In the remote slums of Capri (for even Capri has slums), in tarry little by-lanes and fishy hovels, where barricades of seines and nets hung out to dry impede the passage, and the little children toddle about in bucket-boots and sou'-wester hats, you may discover, grizzling over saucepans or mumping on patchwork counterpanes, preposterous old women in pea-jackets and Welsh-wigs, always infirm, often bed-ridden—magging, obstinate, superstitious, ignorant crones—who yet possess wonderful reputations as doctoresses, and are the holders of dire medicaments; grim recipes, "as was took by his blessed Majesty for the innards," and warranted to work marvellous cures. They cannot read or write, these ancient ladies; they moan in their own sick-beds, and dun the parish surgeon for doctor's stuff; yet they cure all bodily complaints of others. Solemn house-

keepers come to Cod's Head Alley or Hard Roe Lane, sent
by the Marchioness of Capri, to consult these old women. If
they cannot cure, at least they have the consolation of knowing that they thwart the regular physician, and counteract
the effect of his medicines, and render his guinea-visit null
and void. Do I call people simpletons for running after
quacks here at Capri or throughout the mortal world? No—
not I. How do we know—what do we know? Goody Fish-
bone's salted roe of a herring, beaten up in a glass of rhubarb
and gin, and swallowed fasting, may do us good. A man
believes in quacks, as he believes in ghosts; and how many
of the wisest of us have spectres at our bed's-foot every midnight in the year?

Lest quackery, however, left to itself, should quite cure
—or kill—Capri out of hand, it is but justice to remember that
it is the dwelling-place of very many learned and accomplished physicians and surgeons—men whose long lives have
been spent not only in the ardent pursuit of knowledge and
science, but also in doing good to their fellow-creatures
—in healing not only hurts but hearts; and who glorify
by their charity the profession which by their talents they
adorn.

Ought I to say anything of the reverend profession in
Capri? Shall I be impertinent in lightly touching on themes
ecclesiastical? Would not, moreover, a paraphrase of that
which I have said of the doctors serve also for the clergy?
For there are doctors and doctors, and there are parsons and
parsons. Orthodox ecclesiastics—good, pious, charitable,
unostentatious men, doing acts of mercy by stealth; Christian
priests of every denomination, labouring heartily in their

vocation, and earning their reward. And there are also the irregular Cossack corps, the sellers of pious pills, and holy ointments, and polemical plaisters—braying Boanerges, cushion-thumpers—men who jump, and howl, and rave, and throw their arms about, and pipe all hands to repentance as violently and hoarsely as boatswains. When I hear the Reverend Mr. Tinklesimble, who is wonderfully eloquent, but a comb for whose hair and soap for whose face are decidedly (under correction) desiderata—when I hear Mr. Tinklesimble lecture upon the Beast in the Pit, and the Seventh Vial, and the Crystal Sea, proving by word and gesture, plainly though involuntarily, that the study of the Apocalypse hath found him mad or left him so; when in twenty other streets and chapels I hear reverend lunatics gnashing in their padded rooms—I mean pulpits—I am content to pass them by: what would animadversion upon them have to do with Capri, though they dwell there? Are they not common to every nation and every creed, and to all humanity?

Ecclesiastical architecture is of much account in Capri. Tall steeples point upwards like the tall chimneys of Preston, telling of extensive factories of grace. Gothic and Corinthian, Saxon and Byzantine—of every style are these fanes. Yet do I seem to miss a church on a hill I loved twenty years syne: it was the parish church of Capri, when Capri was yet but in the hundred of Herringbone, a poor fishing hamlet. The old church, the natives affectionately called it; that ancient, grey, shingled, moss-grown edifice, with its carved porch and lazy sun-dial. How many, many times when a boy I have played among the green graves, or sat and gazed in childish contemplation at the town beneath, and the blue sea rising straight up at the sky as though to engulph it; or spelt over the inscription on the tomb of the brave sea-captain who took the fugitive Charles the Second over to France after the battle of Worcester, and of that famous old woman who fought in male attire at Blenheim, and Ramilies, and Malplaquet, all through the wars of Queen Anne, and who died when she was more than a hundred years of age, pensioned by the king of Capri.

But the clergy, the doctors, the schools, the aristocracy, all of the proudest features of Capri, culminate on her boulevards, the Cliff.

The stones of the Paris boulevards and my feet are brothers; I know the gardens of the palace at Lacken; I have walked Unter den Linden, and toiled up the Grande Rue of Pera. I have yet to lounge on the Toledo and the Quay Santa Lucia; to smoke a cigarette at the Puerta del Sol; to inhale the evening breeze on the Pincian Hill; to buy sweetmeats on the Ponte Vecchio at Florence, or bargain for a yard of Venice gold-chain on the Rialto at Venice. Regent Street is familiar to me, likewise Ratcliffe Highway; yet I question if any public promenade the wide world through be as pleasant, gay, and picturesque as the Cliff at Capri. The footpath is so narrow, to begin with; the throng is so thick, the people so well dressed; they look so happy; there is so much youth. There are so many smiles. The very commerce is light-hearted and picturesque; jewellery, shells, fancy walking canes, toys, curiosities, French kid-gloves, bonnets and feathers, hot-house fruits and flowers, gay lithographs, gift-books, albums and church-services bound in velvet and gold. None but the amenities of trade find stalls in this gay mart. The bagatelle is triumphant. *Vive la bagatelle !*

If you are unmarried, unhappy, poor, and have no friends, but are withal of a cheerful temperament, and unenvious of the prosperity of others, it is balm to your wounded spirit to walk here on a breezy morning or sunny autumn evening, gliding silently but observantly among the motley, careless crowd. Hundreds of little histories you may weave for yourself, and not one tragic one among them. Here are sweethearts, young couples on their wedding tour, bluff papas of stock-broking tendencies, who have come express from Capel Court to take their young families out walking; stout mammas in gorgeous silks and bonnets, like a page out of Mr. Audubon's natural history book. Here are delicious young ladies blushing to find from the admiring eyes of passers-by how pretty they are; here are wonderful foreigners, whose mustachios, braiding, and mosaic jewellery, would do honour to Verrey's, or the Café Cardinal, and who, disgusted at the turpitude of the Austrian government, the tyranny of the French Emperor, and the tergiversation of the King of Prussia, have come to Capri as to another Patmos; and are not too proud to teach German verbs, and "Do, re, mi, fa, sol," for a livelihood. If you have a becoming British reverence for the Peerage of your country, and for its governing classes, who have done you so much good, you will feel a thrill of pride and gratification when your garments are positively brushed on the cliff by the sweeping silken robes of peeresses in their own right, and the coat-lappets of hereditary legislators.

You meet everybody on the cliff at Capri. The Peers and

the sweet Peeresses, and the Aldermanesses, and the Board of Works. Her Majesty's ministers in plaid shooting-jackets, bishops' wives in green "uglies," gouty old generals in wide-awake hats, archdeacons in waterproof coats, Israelitish millionnaires (very strong is the wealthy Caucasian element at Capri : it dwelleth at Hemp Town in five-storied mansions : it goeth to town in the morning and returneth to dinner by express; grand dinner parties giveth it to the tribe of Benjamin, and of Moses, and of Levi; handsome daughters with ringed fingers hath it, and, curiously, it seems to be continually buying fruit in the market), little city gents, honest florid tradesmen and their families, young dandies, used-up men, fast men, slow men ; fellows of their colleges, from Cambridge, in spectacles; blooming, busy lawyers, with great shirt-frills and watch-chains ; leaders of circuit, in very shabby trousers, with wig-powder yet on their coat-collars, and moving the sea for a rule to show cause why they should not force a transient flush of health into their pallid, tired countenances.

Have I forgotten—no, but I have as yet omitted to mention—two of the strongest classes, and the most constant in their attendance on the cliff. I allude to the canine pets, and the round hats. Every variety of lapdog may you see, O philosopher, in this pretty paradise of puppies. The fat, plethoric, wheezy, long-eared, lolling-tongued, door-mat of a dog, with a pink ribbon round his apoplectic neck, and legs so short that their existence is almost imperceptible. This animal as surely belongs to the Dowager Lady Booterstown, in the peerage of Ireland, as yonder yelping rat-like terrier— or, perhaps, more like a rat that has stolen and caparisoned

himself in a porcupine's panoply—belongs to the austere old
gentleman with the nonconformist countenance, who clutches
his umbrella as though he were going to beat somebody with
it: to this dog enters your silky Blenheim spaniel, a lazy little
cub, but victorious often in his passive obstinacy, turning over
on his back, sticking out his short legs, and, with his head on
one side, humorously defying all the efforts of strenuous footpage, and despairing young lady, although armed with the
poke-inflicting parasol, to make him move on. Then comes
mincing along daintily, as though he had patent leather boots
on, Monsieur Caniche—your French poodle, curled, shaven,
trimmed, pink-nosed, and redolent of Naples soap. And after
him, ambling, but shivering piteously in his plaid paletot,
Signor Lungoshanko, the Italian greyhound. And, sometimes
—the sight is not often seen by human eyes, but is manifest
occasionally — comes there sweeping along the cliff some
dowager of ancient days, bearing in her arms the Lost Book
of Livy, the *ultimus Romanorum*, the Vinegar Bible, the
Samothracian Onagra, the blue diamond, the black swan, the
pearl beyond price of dog-hood—the Dutch Pug:—you see his
coffee-coloured coat, his moist, short, black nose, his snarling
little molars for a moment, and tremble. He departs like a
vision, and you ask the wailing ocean, where you may see
such another dog, alive.

I should like to linger a great while longer on the cliff
at Capri, but my time is come, and to other penal servitude
I must betake myself. You have heard nothing as yet of the
famous pier at Capri, of the pretty horsewomen, of the bold
riding-masters, of the stalwart bathing women, of the doughty
Capri tradesmen. All these things you shall hear some day,

if you are inclined, and time will serve ; likewise of the first mayor of Capri, and how all the town-councillors wanted to be aldermen, and how all the aldermen wanted to be mayor, and failing, each and every of them in the attainment of that high office, moved votes of censure upon everybody, and played the very deuce with the town of the Metamorphosed Pagoda.

XVII.

THE LAND OF NOD, A KINGDOM OF RECONCILED
IMPOSSIBILITIES.

THERE is a kingdom whose boundaries are within the reach of every man's hand, on whose frontiers no heavier entrance-tribute or import-duty is exacted save that comprised in the payment of two-score inflections of the eyelids—or forty winks; a kingdom into which the majority of humanity travel at least once in every twenty-four hours; though the exact time—the precise moment—at which that voyage is commenced is not, and never has been, known to any man alive. Whether we are transported by some invisible agency—on the wings of spirits or in the arms of genii—whether we go to the kingdom or the kingdom comes to us, we cannot tell. Why or how or when we came there we know not; yet, almost invariably, when the tribute of the forty winks has been duly paid, we find ourselves wandering in the Land of Nod—the Kingdom of Reconciled Impossibilities.

Locomotion in this kingdom is astonishingly rapid: we run without moving and fly without wings. Time and space are counted zeros; centuries are skipped at a bound; continents and oceans are traversed without an effort. We are here, there, and everywhere. Grey-headed men, we are little

boys at school, breaking windows and dreading the vindic-
tive cane. Married and settled, we are struggling through
the quickset hedges of our first love. Crippled, we race and
leap; blind, we see. Unlearned, we discourse in strange
tongues and decipher the most intricate of hieroglyphics.
Unmusical, we play the fiddle like Paganini. We pluck fruit
from every branch of the tree of knowledge; the keys of
every science hang in a careless bunch at our girdle; we are
amenable to no laws; money is of no account; Jack is as
good as his master; introductions are not required for
entrance into polite society; the most glaring impossibilities
are incessantly admitted, taken for granted, and reconciled.
Whence the name of this kingdom.

Much more wondrous and full of marvels is it than the
famed land of Cockaigne, than the country of Prester John,
than the ground of Tom Tidler (whose occupation is now
gone in consequence of the discovery of rival grounds in
California and Australia), than Raleigh's Dorado, than the
Arcadia of Strephon and Corydon, Celia, and Sacharissa;
than the fearful country where there are men

> " —— whose heads
> Do grow beneath their shoulders,"

than even the mirabolant land that Jack saw when he had
gotten to the top of the beanstalk. The only territorial
kingdom that I can compare it to is one—and even the
duration of *that* one is fleeting and evanescent, appearing
only for a season, like specks upon the sun or the floating
islands in Windermere—visible and to be travelled in from
the end of December to the end of the following February,
called the Kingdom of Pantomime. This kingdom, which,

at other seasons of the year, is almost as rigorously barred and closed against strangers as China or Japan or the Stock Exchange, offers many points of resemblance to the Kingdom of Reconciled Impossibilities. There is a voyager therein, one Clown, who, with Pantaloon, his friend and dupe and scapegoat, dances about the streets, insults and beats respectable shopkeepers, swindles and robs ready furnished lodgings, leers at virtuous matrons, commits burglaries and larcenies in the broad day (or lamp) light, and perpetrates child-murders by the dozen, yet goes "unwhipp'd of justice:" nay, he and his confederate are rewarded, at last, by an ovation of fireworks and revolving stars; as are also Harlequin, a prancing scapegrace in a spangled jerkin and hose, and a dancing girl they call Columbine; who together play such fantastic tricks before the footlights as make the gallery roar —such tricks as would be tolerated nowhere but in a Kingdom of Impossibilities. For in all other kingdoms, theft of fish or sausage—be it even the smallest gudgeon or an infinitesimal saveloy—is three months' incarceration at least, and robbery in a dwelling-house is felony; and to force a respectable white-bearded man with a crutch stick and an impediment in his speech to cast involuntary sommersaults, and to make him sit down oftener on a hard surface than he wishes, is an assault punishable by fine and imprisonment; while the cutting up, mutilating, smothering, or thrusting into a letter-box of a baby is Murder.

In all other kingdoms, likewise, as we are well aware, vice is always vanquished and virtue rewarded—ultimately; but in the Kingdom of Reconciled Impossibilities, as well as in that of Pantomime, nothing of the kind takes place. In this former one, innocent, we are frequently condemned to death, or to excruciating tortures. Masters, we are slaves; wronged and oppressed, we are always in the wrong and the oppressors. Though in the every day kingdom we are perhaps wealthy, at least in easy circumstances, we are in the Realms of Impossibility perpetually in difficulties. Moments of inexpressible anguish we pass, from the want of some particular object or the non-remembrance of some particular word; though what the object or the word may be, we never have and never had the remotest idea. Spectres of duties omitted, ghosts of offences committed, sit at banquets with us; and, under circumstances of the greatest apparent gaiety and joviality, we are almost always in sore perturbation of mind and vexation of spirit.

The kingdom, indeed, is full of tribulations, impossible yet poignant. Frequently, when we attempt to sing, our voice dies away in an articulate murmur or a guttural gasp. If we strive to run, our legs fail under us; if we nerve our arm to strike, some malicious influence paralyses our muscles, and the gladiator's fist falls as lightly as a feather; yet, powerless as we are, and unable to beat the knave who has wronged us, we are ourselves continually getting punched on the head, beaten with staves, gashed with swords and knives. Curiously, though much blood flows, and we raise hideous lamentations, we do not suffer much from these hurts. Frequently we are killed—shot dead—decapitated; yet we walk and talk shortly afterwards, as Saint Denis is reported to have done. Innumerable as the sands of the sea are the disappointments we have to endure in the Kingdom of Impossibilities. Get up as early as we may, we are sure to miss the train ; the steamboat always sails without us ; if we have a cheque to get cashed, the iron-ribbed shutters of the bank are always up, when our cab drives to the door, and somebody near us always says, without being asked, " Stopped payment!" All boats, carriages, beasts of burden and other vehicles and animals, behave in a similar tantalising and disappointing manner ; tall horses that we drive or ride, change unaccountably into little dogs, boats split in the middle, coaches rock up and down like ships. We walk for miles without advancing a step, we write for hours without getting to the end of a page, we are continually beginning and never finishing, trying and never achieving, searching and never finding, knocking and never being admitted.

The Kingdom of Impossibilities must be the home of Ixion, and the Danaïdes, and Sisyphus, and peculiarly of Tantalus. The number of tubs we are constantly filling, and which are never full; and the quantities of stones which, as soon as we have rolled them to the top of a hill, roll down again, are sufficiently astonishing : but it is in a tantalizing point of view that the kingdom is chiefly remarkable. We are for ever bidden to rich banquets—not Barmecide feasts, for the smoking viands and generous wines are palpable to sight and touch. But, no sooner are our legs comfortably under the mahogany, than a something far more teazing and vexatious than the ebony wand of Sancho's physician sends the meats away untasted, the wines unquaffed, changes the *venue* to a kingdom of realities. Dear me ! When I think of the innumerable gratuitous dinners I have set down to in the Land of Impossibilities, of the countless eleemosynary spreads to which, with never a dime in my pocket, I have been made welcome,—of the real turtle, truffled turkeys, Strasbourg pies, and odoriferous pine apples that have tempted my appetite,—of the unhandsome manner in which I have been denied the enjoyment of the first spoonful of soup, and of the rude and cavalier process by which I have been suddenly transported to another kingdom where I am usually expected to pay for my dinner—when I think of these things, I could weep.

Sometimes, though rarely, the rulers of the Impossible Kingdom permit you to drink—provided always that you have tumbled (which is always your mode of entrance) into their domains in a desperately parched and thirsty condition. Cold water is the general beverage provided, and you are liberally allowed to drink without cessation—to empty water-jugs, pitchers, decanters, buckets, if you choose. I have known men who have sucked a pump for days, nay, who have lapped gigantic quantities of the Falls of Niagara; but the ruler of the Impossible Kingdom has mingled one cruel and malicious condition with his largesse. You may drink as much as you like, but you must never quench your thirst, and you must always wake—tumble out of the kingdom I mean—thirstier than you was before.

Travelling in this strange country is mostly accomplished in the night season—"in thoughts from the visions of the night, when deep sleep falleth upon men." It is when the Kingdom of Life is hushed and quiescent, when the streets are silent, and there are none abroad but the watchers and the houseless, that the Kingdom of Impossibilities wakes up in full noise, and bustle, and activity. Yet betimes we are favoured with a passport for this kingdom in the broad day

season, in the fierce summer heat, when we retire to cool
rooms, there to pay the tribute of forty winks to the Monarch
of the Impossible Kingdom ; when, as we travel, we can half
discern the green summer leaves waving through our trans-
lucent eyelids,—can hear the murmuring of fountains, and the
singing of birds, in the kingdom we have come from. Very
pleasant are these day voyages, especially when we can
drowsily hear the laughter of children playing on a lawn outside.

The Kingdom of Reconciled Impossibilities is a land of
unfulfilled promises, of broken engagements, of trees for
ever blossoming but never bearing fruit, of jumbles of
commencements with never a termination among them, of
prefaces without a finis, of dramas never played out. The
unities are not observed in this kingdom. There are a great
many prologues, but no epilogues. It is all as it should not
and cannot be. It snows in July, and the dog-days are in
January. Men sneeze with their feet, and see with their
thumbs, like Gargantua. The literature of the country consists
of tales told by idiots, full of sound and fury, signifying
nothing. The houses are all built without foundations ; they
are baseless fabrics, which vanishing leave not a wreck behind.
Everything in the kingdom is impossible.

Impossible, yet reconciled. In no other land, certainly,
are we so convinced of the truth of the axiom that "whatever
is is right." Against our knowledge, feelings, experience, and
convictions, against all evidence, oral or ocular, against truth,
justice, reason, or possibility, we smilingly confess that black
is white, that clouds are whales, that the moon is cheese. We
know our brother to be our brother, yet, without difficulty or

reluctance, we admit him to be Captain Cook. With a full
knowledge that what we are doing can't be, we are pleasingly
convinced that it can be, and that it is, and is right. So we
violate all the laws of morality, and decency, and international
justice, honesty, and courtesy, with a comfortable self-
consciousness that it is "all right," and that we are wronging
no one. Quakers have been known, in the Kingdom of
Impossibilities, to lie in wait for men, and murder them; nay,
to have hidden the bodies in corn bins and chemists's bottles.
Moral men have eloped with ballet dancers. Bishops have
found themselves at the Cider Cellars. Judges of the
Ecclesiastical Court create disturbances at the Casino, and
have wrenched off knockers, in company with jovial proctors,
and fast old surrogates, about town. There was a cathedral
verger once, in the Kingdom of Impossibilities, who refused
a fee, there was an Irish Member without a grievance,
there was a Chancery suit decided to the satisfaction of all
parties.

Good men not only become rascals, but rascals turn honest
men in this astonishing country. Captain Mac Swindle paid
me, only last night, the five pounds he has owed me for fifteen
years. I saw the unjust steward render up a faultless account.
All is not vexatious and disappointing in the Impossible Kingdom. If it be a kingdom of unfulfilled promises, it is one of
accomplished wishes. Sorely pressed for cash in this possible kingdom, no sooner are we in the impossible one than the
exact sum we wished for, chinks in golden sovereigns, rustles
in crisp notes, mellifluously whispers in soft-paper cheques
before our eyes, within our gladsome pockets, or our rejoicing
fingers. We shall be able to meet the little bill; streets are

no longer stopped up; the tailor shall cringe again; Caroline shall have the velvet mantle trimmed with sable. Hurrah! But alas! the money of the kingdom that never can be, and yet always is and will be, is as treacherous and deceitful as a will-of-the-wisp, or an Eastern mirage; no sooner do we possess it than we have it not. We wake, and the shining sovereigns and the rustling notes have turned into dry leaves, like the money paid by the magician in the Arabian Nights.

If the kingdom (to expatiate further on its advantageous features) be one of tribulations and disappointments, it is also one of great and extended privileges. We are privileged to walk about unwashed, unshaven, and undressed, to clap kings upon the back, to salute princesses if we list, to ride blood horses, to fly higher than the skylark, to visit foreign lands without a Foreign Office passport, the reference of a banking firm, or the necessity of being personally known to the Foreign Secretary. We have the privilege of being a great many people and in a great many places at one and the same time. We have the privilege of living our lives over again, of un-doing the wrongs we have done, of re-establishing our old companionship with the dead, and knowing their worth much better than we did before we lost them.

Yes, pre-eminent and radiant stands one privilege, to the enjoyment of which every traveller in the land of Reconciled Impossibilities is entitled. He is privileged to behold the Dead Alive. The King of Terrors has no power in the do-mains of the Impossible. The dead move and speak and laugh, as they were wont to speak and move and laugh, in the old days when they were alive, and when we loved them. They have been dead—of course—we know it and they say

T

so—but they are alive now; and, thanks to the irresistible
logic of the Impossible kingdom, we slightly question how.
These visitors have no grim tales to tell, no secrets of their
prison-house to reveal. Here, joyful and mirthful as ever,
are the old familiar faces; the life-blood courses warmly
through the old friendly hands; dead babies crow and battle
valorously in nurses' arms; dead sweethearts smile and blush;
dead aunts scold; dead schoolmasters awe; dead boon companions crack the old jokes, sing the old songs, tell the old
stories, till WE WAKE into the kingdom of the Possible; and
ah me! the eye turns to a vacant chair, a faded miniature, a
lock of soft hair in crumpled tissue paper, a broken toy;
while the mind's vision recurs to a green mound, and a half
effaced stone.

In the regions of the Impossible there is a population
separate, apart, peculiar; possible nowhere but in a land of
impossibilities. Monstrous phantasms in semi-human shape,
horrible creations, deformed giants, dwarfs with the heads of
beasts; shapeless phantoms, hideous life such as the Ancient
Mariner saw on the rotting deep. Such things pursue us
through these regions with grinning fangs, and poisonous
breath; kneel on our chests; wind their sharp talons in our
hair; gnaw at our throats with horrid yells. And, apart
from the every day scenes of every day life brought to the
reductio ad absurdum in the Kingdom of Impossibilities, we
tarry betimes in chambers of horrors, in howling deserts, in
icy caverns, in lakes of fire, in pits of unutterable darkness.
Miserable men are they who are frequent travellers through
these districts of the Impossible kingdom! They may say
with the guilty Thane—

" —— Better be with the dead,
　Whom we to gain our place have sent to peace,
　Than on the torture of the mind to lie
　In restless ecstacy."

If you would leave such countries unexplored, lead virtuous lives, take abundant exercise, be temperate (in the true sense of the word : not choosing in what, but in everything), and take no man's wrong to bed with thee—no, not for one single night.

XVIII.

TWENTY MILES.

HE who travels frequently, sometimes on foot, always humbly, seldom unobservantly, has other and better opportunities, it appears to me, of forming a just notion of the countries he passes through than Mr. Assistant Commissioner Mac Collum, of the Inner Temple, Barrister-at-Law, who scours through the land in the first class *coupé* of an express train; holds his commission in the best sitting room of the best hotel; and, after drawing his three or five guineas a day, scours back again, serves up an elaborate report to my Lords, and is in due course of time rewarded for his arduous services by being made Puisne Judge of Barataria, or Lieutenant-Governor of the Larboard Islands.

It is astonishing how little a man may see while travelling, if he will only take the trouble to shut the eyes of his mind. The Sir Charles Coldstreams who go up to the top of Vesuvius and see nothing in it; who in their ideas of Grand Cairo do not condescend to comprise the pyramids, but confine themselves to complaints of the bugs and fleas at Shepherd's hotel: who have no recollections of Venice, save that there was no pale ale to be got there; are not so un-

common a class as you may imagine. It is not always necessary for a man to be "used-up" to visit a country, and see
nothing in it; nay, that noble lord is not quite a *rara avis*,
who, having just returned from Greece, and being asked at a
dinner party " what he thought of Athens?" turned to the
valet, standing behind his chair, and calmly said, " John,
what did I think of Athens? "

It was once the lot of your humble servant to travel
twenty miles by railway, and in the depth of winter, in company with one single traveller.   The scenery through which
we were passing was among the most beautiful in the world;
and in its wintry garb was so exquisitely fair, that it might
have moved even the taciturn Mr. Short, in Captain Marryat's
" Snarley-yow," to grow eloquent upon it. But your servant's
companion, a hard-featured man in a railway rug, was a dumb
dog, and made no sign.   In vain did your servant try him
upon almost every imaginable subject of conversation—the
weather, the country, politics, the speed of the train, the am-
biguities of Bradshaw, the electric telegraph, the number of
stations, and the prevalence of influenza. He was mum. He
could scarcely be silently observing and commenting upon
the works of Nature in the landscape without, or of art in
your servant's dress within, for he never looked out of the
window, and kept his eyes (staringly wide awake they were)
upon one particular check of his railway rug. He could
scarcely have been a philosopher, looking, as he did, like a
tub, without a Diogenes in it ; and, unless he was speculating
upon the development of textile fabrics, or counting the
number of pulsations of the engine to himself (I did once
travel from Liverpool to London, two hundred and twenty

miles, with a gentleman whose sole occupation was in checking off the number of telegraph posts, but who, getting confused between them and a white paling, lost count at Tring, in Hertfordshire, and relapsed into absolute silence), his mind must have been a blank. At last, on a stoppage at some station, I remarked, desperately scraping the gelid rime from the carriage window, that "it froze:" whereupon, speaking for the first and last time, he responded solemnly, "Hard;" immediately afterwards, drew from underneath the seat a black cow-skin travelling-bag, as hard, cold, and silent as himself, and slid out of the carriage. Some angular female drapery, surmounted by the ugliest bonnet that ever existed, was waiting for him on the platform; and my hard friend went on his way, and I saw him no more. I would rather not dine with him and the drapery, next Christmas day.

Yet there is much virtue in twenty miles. Along the dreariest railway; up to the loneliest turnpike road; across the darkest, barrenest, rainiest sea; there are to the observant twenty score of lessons in every mile of the twenty. To bring this enjoyment to every door, I would have all travellers taught to Draw. I would not insist that they should become proficients in Poonah painting, or that they should attend Professor Partridge's lectures upon anatomy: I would not make it a *sine quâ non* that they should visit Rome, and copy all the frescoes in the Loggie and Stanze of the Vatican; but some rudimentary education in design and colour, I would cause to be given to every man, woman, and child (able and willing to learn) who intends to travel twenty miles. He who can draw, be it ever so badly, has a dozen extra preference-shares in every landscape—shares that are perpetually paying

golden dividends.   He can not only see the fields and the
mountains, the rivers and the brooks, but he can eat and
drink them.   The flowers are a continual feast: and when
the rain is on them, and after that the Sun, they may be
washed down with richest wines, hippocras, hydromel, aqua-
d'oro, what you will.   Every painter is, to a certain extent, a
poet; and I would have every poet taught to paint.   Charles
Lamb asked, " why we should not say grace, and ask a blessing before going out for a walk, as before sitting down to
dinner ? "   Why should we not ?   The green meat of the
meadows is as succulent a banquet to the mind, as ever the
accloyed Lucullus stretched himself upon his couch to devour
To the artistic eye there are inexhaustible pleasures to be
found in the meanest objects.   There are rich studies of colour
in a brick wall; of form in every hedge and stunted pollard
of light and shade in every heap of stones on the Macadam-
ised road; of more than Præ-Raphaelite stippling and finish
in every tuft of herbage and wild flowers.   The shadow cast
by a pig-stye upon a road, by an omnibus driver's reins on
his horses' backs; the picturesque form of a donkey cart; the
rags of a travelling tinker; the drapery folds in a petticoat
hung out to dry on the clothes' line in the back yard; the
rugged angularities of the lumps of coal in the grate; the
sharp lights upon the decanter on the table at home; all these
are fruitful themes for musing and speculative pleasure.   The
fisherman who can draw, has ten times more enjoyment in his
meditative pursuit than the inartistic angler.   An acquaintance with art takes roods, perches, furlongs from the journey;
for however hard the ground may be; however dreary the
tract of country through which we journey ; though our twenty

miles may lie in the whole distance between two dead walls ;
have we not always that giant scrap-book, the sky above us ?
—the sky with its clouds that sometimes are dragonish ; with
its vapours sometimes—

> " Like a bear or lion,
> A tower'd citadel or a pendant rock,
> A forkèd mountain or blue promontory
> With trees upon 't that nod unto the world,
> And mock our eyes with air,"

—the sky with all its glorious varieties of colour, its rainy
fringes, its changing forms and aspects ? I would not have
a man look upon the Heavens in a purely paint-pot spirit. I
would not have him consider every sky as merely so much
Naples yellow, crimson lake, and cobalt blue, with flake-white
clouds spattered over it by a dexterous movement of the
palette-knife ; but I would have him bring an artist's eye and
an artist's mind to the Heavens above. So shall his twenty
miles be one glorious National Gallery of art, and every
square plot of garden-ground a Salon Carré, and every group
of peasant children a Glyptothek.

There are many many twenty miles that have left green
memories to me, and that have built themselves obelisks surmounted by *immortelles* in the cemetery of my soul. Twenty
miles through the fat green flats of Belgium, enlivened by the
horn of the railway guard, the sour beer, the lowly pipe, the
totally incomprehensible, but no less humorous, Low Dutch
jokes of Flemish dames in lace caps and huge gold ear-rings,
and bloused farmers, and greasy curés. Twenty miles through
that heavenly garden, that delicious lake country of England,
in the purple shadow of the great crags and fells. Twenty
miles along the dusty roads of Picardy with the lum-

bering diligence, the loquacious *conducteur*, the swift-scudding beggars, the long, low stone cottages, the peasantry in red night-caps and *sabots*, singeing pigs iu the wide unhedged fields. Twenty miles along the trim English Queen's highway; on the box-seat of the Highflier coach, with the driver who knew so much about every gentleman's seat we passed, and had such prodigious stories to tell about horses present and past; with the comfortable prospect of the snug hotel and the comfortable dinner at our journey's end. Twenty miles through the Kentish hop-gardens and orchards radiant with their spring-snow of blossoms. Twenty miles through the grim black country round Wolverhampton, with its red furnaces glaring out from the darkness like angry eyes. Twenty miles in a certain omnibus hired for the day, in which there was much shouting, much laughing, much cracking of jokes, and munching of apples; in which there were twenty happy schoolboys going twenty miles to see the grand royal Castle of Windsor, and play cricket afterwards, in the royal park; in which there was a schoolmaster so smiling, so urbane, so full of merry saws and humourous instances, that his scholars quite forgot he had a cane at home; in which there was a bland usher, who had brought a white neckcloth and a pocket Horace with him for the sake of appearances, but who evidently longed to cut off the tails of his black coat, and be a boy immediately; in which there was one young gentleman who thought the twenty miles the happiest and most glorious he had ever journeyed, and began to write in his mind volume the first of a romance, strictly historical, of which he was the hero, Windsor Castle the scene, and all Miss Strickland's Queens of England the heroines.

Yes; and the twenty miles in that barouche of glory, drawn by four grey horses, with pink postboys, which dashed round Kennington Common about eleven in the forenoon on a certain Wednesday in May; the barouche that stopped so long at Cheam Gate, and had a hamper strapped behind it containing something else besides split peas and water; which coming home had so many satiric spirits and Churchills hitherto unknown to fame in it, and was so merry a barouche, so witty a barouche, not to say so inebriated a barouche. Ah me! the miles and the minutes have glided away together.

There dwells upon my mind a twenty miles journey that I once performed on foot—the dullest, most uninteresting, most uneventful twenty miles that ever pedestrian accomplished. It was a stupid walk indeed. There was literally "nothing in it;" so it is precisely for that reason (to bear out a crotchet I have) that I feel inclined to write a brief chronicle of the twenty miles I walked along the highroad from Lancaster to Preston.

When was it? Yesterday, last week, a dozen years ago? Never mind. For my purpose, let it be Now; put on your sparrow-bills; gird up your loins with the blue bird's-eye handkerchief, dear to pedestrians, and walk twenty miles with me.

It is a very threatening summer's morning. Not threatening rain or thunder; the glass and the experience of the last ten days laugh *that* idea to scorn. But the morning threatens nevertheless. It threatens a blazing hot day. General Phœbus has donned his vividest scarlet coat, his brightest golden epaulettes (epaulettes were worn when I walked twenty miles), his sheeniest sword, his hat with the red and white cocks' feathers. He is determined upon a field-day, and serves out redhot shot to his bombardiers. I leave the grey old legendary town of Lancaster, with its mighty castle, its crumbling church, its steep quaint streets. I |leave the tranquil valley of the Lune; the one timber-laden schooner, and row of dismantled warehouses which now represent the once considerable maritime trade of Lancaster (oh, city of the Mersey, erst the haunt of the longed-legged Liver, you have much to answer for!); I leave the rippling waters of Morecambe Bay, with its little pebbly watering-place of Poulton-le-Sands. I leave the blue shade of the mountains of Westmoreland and Cumberland; the memories of Peter Bell and his solitary donkey and the white doe of Rhylstone; the thousand beautiful spots in the loved district, sunlighted by the memories of learned Southey, and tuneful Wordsworth, and strong John Wilson, and gentle, docile, erring Hartley Coleridge (there is not a cottager from Lan-caster to Kendal, from Kendal to Windermere, but has stories to tell about "puir Hartley," affectionately recalling his simple face and ways); I leave all these to walk twenty miles to the town of spindles and smoke, bricks and cotton-bales. I can give but a woman's reason for this perverse walk. I *will* walk it.

There is a place called Scotforth, about two miles out, where I begin to fry. There is a place called Catterham (I think) two miles further, where I begin to broil. Then I begin to feel myself on fire. There is a place where there is a merciful shadow thrown by a high bank and hedge, and there, in defiance of all the laws of etiquette and the usages of society, I take off my coat and waistcoat, and walk

along with them thrown over my arm, as though I were a
tramp. I wonder what the few people I meet think of me,
for I am decently attired, and have positively an all-round
collar. How inexpressibly shocked that phaeton-full of Lan-
castrians that has just passed me (I have a strong idea that
I took tea with some of them last week) must be. What
can the burly farmer in the chaise-cart who pulls up and says
interrogatively, " teaaking a weauork ? " think. I wonder at
all this ; but much more do I wonder where the next beer-
oasis in this dusty desert. is.

I had fortified myself with a good breakfast, and a
" dobbin " of brown ale before I left Lancaster, and had
sternly said to myself, " no beer till Garstaing," which is
half way. But at the very cutset of my twenty miles, at
Scotforth, I was sorely tempted to turn aside (two roads
diverge there) towards the pleasant village of Cockerham, on
the road to which I know of a beery nook, where there is a
little woman, licensed to be drunk on the premises, in a tiny
house, of which the back-door opens into a green churchyard,
with tombstones hundreds of years old ; a little dame, who,
though a Catholic herself, has, in her little library on the
hanging shelf beside her missal and Thomas A'Kempis, a
copy of " Fuller's Worthies," and Barclay's " Apology for the
Quakers." Oh ! for a mug of brown beer at the sign of the
Travellers' Joy. Oh ! for the sanded floor, the long clean
pipe, the *Kendal Mercury* three weeks old, the " Worthies,"
the " Quakers ! " Beer and happiness ? Why not ? There
are times when a mug of ale, a pipe, and an old newspaper
may be the essence of mundane felicity. Get away, you
luxurious Persians. I hate your epicurean splendours ; and,

little boy, bind my brow with a simple hop-garland, and bring me some more beer.

I did not turn off towards Cockerham, however, because I was ashamed. When I am on fire, however, and my stomach so full of hot dust, I throw shame to the winds, and say to resolution, " get thee behind me." (I am always leaving that tiresome resolution behind.) In this strait I meet a tinker. He is black, but friendly. He is a humourist, as most tinkers are, and sells prayer-books besides tin-pots, which most tinkers do. Straightway he knows of the whereabouts of beer, and proposes a libation. I accept. More than this, he insists upon " standing a pot." Am I to insult this tinker by refusing to accept his proffered hospitality? No! He and I dive down a cunning lane, which none but a tinker could discover, and the foaming felicity is poured out to us. The tinker drinks first : I insist upon his drinking first. When he hands me the pot he points to the side of the vessel on which he has himself drunk, and suggests that I should apply my lips to the opposite side. " My mouth it may be sawdery," he says. Could Lord Chesterfield, in all his wiggishness and priggishness, have been politer than this? When we get into the high road again the tinker sings me a Cumberland song, in which there are about nineteen verses, and of which I can understand about four lines. I can only make out that " th' Deil's i' th' lasses o' Pearith " (probably Penrith), and that " Sukey, th' prood mantymecker, tu luik at a navvy thowt sin," which is gratifying to know, surveying the society of navvies (excellent persons as they may be in their operative way) from a genteel point of view. I am dimly given to understand, however, in a subsequent stanza, that the haughty Sukey so far changed her opinion of navvies as to elope with one; and while I ponder over this sad decadence, and instance of how the mighty are fallen, the tinker bids me good day and leaves me. He is a worthy man.

There is a lull just now in the heat. General Phœbus has sheathed his sword for the moment, and is refreshing himself in his golden tent. The sky is almost colourless; the trees are dark and ominous; broad gray-green shadows are cast across the landscape. Perhaps, it is going to rain. How glad I am that I have not got an umbrella! But the hope is fallacious. All at once the sudden sun darts out again, General Phœbus is on horseback giving the word to fire and reload, and I begin to fry again.

Five miles and a half to Garstaing. Four miles and a half to Garstaing—two—three—one mile to Garstaing. The milestones are obliging, and run on manfully before me. It is just one o'clock in the afternoon when I enter Garstaing itself; much to my own satisfaction, having attained my half-way house, and accomplished ten of my appointed twenty miles. I think I am entitled to bread and cheese at Garstaing, likewise to the pipe of peace, which I take on a gate leading into a field, solacing myself meanwhile with a view of a *pas-de-deux* between a young peasant woman in a jacket, and a lively mottled calf, which will not submit to be caught and bound with cords to the horns of a cart, on any terms; frisking, and dodging, and scampering about, either with an instinctive prescience of the existence of such a thing as roast fillet of veal with mild stuffing, or rioting in that ignorance of the possibility of the shambles which is bliss to butcher's meat. I find Garstaing a little market town—a big village rather, with many public-houses, and an amazing juvenile population. The children positively swarm; and, musing, I am compelled to dissent from the moralist who asserts that poor men are not fond of children. It is not only the rich Numenius who glories in multiplying his offspring; and though the days are gone when " a family could drive their herds, and set their children upon camels, and lead them till they saw a fat soil watered with rivers, and there sit them down without paying rent, till their own relations might swell up into a patriarchate, and their children be enough to possess all the regions that they saw, and their grandchildren become princes, and themselves build cities and call them by the name of a child and become the fountain of a nation; " —though these happy patriarchal days are fled, I can never find any disinclination among the veriest poor to have great families. Bread is hard to get, God knows; but the humble meal never seems scantier for a child the more or less. I have heard of men who thanked Heaven they had no children, and prayed that they might not have any; but I never knew one who so misused a prayer. Far more frequently have I met the father mourning and refusing to be comforted for the loss of one of his twelve children—though that twelfth were the youngest, and an idiot.

So, farewell Garstaing, and farewell temptation; for Garstaing, though small, though rural, though apparently innocent, has its temptations. It possesses a railway station; and when I have finished my pipe, the train bound for Preston has pulled up, and is ready to start again. I am sorely moved to abandon my twenty miles project, and take a second-class

ticket for the rest of the journey. But, self-shame (the strongest of all, for no man likes to look ridiculous in his own eyes),
comes to my aid. The day seems lowering somewhat, and
promises a cool afternoon, and I dismiss the locomotive as a
mere figment—a puffing, drinking, smoking, superficial, in-
consequential surface-skimmer, skurrying through the country
as though he were riding a race, or running away from a
bailiff, or travelling for a house in the cotton trade.

I walk resolutely on my journey from Garstaing : the milestones altering their tone now, and announcing so many miles
and a half to Preston. The treacherous sun which has been
playing a game of hide-and-seek with me all day, comes out
again with a redoubled fury, and burns me to a white heat.
Worse than this, I am between two long stages of beer, and
a rustic, in a wide-awake hat, informs me that the next house
of entertainment is at Cabus, "a bad fower mile fadder an."
Worse than all, there is no cottage, farm-house, lodge-gate,
to be seen where I can obtain a drink of water. I am
parched, swollen, carbonised. A little girl passes me with
an empty tin can in which she has carried her father's beer
with his dinner to the hay-field. The vacuity of the vessel
drives me to frenzy. My nature abhors such a vacuum.
There are certainly pools where geese are gabbling, rivulets
whither come the thirsty cows to drink, ditches where the
lonely donkey washes down his meal of thistle. But I have
no cup, waterproof cap, not even an egg-shell, in which I
could scoop out water enough for a draught. I have broken
my pipe, and cannot, even if I would, drink out of its bowl.
l am ashamed of using my boot as a goblet. I might, it is
true, lie down by the side of a ditch, and drink like a beast

of the field ; but I have no fancy for eating, while I drink, of
the toad, the tadpole, the water-newt, the swimming-frog,
the old rat, the ditch dog, and the green mantle of the standing pool.   Poor Tom could do no more than that, who was
whipped from tything to tything, and whose food for seven
long years was " mice, and rats, and such small deer."

I lean over a bridge, beneath which ripples a little river.
The channel is partially dry, but a clear, sparkling little
stream, hurries along over the pebbles most provokingly.   I
groan in bitterness of spirit as I see this tantalising river, and
am about descending to its level, and making a desperate
attempt to drink out of the hollow of my hands, at the risk
of ruining my all-round collar, when, in my extremity on the
river's bank, I descry Pot.   Pot is of common red earthen-
ware—broken, decayed, full of dried mud and sand—but I
hail Pot as my friend, as my deliverer.   I descend.   I very
nearly break my shins over a log of timber.   I incur the peril
of being indicted for poaching or trespassing in a fishing preserve.   I seize Pot.   Broken as he is, there is enough con-
vexity in him to hold half-a-pint of water.   I carefully clean
out his incrustation of dried mud.   I wipe him, polish him
tenderly, as though I loved him.   And then, oh, all ye water
gods, I Drink!   How often, how deeply, I know not; but I
drink till I remember that the water swells a man, and that
I should be a pretty sight if I were swelled ; whereupon with
a sigh I resign Pot, give him an extra polish, place him in a
conspicuous spot for the benefit of some future thirsty wayfarer, and leave him, invoking a blessing upon his broken
head.   This done, I resume my way rejoicing.   I catch up
the milestones that were getting on ahead, and just as the

cool of the afternoon begins, I am at my journey's end. I have walked my twenty miles, and am ready for the juicy steak, the cool tankard, the long deep sleep, and the welcome railway back to Lancaster.

I beg to state that from Lancaster, whence I started at nine A.M., to Preston, where I arrive about five P.M., in this long, hot walk of twenty miles, I see no castle, tower, gentleman's mansion, pretty cottage, bosky thicket, or cascade. The whole walk is eminently common-place. A high road, common hedges, common fields, common cows and sheep, common people and children—these are all I have seen. The whole affair is as insipid as cold boiled veal. How many insipid things there are! A primrose by the river's brim was a yellow primrose to Peter Bell, and it was nothing more; but take the primrose, the cold boiled veal, even my tiresome walk of twenty miles, in an artistic light, and something may be gained from each.

XIX.

LITTLE SAINT ZITA—A CULINARY LEGEND.

THERE is a collection of horrible, though admirably executed, etchings, by the "noble Jacques Callot," extant called " Images des Martyrs, Les Saincts et Sainctes de l'Année." It is a complete pictorial calendar of the Romish martyrology. No amount of indigestion, caused by suppers of underdone pork-chops; no nightmares, piled one on another; no distempered imaginings of topers in the worst state of delirium tremens; no visions of men with guilt-laden consciences—could culminate into a tenth part of the horrors that the noble Jacques has perpetuated with his immortal graver. All the refinements of torture, invented by the ruthless and cruel pagans, and inflicted by them on the early confessors, are here set down in minute detail; not a dislocate dlimb is omitted, not a lacerated muscle is passed over. The whole work is a vast dissecting-room—a compendium of scarifications, maimings, and dismemberments—of red-hot pincers, scalding oil, molten lead, gridirons, wire scourges, jagged knives, crowns of spikes, hatchets, poisoned daggers, tarred shirts, and wild beasts.

The blessed saints had a bad time of it for certain. How

should we, I wonder, with our pluralities, our Easter-offerings, and *regium donum*, our scarlet hats and stockings, and dwellings in the gate of Flam ; our Exeter Hall meetings and buttered muffins afterwards ; our first-class missionary passages to the South Seas, and grants of land and fat hogs from King Wabashongo ; our dean and chapter dinners, and semi-military chaplains' uniforms (Oh, last-invented, but not least scorn-worthy of humbugs !) ; how should we confront the stake, the shambles, and the executioner, the scourge, the rack, and the amphitheatre ? Surely the Faith must have been strong, or the legends untrue !

Yet there are more saints than the noble Jacques ever dreamed of in his grim category, crowded as it is. Saint Patrick, if we may credit the Irish legend, had two birthdays ; still, the number of saints, all duly canonised, is so great, that the year can scarcely spare them the sixth of a birthday apiece. Only yesterday, the postman (he is a Parisian postman, and, in appearance, is something between a policeman and a field-marshal in disguise) brought me a deformed little card, on which was pasted an almanac with a whole calendar-full of saints, neatly tied up with cherry-coloured riband, accompanying the gift with the compliments of the season, and an ardent wish that the new year might prove *bonne et belle* to me ; all of which meant that I should give him two francs, on pain of being denounced to the door-porter as a curmudgeon, to the landlord as a penniless lodger, and to the police as a suspicious character. Musing over the little almanac, in the futile attempt to get two francs' worth of information out of it, I found a whole army of saints, of whom I had never heard before, and noticed the absence of a great many who are duly set down in another calendar I possess. Would you believe that neither Saint Giles nor Saint Swithin was to be found in my postman's hagiology— that no mention was made of Saint Waldeburga, or of the blessed Saint Wuthelstan; while on the other hand I found Saint You, Saint Fiacre, Saint Ovid, Saint Babylas, Saint Pepin, Saint Ponce, Saint Frisque, Saint Nestor, and Saint Pantaloon? What do we know of these saints in England? Where were Saint Willibald, Saint Winifred, Saint Edward the Confessor, and Saint Dunstan, the nose-tweaker? No- where! Yet they must all have their days, their eves, and morrows. Where, above all, was my little Saint Zita?

If one of the best of Christian gentlemen—the kindly humourist, who wrote the Ingoldsby Legends—could tell us, without scandal to his cloth or creed, the wondrous stories of Saint Gengulphus and Saint Odille, Saint Anthony and Saint Nicholas, shall I be accused of irreverence, if, in my own way, I tell the legend of little Saint Zita? I must premise that the first discovery of the saintly tradition is due to M. Alphonse Karr, who has a villa at Genoa, the birth-place of the Saint herself.

I have no memory for dates, and no printed informa- tion to go upon, so I am unable to state the exact year, or even century, in which Saint Zita flourished. But I know that it was in the dark ages, and that the Christian religion was young, and that it was considerably more than one thousand five hundred years ago.

Now, Pomponius Cotta (I give him that name because it is a sounding one—not that I know his real denomination) was a noble Roman. He was one of the actors in that drama

which Mr. Gibbon of London and Lausanne so elegantly described some centuries afterwards : "The Decline and Fall of the
Roman Empire." It must have been a strange time, that
Decline and Fall. Reflecting upon the gigantic, overgrown,
diseased civilisation of the wonderful empire, surrounded and
preyed upon by savage and barbarous Goths and Visigoths,
Vandals, Dacians, and Pannonians, I cannot help picturing to
myself some superannuated old noble, accomplished, luxurious,
diseased, and depraved—learned in *bon-mots* and scandalous
histories of a former age, uselessly wealthy, corruptly culti-
vated, obsoletely magnificent, full of memories of a splendid
but infamous life, too old to reform, too callous to repent, cyni-
cally presaging a deluge after him, yet trembling lest that
deluge should come while he was yet upon the stage, and
wash his death-bed with bitter waters; who is the sport and
mock, the unwilling companion and victim unable to help
himself, of a throng of rough, brutal, unpolished youngsters
—hobbedehoys of the new generation—who carouse at his
expense, smoke tobacco under his nose, borrow his money,
slap him on the back, and call him old fogey behind it, sneer
at his worn out stories, tread on his gouty toes, ridicule his
old-fashioned politeness, and tie crackers to the back of his
coat collar. Have you not seen the decline and fall of the
human empire?

But Pomponius Cotta never recked, it is very probable, of
such things. He might have occasionally expressed his belief,
like some noble Romans of our own age and empire, that the
country was going to the bad; but he had large revenues,
which he spent in a right noble and Roman manner; and he
laid whatever ugly misgivings he had in a red sea of Falernian

and Chiajian (if, indeed, all the stock of those celebrated vintages had not already been drunk out by the thirsty Visigoths and Vandals). He had the finest house in Genoa; and you who know what glorious palaces the city of the Dorias and the Spinolas can yet boast of, even in these degenerate days, may form an idea of what marvels of marble, statuary, frescos, and mosaics owned Pomponius Cotta for lord, in the days when there was yet a Parthenon at Athens, and a Capitol at Rome.

The noble Pomponius was a Christian, but I am afraid only in a very slovenly, lukewarm, semi-pagan sort of way. As there are yet in France some shrivelled old good-for-nothings whose sympathies are with Voltaire and d'Alembert—who sigh for the days of the Encyclopedia, the Esprits-forts, and the Baron d'Holbach's witty, wicked suppers, so Pomponius furtively regretted the old bad era before creation heard the voice that cried out that the god Pan was dead*—the days when there were mysteries and oracles, sacrifices and *Lares*, and *Penates*, and when laziness and lust, dishonesty, and superstition, were reduced into systems, and dignified with the name of philosophy. So Pomponius half believed in the five thousand gods he had lost, and was but a skin-deep worshipper of the One left. As for his wife, the Domina Flavia Pomponia, she came of far too noble a Roman family, was far too great a lady, thought far too much of crimping her tresses, perfuming her dress, painting her face, giving

---

* This is one of the earliest traditions of the Christian era : that at midnight on the first Christmas-Eve a great voice was heard all over the world, crying, "The God Pan is dead." Milton bursts into colossal melody on this key-note in his magnificent Christmas hymn. See also a learned lyric by the late Mrs. Browning.

grand entertainments, and worrying her slaves, to devote herself to piety and the practice of religion; and though Onesimus, that blessed though somewhat unclean hermit, did often come to the Pomponian house and take its mistress roundly to task for her mundane mode of life, she only laughed at the good man; quizzed his hair, shirt, and long thickly-peopled beard; and endeavoured to seduce him from his recluse fare of roots and herbs and spring-water, by pressing invitations to partake of dainty meals and draughts of hot wine.

I am not so uncharitable as to assume that all the seven deadly sins found refuge in the mansion of Pomponious Cotta, but it is certain that it was a very fortalice and citadel for one of them—namely gluttony. There never were such noble Romans (out of Guildhall) as the Pomponii for guzzling and guttling, banqueting, junketing, feasting, and carousing. It was well that plate glass was not invented in those times, for the house was turned out of windows regularly every day, and the major part of the Pomponian revenues would have been expended in glaziers' bills. But there were dinners, and suppers, and after-suppers. The guests ate till they couldn't move, and drank till they couldn't see. Of course they crowned themselves with flowers, and lolled upon soft couches, and had little boys to titillate their noses with rare perfumes, and pledged each other to the sounds of dulcet music; but they were an emerited set of gormandisers for all that, and richly deserved the visitation of the stern Nemesis that sate ever in the gate in the shape of the fair-haired barbarian, with the brand to burn, the sword to slay, and the hands to pillage. Or, like the Philistine lords, they caroused and made merry, unwotting of that stern, moody, blind Samson, sitting apart, yonder, with his hair all a-growing, and soon to arise in his might and pull the house down on their gluttonous heads. Or, like Belshazzer's feasters, they were drunk in vessels of gold and silver, while the fingers of a man's hand were writing on the wall, and the Medes and Persians were at the gate.

It may easily be imagined that in such a belly-god temple—such a house of feasting and wassail—the cook was a personage of great power and importance. Pomponius Cotta had simply the best cook not only in Genoa, but in Magna Græcia—not only in Magna Græcia, but in the whole Italian peninsula. But no man-cook had he—no haughty, stately, *magister coquinæ*, no pedant in Apicius, or bigoted believer in Lucullus. Yet Pomponius was proud and happy in the possession of a culinary treasure—a real *cordon-bleu*, a Mrs. Glasse of the dark ages, a Miss Acton of antiquity, a Mrs. Rundell of Romanity; and this was no other than a little slave girl whom they called Zita.

We have all heard of the cook who boasted that he could serve up a leathern shoe in twenty-seven different phases of sauce and cookery. I never believed in him, and always set him down as a vapouring fanfaroon—a sort of copper-stew-pan captain of cookery. But I have a firm belief that little Zita would have made everything out of anything or nothing culinary; that her stewed pump-handles would have been delicious, her *salmi* of bath-brick exquisite, her *croquettes* of Witney blanket unapproachable, her horsehair *en papillotes* a dish fit for a king. She cooked such irresistible dishes for the noble Pomponius that he frequently wept, and would have given her her freedom had he not been afraid that she would be off and be married : that the noble Domina Pomponia was jealous of her, and that she would have led a sorry life, had the Domina dared to cross her husband; that the guests of the Pomponian house wrote bad sapphics and dactylics in her praise, and would have given her necklaces of pearl and armlets of gold for gifts, but that the Roman finances were in rather an embarrassed condition just then, and that poor trust was dead with the Genoese jewellers.

Little Zita was very pretty; she must have been pretty— and she was. She was as symmetrical as one of Pradier's Bacchantes—as ripe and blooming as the grapes they press; but as pure as the alabaster of which they are made. Her complexion was as delicately, softly tinted as one of Mr. Gibson's Græco-Roman statues; her long hair, when she released it from its confining fillet, hung down about her like a king's mantle; she had wrists and ankles that only gold or gems were worthy to embrace : she had a mouth like a Cupid's bow, and eyes like almonds dyed in ebony; and teeth that were gates of ivory to the dreams of love, and nails like mother of pearl. She danced like Arbuscula, and sang like Galeria Coppiola; and she cooked, like an angel—as she Is.

None could serve up in such style the great standard dishes of Roman cookery. The wild boar of Troy, with honey, oil, flour and *garum ;* the Campanian sow fed from golden troughs, stuffed with chesnuts and spices, and brought to table whole with her nine little sucking pigs disposed around her in sweet sauce; the *vol-au-vents* of peacocks' tongues, and ortolans' eyes, and nightingales' brains.

Yet, though great in these, she excelled in fanciful, ravishing, gem-like dishes—in what the French call *surprises*— in culinary epigrams, edible enigmas, savoury fables, poems that you could eat and drink. She had sauces, the secrets of which have gone to Paradise with her; she had feats of legerdemain in compounding dishes that no life-long apprenticeship could teach. And, withal, she was so saving, so economical, so cleanly in her arrangements, that her kitchen was like a street in the clean village of Brock (I should not like to pass half an hour even in Véfour's kitchen); and her noble master had the satisfaction of knowing that he gave the mightiest "spreads" in Genoa at anything but an unreasonable or ruinous expense.

She was as honest as a child's smile, and quite regardless of kitchen stuff, perquisites, Christmas boxes from tradesmen; and the dangerous old crones who hang about the area and cried hare-skins, as your own cook, madam, I hope may be. And, above all, little Zita had no followers, had boxed the major-domo's ears for offering her a pair of filligree earrings, and was exceeding pious.

Now, a pious cook is not considered, in these sceptical days, as a very great desideratum. A pious cook not unfrequently refuses to cook a Sunday's dinner, and entertains a non-serious grenadier on Sunday evening. I have seen many a kitchen drawer in which the presence of a hymn-book, and the "Cook's Spiritual Comforter" (price ninepence per hundred for distribution) did not exclude the company of much surreptitious cold fat and sundry legs of fowls that were not picked clean. Serious cooks occasionally wear their mistresses' black silk stockings to go to chapel in; my aunt had a serious cook who drank; and there is a legend in our family of a peculiarly evangelical cook who could not keep her hands off other people's pomatum. But little Zita was sincerely, unfeignedly, cheerfully, devotedly pious. She did not neglect her duties to pray: she rose up early in the morning before the cock crew, while her masters were sunk in drunken sleep, and prayed for herself and for them, and then went to her daily labour with vigorous heart of grace. There are some of us who pray, as grudgingly performing a certain duty, and doing it, but no more—some of us as an example (and what an example!) to others—some through mere habit (and those are in a bad case)—some (who shall gainsay it!) in hypocrisy; but do we not all, Scribes and Pharisees, Publicans and Sinners, number among our friends, among those we know, some few good really pious souls who strike us with a sort of awe and reverent respect; who do their good deeds before we rise, or after we retire to rest; creep into heaven the back way, but are not the less received there with trumpets and crowns of glory?

Such was little Saint Zita. She was, I have said, truly pious. In an age when there was as yet but one Ritual, before dissent and "drums ecclesiastic" existed, Zita thought it her bounden duty to abide by and keep all the fasts and festivals of the church as ordained by the bishops, priests, and deacons. For she was not book-learned, this poor little cook-maid, and had but these three watchwords for her rule of conduct—Faith, Duty, and Obedience.

It is in the legend that she would decoy the little white-haired, blue-eyed children of the barbarian soldiers into her kitchen, and there, while giving them sweetmeats and other goodies, teach them to lisp little Latin prayers, and tell over the rosary, and kiss the crucifix appended to it. She bestowed the major part of her wages in gifts to beggars, unmindful whether they were christian or pagan ; and, for a certainty, the strong-minded would have sneered at her, and the wearers of phylacteries would have frowned on her, for she thought it a grave sin to disobey the edict of the church that forbade the eating of flesh on Friday and other appointed fasts. Pomponius Cotta, it must be acknowledged, was troubled with no such scruples. He would have rated his cook soundly, and perchance scourged her, if she had served him up meagre fare on the sixth day of the week ; yet I find it in the legend that little Zita was enabled by her own skill, and, doubtless, by celestial assistance, to perpetrate a pious fraud upon this epicurean Roman. The Fridays' dinners were as rich and succulent, and called forth as loud an encomium as those of the other days, yet not one scrap of meat, one drop of carnal gravy, did Zita employ in the concoction thereof. Fish, and eggs, and divers mushrooms, truffles and catsups, became, in the hands of the saintly cook, susceptible of giving the most meaty flavours. 'Tis said that Zita invented burnt onions—those grand culinary deceptions ! And though they were in reality making meagre, as good Christians should do, Pomponius and his boon companions thought they were feasting upon venison and poultry and choice roasts. This is one of the secrets that died with Saint Zita. I never tasted sorrel pottage that had even the suspicion of a flavour of meat about it ; and though I have heard much of the rice fritters and savoury soups of the Lancashire vegetarians, I doubt much of their ability to conceal the taste of the domestic cabbage and the homely onion.

Now it fell out in the year—which, by the by, has un-luckily escaped me—that P. Maremnius Citronius Ostendius, a great gastronome and connoisseur in oysters, came from Asia to visit his kinsman Pomponius. There was some talk of his marrying the beautiful Flavia Pomponilia, the eldest daughter of the Pomponian house (she was as jealous of Zita as Fleur de Lys was of Esmeralda, and would have thrust golden pins into her, *à-la-mode Romaine*, but for fear of her father); but at all events Ostendius was come down from Asia to Genoa, and there was to be a great feast in honour of his arrival. Ostendius had an aldermanic abdomen under his toga, had a voice that reminded you of fruity port, bees-wings in his eyes, a face very like collared brawn, and wore a wig. Those adjuncts to beauty were worn, ladies and gentlemen, fifteen hundred years ago. Ay! look in at the Egyptian Room of the British Museum, London, and you shall find wigs older than that. He had come from Asia, where he was reported to have partaken of strange dishes —birds of paradise, gryphons, phœnixes, serpents, ele-phants—but he despised not the Persicos' apparatus, and was not a man to be trifled with in his victuals! Pom-ponius·Cotta called his cook into his sanctum, and gave her instructions as to the banquet, significantly telling her what she might expect if she failed in satisfying him and his gas-tronomical guests. Poor Zita felt a cold shudder as she listened to the threats which, in lazy Latin, her noble master lavished upon her. But she determined, less through fear of punishment than a sincere desire of doing her duty, to exert

herself to the very utmost in the preparation of the feast.
Perhaps there may have been a little spice of vanity in this
determination; perhaps she was actuated by a little harmless
desire to please the difficult Ostendius, and so prove to him
that Pomponius Cotta had a slave who was the best cook in
Genoa and in Italy. Why not? I am one who, believing
that all is vanity, think that the world as it is could not
well get on without some vanity. By which I mean an
honest moderate love of and pleasure in approbation. I think
we could much easier dispense with money than with this.
When I see a conceited man, I think him to be a fool; but
when I meet a man who tells me he does not rejoice when
he is praised for the good book he has written, or the good
picture he has painted, or the good deed he has done, I know
him to be a humbug, and a mighty dangerous one to his
fellow-creatures.

Flowers, waxen torches, perfumes, rich tapestries, cunning
musicians—all were ordered for the feast to the guest who
was come from Asia. The *piscator* brought fish in abun-
dance; the *lignarius* brought wood and charcoal to light the
cooking furnaces withal; the *venator* brought game and
venison; the *sartor* stitched unceasingly at vestments of
purple and fine linen; the slaves who fed ordinarily upon
salsamentum or salt meat revelled in blithe thoughts of the
rich fragments that would fall to their share on the morrow
of the banquet. It need scarcely be said that Zita the cook
had a whole army of cook's mates, scullions, marmitons,
plate-scrapers, and bottle-washers, under her command.
These peeled the vegetables, these jointed the meat, these
strained the soups and jellies; but to none did she ever con-

fide the real cooking of the dinner. Her spoon was in every *casserole*, her spatula in every sauceboat ; she knew the exact number of mushrooms to every *gratin*, and of truffles to every turkey. Believe me—in the works of great artists there is little vicarious handiwork. Asses say that Mr. Stanfield painted the scenery of Acis and Galatea by means of a speaking-trumpet from the shilling gallery, his assistants working on the stage. Asses say that Carême used to compose his dinners reclining on a crimson velvet couch, while his nephew mixed the magic ingredients in silver stewpans. Asses say that all the hammering and chiselling of Praxiteles' statues were done by workmen, and that the sculptor only polished up the noses and finger tips with a little marble dust. Don't believe such tales. In all great works the master-hand is everywhere.

On the morning of the banquet, early, Zita went to market, and sent home stores of provisions, which her assistants knew well how to advance through their preparatory stages. Then, knowing that she had plenty of time before her, the pious little cook—though she had already attended matins— went to church to have a good pray. In the simplicity of her heart, she thought she would render up special thanks for all the good dinners she had cooked, and pray as specially that this evening's repast should be the very best and most succulent she might ever prepare. You see she was but a poor, ignorant, little slave-girl, and lived in the dark ages.

Zita went to church, heard high mass, confessed, and then, going into a little dark chapel by herself, fell down on her knees before the shrine of Her whom she believed to be the Queen of Heaven. She prayed, and prayed, and prayed so long, so earnestly, so devoutly, that she quite forgot how swiftly the hours fleet by, how impossible it is to overtake them. She prayed and prayed till she lost all consciousness and memory of earthly things, of earthly ties and duties :—till the vaulted roof seemed to open ; till she seemed to see, through a golden network, a sky of lapis-lazuli all peopled with angelic beings in robes of dazzling white ; till she heard soft sounds of music such as could only proceed from harps played by celestial hands ; till the statue of the Queen of Heaven seemed to smile upon her and bless her ; till she was no longer a cook and a slave, but an ecstatic in communion with the saints.

She prayed till the mortal sky without, from the glare of noonday took soberer hues ; till the western horizon began to blush for Zita's tardiness ; till the great blue Mediterranean sea grew purple, save where the sunset smote it ; till the white palaces of Genoa were tinged with pink, as if the sky had rained roses. She prayed till the lazy dogs which had been basking in the sun rose and shook themselves and raised their shiftless eyes as if to wonder where the sun was ; till the barbarian soldiers, who had been lounging on guard-house benches, staggered inside, and fell to dicing and drinking ; till hired assassins woke up on their straw pallets, and, rubbing their villanous eyes, began to think that it was pretty nearly time to go a murdering ; till cut-purses' fingers began to itch premonitorily ; till maidens watched the early moon, and longed for it to be sole sovereign of the heavens, that the trysting-time might arrive ; till the young spendthrift rejoiced that another day was to come, and the old sage sighed that another day was gone ; till sick men quarrelled with their nurses for closing their casements, and the birds grew drowsy, and the flowers shut themselves up in secresy, and the frog began to speak to his neighbour, and the glow-worm kindled his lamp.

She prayed till it was dusk, and almost dark, till the vesper bell began to ring, when she awoke from out her trance; and not a dish of the dinner was cooked!

And she hurried home, weeping, ah! so bitterly. For Zita knew her duty towards her neighbour as the road towards Heaven. She knew that there were times for all things, and that she had prayed too much and too long. Punishment she did not so much dread as the reproaches of her own conscience for the neglect of her duty. At length, faltering and stumbling in the momentarily increasing darkness, she reached the Pomponian house, which was all lighted up from top to bottom. "Ah!" thought she, "the major domo has, at least, attended to his business." She hurried into a small side court-yard where the kitchen was, and there she found all her army of assistants: the cook's mates, the scullions, the marmitons, the plate-scrapers, and the bottle-washers, all fast asleep, with their ladles, their knives, and their spits on benches and doorsteps, and in corners. "Ah!" cried little Zita, wringing her hands; "waiting for me, and quite worn out with fatigue!" Then, stepping among them without awakening them, she approached the great folding-doors of the kitchen, and tried the handle; but the doors were locked, and through the keyholes and hinges, the chinks and crannies of the portal, there came a rich, powerful, subtle odour, as of the best dinner that ever was cooked. She thought she understood it all. Enraged at her absence, her master had sent for Maravilla, the corpulent female cook of Septimus Pylorus, his neighbour, to prepare the dinner, or, perhaps, the great P. Maremnius Citronius Ostendius had himself condescended to assume the cook's cap and apron, and was at that moment engaged within, with locked doors, in blasting her professional reputation for ever. She was ruined as a cook, a servant—a poor little fatherless girl, with nought but her virtue and her cookery for a dower. Unhappy little Zita !

She ran back, through the court-yard to the great banquetting saloon, and there, lo ! she found the table decked, and the soft couches ranged, the flowers festooned, the rich tapestries hanging, and the perfumes burning in golden censers. And there, too, she found the proud Domina Pomponia, in gala raiment, who greeted her with a smile of unwonted benevolence, saying :

" Now, Zita, the guests are quite ready for the banquet ; and I am sure, from the odour which we can smell even here, that it will be the very best dinner that ever was cooked."

Then came from an inner chamber the fruity Falernian voice of Ostendius, crying,

" Ay, ay, I am sure it will be the very best dinner that ever was cooked ;" and the voice of Pomponius Cotta answered him gaily, that " Little Zita was not the best cook in Genoa for nothing," and that he would not part with her for I don't know how many thousand sesterces. Poor Zita saw in this only a cruel jest. For certain another cook had been engaged in her place, and she herself would be had up after the banquet, taunted with its success, confronted

with her rival, and perhaps scourged to death amid the
clatter of drinking-cups. Her eyes blinded with tears, she
descended again to the court-yard, and fervently, though
despairingly, breathed one more brief prayer to our Lady of
the Chapel. She had scarcely concluded, when the great
folding-doors of the kitchen flew open, and there issued forth
a tremendous cloud of ambrosial vapour, radiant, golden,
roseate, azure, in which celestial odours were mingled with
the unmistakeable smell of the very best dinner that ever
was cooked. And lo! hovering in the cloud, the rapt eye
of little Saint Zita seemed to descry myriads of little airy
figures in white caps and jackets, even like unto cooks, but
who all had wings and little golden knives at their girdles.
And she heard the same soft music that had stolen upon her
ears in the chapel; and as the angelic cooks fluttered out of
the kitchen, it seemed as though each little celestial Soyer
saluted the blushing cheek of the trembling maiden with a
soft and soothing kiss.

At the same time the army of earthly cook's assistants
awoke as one scullion, and without so much as yawning, took
their places at the dresser-board, and composedly began to
dish the dinner. And little Zita hurrying from furnace to
furnace, and lifting up the lids of *casseroles* and *bain-marie*
pans, found, done to a turn, a dinner even such as she with
all her culinary genius would never have dreamt of.

Of course it was a Miracle. Of course it was the very
best dinner ever dressed: what else could it have been with
such cooks? They talk of it to this day in Genoa; though
I am sorry to say the Genoese cooks have not profited by the
example, and do not seek to emulate it. They have the

best maccaroni, and dress it in worse fashion than any other people in Europe.

The legend ought properly to end with a relation of how Pomponius Cotta gave his little cook her freedom, how the guests loaded her with presents, and how she married the major domo, and was the happy mother of many good cooks and notable housewives. But the grim old monkish tradition has it, that little Zita died a Virgin, and, alas, a Martyr! But she was canonised after her death; and even as St. Crispin looks after the interests of Coblers, and St. Barbe has taken Bombadiers under his special patronage, so the patroness of Cooks has ever since been little Saint Zita.

XX.

O F primary causes or primary colours, I am neither philosopher nor optician enough to be enabled profitably to
discourse. Yet there are primaries—first things—in all our
lives very curious and wonderful, replete with matter for
speculation, interesting because they come home to and can
be understood by us all.

That it is "*le premier pas qui coûte*"—that the first step
is the great point—is as much a household word to us, and is
as familiar to our mouths as that the descent of Avernus is
unaccompanied by difficulty, or that one member of the
feathered creation held in the hand is worth two of the same
species in the bush. And, if I might be permitted to add to
the first quoted morsel of proverbial philosophy a humble
little rider of my own, I would say that we *never* forget the
first step, the first ascent, the first stumble, the first fall.
Time skins over the wound of later years, and, looking at the
cicatrice (if, indeed, a scar should remain), we even wonder
who inflicted the wound, where or how, or when it was
inflicted, and when and where healed. But the first-born
of our wounds are yet green, and we can see the glittering

glaive, and feel the touch of the steel, now that our hair is grizzled, and our friends and enemies are dead, and we have other allies and foes who were babies in the old time when we got that hurt.

Many men have as many minds, but we are all alike in this respect. The camera may be costly rosewood or plain deal, the lens of rare pebble or simple bottle glass, but the first impressions come equally through the focus, and are photographed with equal force on the silver tablet or collodionized papyrus of memory. The duke and the dustman, the countess and the costermonger, the schoolboy and the whiteheaded patriarch—for all the dreary seas that flow between the to-day they live in, and the yesterday wherein they began life—still, like the cliffs in Cristabel, bear the "mark of that which once hath been."

Many primaries are locked up in the secret cabinets of the mind, of which we have mislaid (and think we have lost) the keys ; but we have not; and, from time to time, finding them in bunches in old coat pockets, or on disregarded split rings, we open them. From the old desk of the mind we take the first love letter, of which the ink is so yellow now, and was so brilliant once, but whose characters are as distinct as ever. From the old wardrobe of the mind we draw the first tail-coat—threadbare, musty, and worm-eaten, now ; but the first tail-coat for all that. For all that we may have been twice bankrupt and once insolvent ; for all that Jack may have been transported, or Ned consigned to his coffin years ago, or Tom barbecued in Typee or Omoo regions ; for all that we may be riding in golden coaches, and denying that we ever trotted in the mud ; for all that we may have changed our names, or tacked titles to them, or given the hand that was once horny and labour-stained a neat coat of blood-red crimson, and nailed it on a shield, like a bat on a barn door; for all that we eat turtle instead of tripe, and drink Moselle instead of "max;" the primaries shall never be forgotten, the moment when our foot pressed the first step shall never vanish. Cast the stone as far into the river of Lethe as you will, the sluggish tide shall wash it back again, and, after playing duly with it on the sand, ever land it high and dry upon the beach.

Male primaries and female primaries there are, and I am of the ruder sex; but there are many common to both sexes.

Not this one though, the first—well there is no harm in it!—the first pair of trousers. Who does not remember, who can ever forget, those much desiderated, much prized, much feared, much admired, articles of dress? How stiff, angular, hard, wooden, they seemed to our youthful limbs! How readily, but for the proper pride and manliness we felt in them—the utter majority and independence of seven years of age—we would have cast them off fifty times the very first day we wore them, and, resuming the kilt, have once more roamed our little world a young Highlander! How (all is vanity!) we mounted on surreptitious chairs, viewed ourselves in mirrors, and, being discovered in the act by pretty cousins, blushed dreadfully, and were brought thereby to great grief and shame! What inexpressible delight in that first plunge of the hand (and half the arm) into the trousers pocket, in the first fingering of the silver sixpence deposited five fathoms deep, for luck! What bitter pain and humiliation we felt when, first strutting forth abroad in them, rude contumelious, boys mocked us, likened us to a pair of tongs, aimed at our legs with peg-tops ! What agonies we suffered from that wicked youth (he must have been hanged or transported in after years) who, with a nail—a rusty nail—tore the left leg of those trousers into a hideous rent, and then ran away laughing ! what tortures at the thought of what our parents and guardians would say ! Those premier pantaloons were snuff-coloured, buttoning over the trousers, and forming, with an extensive shirt frill, what was then called a "skeleton suit." They shone very much, and had a queer smell of the snuff-coloured dye. They gave the wearer something of a trussed appearance, like a young fowl ready for the spit. It was a dreadful fashion, as offering irresistible temptations to the schoolmaster to use his cane. You were got up ready for him, and abstinence was more than he could bear. We confess to a horrid relish in this wise ourselves at the present time. When we see (rare spectacle now-a-days) a small boy in a skeleton suit, and his hands in his pockets, our fingers itch to be at him !

The first picture book ! We date from the time of the Prince Regent, and remember picture books about dandies—satires upon that eminent personage himself, possibly—but *we* never knew it. In those days there was a certain bright, smooth, cover for picture books, like a glorified surgical plaister. It has gone out this long, long, time. The picture book that seems to have been our first, was about one Mr. Pillblister (in the medical profession, we presume, from the name), who gave a party. As the legend is impressed on our remembrance it opened thus :

"Mr. Pillblister, and Betsy, his sister,
　　Determined on giving a treat ;
　　Gay dandies they call,
　　To a supper and ball,
　　At their house in Great Camomile Street."

The pictures represented male dandies in every stage of preparation for this festival, holding on to bedposts to have their stays laced, embellishing themselves with artificial personal graces of many kinds, and enduring various humiliations in remote garrets. One gentleman found a hole in his stocking at the last moment.

"A hole in my stocking,
　　O how very shocking !
　　Says poor Mr. (Some one) enraged,
　　It's always my fate,
　　To be so very late,
　　When at Mr. Pillblister's engaged !"

If we recollect right, they all got there at last, and passed a delightful evening. When we first came to London (not the least of our primaries), we rejected the Tower, Westminster Abbey, St. Paul's, and the Monument, and entreated to be taken to Great Camomile Street.

About the same period we tasted our first oyster. A remarkable sensation ! We feel it slipping down our throats now, like a kind of maritime castor oil, and are again bewildered by an unsatisfactory doubt whether it *was* the oyster that made that mysterious disappearance, or whether we are going to begin to taste it presently.

The first play ! The promise, the hope deferred, the saving clause of "no fine weather no play," the more than Murphian scrutiny of the weather during the day ! Willingly did we submit, at five o'clock that evening, to the otherwise, and at any other time, detestable ordeal of washing and combing, and being made straight. We did not complain when the soap got into our eyes; we bore the scraping of the comb and the rasping of the brush without a murmur: we were going to the play, and we were happy. Dressed, of course, an hour too soon; drinking tea as a mere ceremony—for the tea might have been hay and hot water (not impossible), and the bread and butter might have been sawdust, for anything we could taste of it; sitting, with petful impatience, in the parlour, trying on the first pair of white kid gloves, making sure that the theatre would be burnt down, or that papa would never come home from the office, or mamma would be prevented, by some special interference of malignant demons, from having her dress fastened, or that (to a positive certainty) a tremendous storm of hail, rain, sleet, and thunder, would burst out, as we stepped into the fly, and send us, theatreless, to bed. We went to the play, and were happy. The sweet, dingy, shabby, little country theatre, we declared, and believed to be, much larger than either Drury Lane or Covent Garden, of which little Master Cheesewright—whose father was a tailor, and always had orders—was wont to brag. Dear narrow, uncomfortable, faded cushioned, flea haunted; single tier of boxes! The green curtain, with a hole in it, through which a bright eye peeped; the magnificent officers, in red and gold coats (it was a garrison town), in the stage box, who volunteered, during the acts, the popular catch of—

> " Ah, how, Sophia, can you leave
> Your lover, and of hope bereave ?"

—for our special amusement and delectation, as we thought

then, but, as we are inclined to fear now, under the influence of wine. The pit, with so few people in it; with the lady, who sold apples and oranges, sitting in a remote corner, like Pomona in the sulks. And the play when it did begin—stupid, badly acted, badly got up as it very likely was. Our intense, fear-stricken admiration of the heroine, when she let her back hair down, and went mad, in blue. The buff boots of Runt, the manager. The funny man (there never was such a funny man) in a red scratch wig, who, when imprisoned in the deepest dungeon beneath the castle moat, sang a comic song about a leg of mutton. The sorry quadrille band in the orchestra, to our ears as scientifically melodious as though Costa had been conductor; Sivori, first fiddle; Richardson, flute; or Bottesini, double bass. The refreshment, administered to us by kind hands during the intervals of performance, never to be forgotten—oranges, immemorial sponge-cakes. The admonitions to "sit up," the warnings not to "talk loud," in defiance of which (seeing condonatory smiles on the faces of those we loved) we screamed outright with laughter, when the funny man, in the after-piece, essaying to scale a first floor front by means of a rope ladder, fell, ladder and all, to the ground. The final fall of the green curtain, followed by an aromatic perfume of orange-peel and lamp-oil, and the mysterious appearance of ghostly brown Holland draperies from the private boxes. Shawling, cloaking, home, and more primaries—for then it was when we for the first time "sat up late," and for the first time ever tasted sandwiches after midnight, or imbibed a sip, a very small sip, of hot something and water.

Who can lay his hand upon his waistcoat pocket, and say

he has forgotten his first watch? Ours was a dumpy silver one, maker's name Snoole, of Chichester, number seventeen thousand three hundred and ten. Happy Snoole, to have made so many watches; yet we were happy—oh, how happy! to possess even one of them. We looked at that watch continually; we set it at every clock, and consulted it every five minutes; we opened and shut it, we wound it up, we regulated it, we made it do the moſt amazing things, and suddenly run a little chain off a wheel in a tearing manner—after which it stopped. How obliging we were to everybody who wished to know what o'clock it was! Did we ever go to bed without that watch snug under the pillow? Did not a lock of our sweetheart's hair have a sweet lurking place between the inner and outer cases? Where is that dumpy silver watch—where the more ambitious pinchbeck (there are no pinchbeck watches now) that followed? Where is the gold Geneva, the highly finished hunter, with compensation balance and jewelled in a thousand and one holes, from Benson of Ludgate Hill, the silver lever? How many watches have we bought, sold, swopped, and bartered, since then; and which of them do we remember half so well as the dumpy silver, maker's name Snoole, Chichester, seventeen thousand three hundred and ten!

And the first lock of a sweetheart's hair brings me to the primary of primaries—First love. We don't believe, we can't believe, the man who tells us he has never been in love, and can't remember with delicious, and yet melancholy distinctness, all about it. We don't care whether it was the little girl with plaited tails, in frilled trousers, and a pinafore (though we never truly loved another); or your schoolmaster's daughter, or the lady who attended to the linen department, whom we thought a Houri, but who was, probably, some forty years of age. You may have loved Fanny, Maria, Louisa, Sarah, Martha, Harriet, or Charlotte, or fancied that you loved them, since then; but in your heart of hearts you still keep the portrait of your first love, bright.

By first love, we mean what is commonly known as " calf love." Our reminiscences öf real first love are indissolubly connected with a disrelish for our victuals, and a wild desire to dress, regardless of expense ; of dismal wailings in secret; of a demoniacal hatred of all fathers, cousins, and brothers ; of hot summer days passed in green fields, staring at the birds on the boughs, and wishing—oh, how devoutly wishing !— that we were twenty-one years of age.

The first baby ! The doctor, the imperious nurse, the nervous walking up and down the parlour, the creaking stairs, the nurse again, imperious still, but now triumphant. The little stranger sparring like an infant Tom Cribb in long clothes. That baby's acts and deeds for months ! His extraordinary shrewdness, his unexampled beauty, his super-human capacity for " taking notice," his admirable Crich-tonian qualities. He *was* a baby ! Another and another little stranger have dropped in since then. Each was *a* baby, but not *the* baby !

We hope and trust you may never have had this primary we are about to speak of. But there *are* some persons of the male sex who may remember with sufficient minuteness the first time they ever got—elevated. If *you* do, the impression will never be eradicated from your mind. Competent persons have declared you, on several subsequent occasions, to have

been incapable of seeing a hole in a ladder. The earth seemed
to spin round in an inconsistent manner; the pavement was
soft—very soft—and felt, you said, as though you were walking
on clouds; until suddenly, without the slightest provocation,
it came up and smote you on the forehead. Of course, you
didn't fall down—that would have been ridiculous. Slan-
derers declared that you attempted to climb up the gutter,
under the impression that it was a lamp-post; and, being
dissuaded therefrom, vehemently endeavoured to play the harp
upon the area railings. How distinctly you remember to this
day how completely you forgot everything; how you dreamt
you were a water-jug with no water in it—Tantalus, Prome-
theus, Ixion, all rolled into one; how you awoke the next
morning without the slightest idea of how you got into bed;
how sick, sorry, and repentant you were!

Being in genteel society, we would not, of course, hint
that any one of our readers can remember so very low and
humiliating a thing as the first visit to "My Uncle"—the
first pawnbroker. We have been assured though, by those
whose necessities have sometimes compelled them to resort,
for assistance, to their avuncular relation, that the first visit
—the primary pawning — can never be forgotten. The
timorous, irresolute glance at the three golden balls; the
transparent hypocrisy of looking at the silver forks, watches
jewelled in an indefinite number of holes, china vases, and
Doyley and Mant's Family Bible ("to be sold, a bargain"),
in the window; the furtive, skulking slide round the corner,
to the door in the court where the golden balls are emblazoned again, with announcements of "Office," and "Money
Lent;" the mental perplexity as to which of the little cell

doors looks the most benevolent ; and the timorous horror of finding the selected one occupied by an embarrassed shoemaker raising money by debentures, on soleless Wellingtons and Bluchers. All these, we have been told, are memorable things.

Another primary—the first death. The tan spread on the street before the door ; its odour in the house ; the first burst of grief when all was over ; the strange instinctive way in which those who seemed to know nothing of Death went about its grim requirements. The one appalling never-to-be-forgotten undertaker's knock at nine in the evening. The steps on the stairs ; the horrible agility and ghostly quietness. Then, the gentle melancholy that succeeded to the first bitterness of sorrow.

XXI.

OLD CLOTHES.

A STERN legislature has laid its red, or rather blue, right hand, in the shape of police enactments, upon many of the Cries of London. No more may the portly dustman toll his bell, and with lusty lungs make quiet streets re-echo to the cry of "Dust-ho!" The young sweep's shrill announcement of his avocation is against the law; and the sweep himself—first mute, perforce—has now ceded his place to the Ramoneur voluntarily, and has vanished altogether. Of the Cries which the New Police Act has not included in its ban, many have come to disuse, and must be numbered now with old fashions and old-fashioned people. The Cries are dead, and the criers, too. The "small-coal-man," and the vender of saloop; the merchant who so loudly declared in his boyhood, that if he had as much money as he could tell, he would not cry young lambs to sell; the dealer in sweet-stuff, who sung in so fine a baritone voice, and with so unctuous an emphasis, the one unvarying refrain, "My brandy-balls! my brandy-balls! My slap-up, slap-up brandy-balls!" the seller of rotten-stone and emery, who, by way of rider to the announcement of his wares, added strong adjurations; the reduced gentlewoman, who cried, "cats' meat!" in so sub-- dued a tone (*she* flourished before my time, and I only regard her in a traditional light);—all these are gone. There was a work published towards the close of the last century, full of copperplate pictures of the various London street-sellers, with notices of their "Cries." Look through the book now, and you will find few that are not obsolete. We have grown luxurious, and cry, "Pine apples, a penny a slice!"—moral, and have superseded the tossing pieman, who cried, "Toss or buy! up and win 'em!" by a gaudy hot-pie "Depôt," with plate-glass window and mahogany fixtures. We have grown fastidious, and have deserted "'Taters, all hot!" for the Irish fruit warehouse." The voice of him who cried, "One a penny, two a penny, hot cross-buns!" is hushed, goodness help us! where are we going to? The cry of "kearots" and "sparrow-grass" will go next, I suppose; "cats'-meat" will no longer be allowed to be cried; "milk ho!" is doomed; the cries of "butcher!" and "baker!" will be rendered illegal, and contrary to the statute.

But as I write, floats on the ambient air, adown the quiet street in which I live, softly through the open window, gently to my pleased ears, a very familiar and welcome cry. I have always heard *that* cry, and always shall, I hope. It was cried in London streets years before I was born, and will be cried years after I am dead. It never varies, never diminishes in volume or sonorous melody, this cry; for, as the world wags, and they that dwell in it live and die, they must be clothed—and, amidst the wear and tear of life, their clothes become worn and torn, too;—so we shall always have Old Clothes to buy or sell; and for many a year, down many a quiet street, through many an open window, shall float that old familiar cry—"Old Clo'!"

My first recollections of Old Clo' are entwined with the remembrance of a threat, very awful and terrifying to me then, of being imprisoned in the bag of an old clothesman, and forthwith conveyed away. My threatener was a nurse-maid, who, if I remember right, left our service in conse-quence of the mysterious disappearance of a new silk dress, which she solemnly averred my mother to "have worn clean out;" and the clothesman was a dreadful old man, with a long, tangled, grey-reddish beard, a hawk nose, which, like the rebuke of the nautical damsel in Wapping Old Stairs, was never with-out a tear. This dreadful personage carried a bag of alarming size. I am not ashamed to say, now, that I perfectly believed this clothesman (a harmless Israelite, no doubt), to be capable of effecting my capture and abduction on the commission of any juvenile indiscretion whatsoever; and that he, and "the sweep,'" a mysterious phantom I was often menaced with, but never saw; a black dog, addicted to sitting on the shoulders of naughty children; and a "big black man," supposed to be resident in the back kitchen, whence he made periodical irruptions for the purpose of devouring insubordinate juve-niles, formed in their glomerate natures the incarnation, to my youthful mind, of a certain personage who shall be name-less, but who has been likened to a roaring lion.

Strangely enough, this old clothesman of mine (he was dreadfully old when I first knew him) doesn't seem to get any older, and cries "Clo'!" to this day with undiminished voice and bag. I am not afraid of him now, and have even held conversations with him touching the statistics and profits of his trade. But I dream about him frequently, and never look at that very large bag of his without a certain sort of awed and hushed curiosity. Very curious are early impressions in their ineffaceability. We can remember the father or the sister who died when we were babes, almost with minute distinctness; and yet forget what happened the day before yesterday. How well we can remember the history of Jack Horner, and the adventures of the other Jack, who rose in life through the instrumentality of a bean-stalk; and yet, how often we forget the matter of the first leader in the *Morning Bellower*, before we have got half through the second one!

The subject of left-off garments has always been an interesting one to me, for it is fertile in the homely-picturesque. Yet there are many mysteries connected with the old clothes question; which, though I have studied it somewhat profoundly, I am as yet unable to fathom. To what I do know, however, the reader is perfectly welcome to.

The statistics of ancient habiliments have already been fully and admirably touched upon, in " another place," as honourable Members say. The aspect of Rag Fair, Cloth Fair, Petticoat Lane, and Holywell Street, have, moreover, been described over and over again; so that my lay will be, perhaps, only an old song to a questionably new tune, after all. But there is nothing new under the sun to speak of, and to be entirely original would be, too, as out of the fashion, as it is out of my power to be so.

Imprimis, of old clothesmen. Why should the Hebrew race appear to possess a monopoly in the purchase and sale of dilapidated costume? Why should their voices, and theirs alone, be employed in the constant iteration of the talismanic monosyllables " Old Clo' ? " In Glasgow, they say, the Irish have commenced the clothes trade, and have absolutely pushed the Jew clothesmen from their stools. I can scarcely believe so astonishing an assertion. I could as soon imagine an Israelitish life-guardsman as an Hibernian old clothesman. I can't—can you—can anybody—realise the strident, guttural " Ogh Clo' " of the Hebrew, the *mot d'ordre*, the shibboleth, the password of the race, transposed into the mellifluous butter-milky notes of the sister isle?

My old clothesmen are all of the " people." Numerous are they, persevering, all-observant, astute, sagacious, voluble yet discreet, prudent and speculative. They avoid crowded main streets, and prefer shadier and quieter thoroughfares. These do they perambulate indefatigably at all seasons, in all weathers. Lives there the man who ever saw an old clothesman with an umbrella? I mean using it for the purpose an umbrella is generally put to. He may have, and very probably has, half-a-dozen in his bag, or somewhere about him, but never was he known to elevate one above his head.

I am sorry to gird at an established idea, but duty compels me to do so. Artists generally represent the old clothesman with three, and sometimes four, hats superposed one above the other. Now, though I have seen him with many hats in his hands or elsewhere, I never yet saw him with more than one hat on his head ; and I have been assured by a respectable member of the fraternity, with whom I lately transacted business, that the three-hat tradition has no foundation whatever ; in fact, that it is a mere device of the enemy, as shallow a libel as the ballad of "Hugh of Lincoln," or the assertion that Jews cannot expectorate, but must, *nolens volens*, slobber. The three-hatted clothesman, if he ever existed, is obsolete; but I incline to consider him a myth, an æsthetic pre-Raphaelite abstraction, like the Sphinx, or the woman caressing her Chimæra.

The *old* old clothesman is, I am sorry to say, becoming every day a swan of blacker hue. Young Israel has taken the field, and Old Jewry—old, bearded, gabardined, bent-backed Jewry is nearly extinct. It may be, perhaps, that after a certain age he abandons the bag, and laying in a large stock of crockery-ware, and vouchers for enormous sums, retires to the East, where he awaits the goods which the gods of diplomacy provide him.

Very rarely now is this gabardine—that long, loose, shapeless garment, the same on which Antonio spat—to be seen in London streets. I recollect the time when nearly all the old clothesmen wore it, and I am certain *my* clothesman —the bogey of my childhood—was wont to be habited therein. Young Israel wears cut-away coats, and chains, and rings; has eschewed the beard for the curl known as the aggravator, the chin tuft, and the luxuriant fringe of whisker; carries the bag jauntily, not wearily and cumbrously, as Old Jewry did. But the *inside* is the same, the sagacity, the perseverance, the bargaining—oh! the keen bargaining is as keen as ever.

Then there is the bagless clothesman—the apparently bag-less one at lest—the *marchand sans sac*. You may be in the street, and meet a gentleman attired in the first style of fashion, walking easily along, twirling his cane, and thinking, it would seem, of nothing at all. Passing him, you catch his eye ; you find out that he has not got that piercing black eye, and that acutely aquiline nose, for nothing. He slides up to you, and in an insinuating *sotto voce,* something between a stage " aside " and an invitation to " buy a little dawg " from a Regent-street fancier, asks you the momentous question, " Have you anything to shell, sir ? "

The interrogatory may have been put in Kensington, and you may live at Mile-end; but the bagless clothesman will not be deterred by any question of distance from accompanying you. He would walk by your side from Indus to the Pole, with that peculiar sidling, shuffling gait of his, on the bare chance of the reversion of a single pair of pantaloons. And, should you so far yield to his seductive entreaties as to summon him to your domicile, he will produce, with magical rapidity, from some unknown receptacle, a BAG—when, or where, or whence, or how obtained, it is not within the compass of human ken to know.

A marvellous article is that bag. . It will hold everything and anything : always stuffed to repletion, it will hold more. The last straw, it has been aphoristically observed, breaks the camel's back; but trussess of trousers, stacks of paletôts, ricks of waistcoats, thrust into this much-enduring bag, seem not to tax its powers of endurance to anything above a moderate degree. As to breaking the bag's back, it is far more likely that it would dislocate the dorsal vertebræ of any novice bold enough to carry it than its own.

A friend of mine met with a bagless clothesman on the Queen's highway, and in his habit as he lived. Being about to leave London, he acknowledged the soft impeachment of having a few old clothes to dispose of, and of which he thought he might as well make a few shillings. Trousers, waistcoats, and coats were produced, and passed in review, and then my friend yielded to a Machiavelian suggestion of the clothesman relative to old boots. Remembering the existence of a decayed pair of Wellingtons under the parlour sofa, he descended to fetch them, leaving—*infelix puer !*—the clothesman alone. He reascended : the usual chaffering, bickering, and eventual bargain-driving took place. The money agreed on was paid, and the clothesman departed. But—oh, duplicity of clothesmankind!—the nefarious Israelite had stuffed into his bag the only pair of evening dress continuations my friend possessed. There was likewise a blue satin handkerchief with a white spot—what is popularly, I believe, known as a bird's-eye fogle—which was missing ; and though, of course, *I* would not insinuate anything to the disadvantage of the carriers of the bag, the disappearance will be allowed to be strange. Mrs. Gumm, however, my friend's landlady (who has sheltered so many medical students beneath her roof that she may almost be considered a member of the profession, and who reads the " Lancet " on Sunday afternoons with quite a relish), Mrs. Gumm now stoutly avers that he *did* annex them ; declaring, in addition, her firm belief that he appropriated at the same time, and stowed away in his bag, a feather-bed of considerable size, and a miniature portrait of the Otaheitan chief who was supposed to have eaten a portion of Captain Cook : which portrait was presented to her by the Rev. Fugue Trumpetstop, an earnest man, and now minister of finance to King Kamehameha XXXIII. of the Sandwich Islands. I think that if there had been a chest of drawers or a four-post bed missing, the dealer in worn out apparel would have been suspected as the spoliator.

Carrying the bag, and crying " ogh clo ! " seems a sort of novitiate, or apprenticeship, which all Hebrews are subjected to. They can flesh their maiden swords in the streets, without its being at all considered derogatory. I please myself with the theory, sometimes, that of the millionnaires I see rolling by in carriages ; read of as giving magnificent balls and suppers ; hear of as the pillars of commerce and the girders of public credit ; many have in their youth passed through the dusky probation of the bag. Keen chaffering about ragged paletots and threadbare trousers prepared them, finished them, gave them a sharper edge for the negotiation of the little bill and the sale of the undoubted specimens of the old masters. And from these to millions there were but few steps. There is a dear old dirty, frowsy, picturesque, muddy, ill-paved, worse-lighted, immensely rich old street in Frankfort, called the " Judengasse," a kind of compound of the worst parts of Duke Place and St. Mary Axe, and the best parts of Petticoat Lane, and Church Lane, St. Giles's. Here dwell the Jews of Frankfort—as dirty, as dingy, and as wealthy as their abiding-place. Departing at morn, and returning at eve, with the never-failing bag, you may see' the young Israelites. Sitting at the doors, smoking their pipes in tranquillity, are the patriarchs ; gossiping at the windows are the daughters of Judah, in robes of rainbow-hued silks or satins, but with under-garments of equivocal whiteness ; sprawling in the gutters amidst old clothes, pots, pans, household furniture, and offal, are the bright-eyed little children. I like much to walk in the Judengasse (after a good dinner at the Hotel de Russie), smoking the pipe of peace and Hungarian tobacco; glancing now at the old clothes, now at the clothesmen; now at the little babies in the kennel—peeping cunningly at the heavy iron-stanchioned doors and the windows, protected at night (and for reasons, the rogues!) with iron-bound shutters. I conjecture how many colossal fortunes have been made out of that shabby, grubby, ill-smelling old street. How many latent Rothschilds there may be in its back attics; how many Sampayos yet to come are sprawling in its kennels! The discipline of the bag is well observed in the Judengasse, and prospers as it does everywhere else.

And this only brings me back to my starting point, and makes me perplexed, confused, bothered. Why should the Jews deal in old clothes? Not only in London or Frankfort; who has not heard the nasal chant of the *Marchand d'habits* in Paris, crying, "*Vieux habits, vieux galons!*" Who has not seen him bartering with the grisette for the sale of her last Carnival's Debardeur dress? Who has not seen him slouching along, with a portion of the said Debardeur dress, in the shape of a pair of black velvet trousers, hanging over his arm; a pair of gold epaulettes sticking out of his coat-pocket; a cavalry sabre tucked under his arm, and an advocate's robe protruding from his as usual crammed bag? Who have not heard of the Gibraltar old clothesmen, or of the fights on board the Levant steamers between the Greeks and the Jews, on disputed questions, relative to the value of cast-off caftans and burnouses? I knew a young Turk once at Marseilles, who wore patent-leather boots, and perfumed himself indefatigably, but was not quite civilised for all that;

for I remember making him a present of a large bottle of West India pickles, which, desiring him to *taste*, he *ate*, from the first Capsicum to the last Chili ; from the first to the last drop of the red-hot pickling vinegar, which he drank, all without one morsel of bread or meat ; smacking his lips meanwhile, and saying, " *Mi piace, questo bastimento !* " his usual expression when pleased. I remember asking him, when we were better acquainted, and he had acquired a more extended knowledge of the European languages, what were the characteristics of the Jews in Constantinople ? " They are dogs," he said, simply, " and wear yellow handkerchiefs, and *go about the streets of Stamboul selling old clothes.*" If in Turkey, why not in Persia, in Abyssinia, in Crim Tartary—everywhere? There is something more in it than is dreamt of in my philosophy. For aught I know, though I believe it without knowledge, the Jews of Honan in China, or the black Jews of India, may deal in cast-off wearing apparel. Every Jew, millionnaire as he may become afterwards, seems to begin with the bag. A fabulously rich Israelite of whom I know something, was once solicited for some favour by a poorer member of his tribe. He declined acceding to the applicant's request. " Ah ! " said his petitioner, spitefully (he was an ill-favoured old man, in a snuff-coloured coat, and a handkerchief tied round his head under his hat), " you're a very great man, no doubt, now ; *but I recollect the time when you used to sell pocket-handkerchiefs in the public houses!*" And so, no doubt, he had.

From the sublime to the ridiculous there is but one step ; and from old clothesmen to old clothes there is but half a one. Let us consider old clothes.

Under which head, I beg to be understood, I include old hats, old boots, old linen, old anything, in fact, in which man delighteth to array himself. With the ladies (bless them!) I will not pretend, just now, to meddle; they have their own distinctive old clothes dealers—their *Revendeuses à la toilette,* their proprietors of shops where ladies' wardrobes are purchased. There are Eleusinian mysteries connected with this branch of the clothes trade; dark stories of duchesses' white satin dresses, and dowager countesses' crimson velvet robes, about which I must have more certain information ere I discourse thereon. To the uninitiated, the "Ladies' Wardrobe" is, as no doubt it is proper it should be, a mystery—a glimmering haze of dusky little shops in back streets, pink silk stockings, white satin shoes, soiled ostrich feathers, ladies' maids, and ladies themselves, shawled and muffled, and with a cab waiting at the corner of the street. Fubsy women in printed gowns and aprons are dimly visible through the haze, sometimes; and the tallyman has something mysteriously to do with the matter. I will inquire into it.

But of the old clothes appertaining to the masculine gender. If you want to see old clothes and old clothesmen in their glory, go to Cloth Fair or the Clothes Exchange. You will have to pay a small toll on entrance, towards the support of the building, but that is nothing. I should not so particularly advise you to take care of your pockets on this occasion; but I should most decidedly caution you to take care of the clothes of which those pockets form a part; for it is by no means improbable that half-a-dozen Jews will fall on you at once, and tug fiercely at your garments; not with any bellicose intention, but simply with the understanding that you *must* have something to sell ; and that, having no bag, and being somewhat eccentric, you are actuated by a desire to sell the clothes you stand upright in.

During the whole of the time the market lasts, one incessant series of pacific fights takes place. Rapidly, in twos and threes, sometimes by dozens and half-dozens, swarm in the clothesmen, who have been perambulating the streets since early morn. In a trice, on these erst buyers, now sellers, fall new buyers. What have they got to shell ? For Moses' shake, vat have they got to shell ? For all the Prophets's shake, give them the refusal ! Oh ! versh the bagsh ? Oh ! vat ish there in it ? Oh ! vat you vant ? Oh ! vat you give ? The gigantic bag is forcibly removed from the shoulders of the resisting clothesman ; it and he are tugged, hauled, hustled, jostled about. At last, he selects the merchant with whom he is desirous of doing business, and on that merchant's shopboard the multifarious contents of the wondrous bag will be vomited forth. Gracious ! will it never have done disgorging garments ? More coats, more waistcoats, more continuations ; a shower of hats ; any quantities of pairs of boots, silk handkerchiefs, umbrellas, boys' caps, pattens ; and, sir, I am not exaggerating when I state, that this marvellous sack may, and has been very often known to, contain, and subsequently disgorge, such miscellaneous trifles as a few pounds of dripping, a birdcage, a live poodle, a theodolite, and an ormolu clock. All is fish that comes to the clothesman's net—all clothes that come to his bag. He would buy your head if it were loose.

On every merchant's shopboard similar heaps of hydranatured garments are tumbling out of similar sacks. Then ensues frantic yelling, screeching, lung-tearing, ear-piercing bargain-making. They gibber, they howl, they clutch each other fiercely, and grapple over a farthing like wolves. See yonder yellow-visaged old mercator, with salt rheum in his eye, and a beard like the beard of an insolvent goat, grown careless of his personal appearance. He is from Amsterdam, and can speak no English; yet he gibbers, and clutches, and grapples with the keenest of his British brethren. He holds up his fingers to denote how much he will give, and no more. For Moses' sake, another finger! S'help me, you 're robbing me! S'help me, it's yoursh! And the mercator has the best of the bargain, for your Jew, when a seller, is as loth to refuse money as he is, when a buyer, to part with it.

Now the air is darkened with legs and arms of garments held up to be inspected as to their condition. The buyer pokes, and peers into, and detects naplessness, and spies out patches, and is aware of rents, and smells out black and blue reviver, and noses darns, and discovers torn linings; the seller, meanwhile, watching every movement with lynx-eyed inquietude. A lull takes place—a very temporary lull, while this inspection is going on; but only wait an instant, and you shall hear the howling, screeching, and see the clutching and grappling commence *de novo*. The air feels hot, and there is a fetid, squalid odour of rags. Jew boys stand in the midst of the market calling sweet-stuff and hot cakes for sale. Hark at Mammon and Gammon yelling at each other, browbeating, chaffering in mutilated English and bastard Hebrew. They *do* make a great noise, certainly; but is there not a little buzz, a trifling hum of business in the area of the Royal Exchange just before the bell rings? Does not

Capel Court resound sometimes to the swell of human voices ?
Is not the immaculate Auction Mart itself occasionally anything but taciturn, when the advowson of a comfortable living
is to be sold ? We can make bargains, and noises about them,
too, for other things besides old clothes.

Look at that heap of old clothes—that Pelion upon Ossa
of ostracised garments. A reflective mind will find homilies,
satires, aphorisms, by the dozen—thought-food by the ton
weight, in that pile of dress-offal. There is my lord's coat,
bespattered by the golden mud on Fortune's highway;
threadbare in the back with much bowing; the embroidery
tarnished, the spangles all blackened; a Monmouth Street
laced coat. Revivified, coaxed, and tickled into transitory
splendour again, it may lend vicarious dignity to some High
Chamberlain, or Stick-in-Waiting, at the court of the Emperor Soulouque. There is a scarlet uniform coat, heavily
embroidered, which, no doubt, has dazzled many a nursemaid
in its day. It will shine at masquerades now; or, perchance,
be worn by Mr. Belton, of the Theatre Royal; then emigrate,
may be, and be the coat of office of the Commander-in-Chief
of King Quashiboo's body-guard; or, with the addition of a
cocked hat and straps, form the coronation costume of King
Quashiboo himself. And there is John the footman's coat,
with ruder embroidery, but very like my lord's coat for all
that. There, pell-mell, cheek by jowl, in as strange juxta-
position, and as strange equality, as corpses in a plague-pit,
are the groom's gaiters and my Lord Bishop's spatterdashes;
with, save the mark! poor Pat's ill-darned, many-holed
brogues, his bell-crowned felt hat, his unmistakeable blue
coat with the brass buttons, high in the collar, short in the

waist, long in the tails, and ragged all over. There is no distinction of ranks ; no precedence of rank, and rank alone, here. Patrick's brogues, if they were only sound and whole, instead of holey, would command a better price than my lord's torn black silk small clothes , you groom's gaiters are worth double the episcopal spatterdashes ; and that rough fustian jacket would fetch more than the tattered dress-coat with only one sleeve, albeit 'twas made by Poole, and was once worn by Beau Smith.

Where are the people, I wonder, to whom these clothes belonged ? Who will wear them next ? Will the episcopal spatterdashes grace the calves of a Low Church greengrocer ? Will John the footman's coat be transferred to Sambo or Mungo, standing on cucumber-shinned extremities on the foot-board of a chariot belonging to some militia field-marshal or other star of the Upper Ten Thousand of New York ? Who was John, and whose footman was he ? How many a weary mile the poor Jews have walked to get these sweepings of civilisation together, and make for a moment a muck-heap of fashion in Cloth Fair—a dunghill of vanity for chapmen to huckster over ! All the lies and the subterfuges of dress, the padded coats and whaleboned-waistcoats, the trousers that were patched in places where the skirts hid them, have come naked to this bankruptcy. The surtout that concealed the raggedness of the body-coat beneath ; the body-coat that buttoned over the shirtless chest ; the boots which were not Wellingtons, as in their strapped-down hypocrisy they pretended to be, but old Bluchers ; all are discovered, exposed, turned inside out, here. If the people who wore them could only be treated in the same manner—

what remarkably unpleasant things we should hear about one another, to be sure !

The Nemesis of Cloth Fair is impartial, unyielding, inexorable. She has neither favourites nor partialities : a dress-coat—be it the choicest work of a Nugee or a Buckmaster—is to her an abomination, unless something can be made of it. She regardeth not a frock-coat, unless there is enough good cloth left in the skirts to make boys' caps of; a military stripe down a pair of trousers has no charms in her eyes ; she is deaf to the voice of the embroidered vest, unless that vest be in good condition.

There are three orders of " Old Clothes," as regards the uses to which they may be applied : First class, clothes good enough to be revivered, tricked, polished, teased, re-napped, and sold, either as superior second-hand garments, in second-hand-shop streets, or pawned for as much as they will fetch, and more than they are worth. Second class, Old Clothes, which are good enough to be exported to Ireland, to Australia, and the Colonies generally. Great quantities are sent to the South American Republics ; and a considerably brisk trade in left-off wearing apparel is driven with that Great Northern Republic which asserts itself capable of inflicting corporal punishment on the whole of the universe. Wearing appared is unconscionably dear in the land of freedom, and the cheap " bucks " of the model republic cannot always afford bran-new broad-cloth. Third-class, or very Old Clothes, include those that are so miserably dilapidated, so utterly tattered and torn, that they would have been, I am sure, despised and rejected even by the indifferently-dressed man who married " the maiden all forlorn." These tatters — " *haillons* " the

z

French call them — have a glorious destiny before them. Like the phœnix, they rise again from their ashes. Torn to pieces by a machine, aptly called a "devil," in grim, brick factories, northwards, they are ground, pounded, tortured into "devil's dust," or "shoddy;" by a magic process, and the admixture of a little fresh wool, they burst into broadcloth again. I need say no more. When I speak of broadcloth and "devil's dust," my acute readers will know as much about it as I do: plate-glass-shops, middlemen, sweaters, cheap clothes, and nasty. Who shall say that the Marquis of Camberwell's footman—those cocked-hatted, bouquetted, silk-stockinged Titans—may not have, in their gorgeous costume, a considerable spice of Patrick the bog-trotter's ragged breeches, and Luke the Labourer's fustain jucket?

We have traditions and superstitions about almost everything in life, from the hogs in the Hampstead sewers to the ghosts in a shut-up house. There are traditions and superstitions about old clothes. Fables of marvellous sums found in the pockets of left-off garments are current especially among the lower orders. There was the Irish gentleman who found his waistcoat lined throughout with bank-notes; and the youth who discovered that all the buttons on a coat he had bought in Petticoat Lane, were sovereigns covered with cloth. Then there was Mary Jenkins who, in the words of the *Public Advertiser*, of February 14th, 1750, "deals in old clothes in Rag Fair, and sold a pair of breeches to a poor woman for sevenpence and a pint of beer. While they were drinking it in a public house, the purchaser, in unripping the breeches, found, quilted in the waistband, eleven guineas in gold—Queen Anne's coin, and a thirty pound bank-note dated 1729 ; which last she did not know the value of, till she had sold it for a gallon of twopenny purl." There are so many stories of this sort about, in old newspapers and in old gossips' mouths, that a man, however credulous, is apt to suspect that a fair majority of them may be apocryphal. There is a tinge of superstition in the connection of money or fortune with clothes. Don't they put sixpence into a little boy's pocket, when he is first indued with pantaloons the *toga virilis* of youthful Britons? Don't we say that a halfpenny with a cross on it will keep the deuce out of our pockets? Don't we throw old shoes after a person for luck? and what is luck but money?